Visual Word Recognition

Word recognition is the component of reading which involves the identification of individual words. Together the two volumes of *Visual Word Recognition* offer a state-of-the-art overview of contemporary research from leading figures in the field.

This first volume outlines established theory, new models and key experimental evidence used to investigate visual word recognition: lexical decision and word naming. It also considers methodological concerns: new developments in large databases, and how these have been applied to theoretical questions; and control considerations when dealing with words as stimuli. Finally, the book considers the visual-orthographic input to the word recognition system: from the left- and right-hand sides of vision, through the processing of letters and their proximity, to the similarity and confusability of words, and the contribution of the spoken-phonological form of the word.

The two volumes serve as a state-of-the-art, comprehensive overview of the field. They are essential reading for researchers of visual word recognition, as well as undergraduate and postgraduate students of cognition and cognitive psychology, specifically the psychology of language and reading. They will also be of use to those working in education and speech-language therapy.

James S. Adelman first became involved in visual word recognition research whilst reading for a degree in Mathematics and Psychology at the University of Liverpool. From there, he went on to complete a PhD and various externally funded research projects at the University of Warwick, where he has been an Assistant Professor since 2010.

Current Issues in the Psychology of Language
Series Editor: Trevor A. Harley

Current Issues in the Psychology of Language is a series of edited books that will reflect the state-of-the-art in areas of current and emerging interest in the psychological study of language.

Each volume is tightly focused on a particular topic and consists of seven to ten chapters contributed by international experts. The editors of individual volumes are leading figures in their areas and provide an introductory overview.

Example topics include: language development, bilingualism and second language acquisition, word recognition, word meaning, text processing, the neuroscience of language, and language production, as well as the inter-relations between these topics.

Visual Word Recognition Volume 1
Edited by James S. Adelman

Visual Word Recognition Volume 2
Edited by James S. Adelman

Forthcoming Titles:

Sentence Processing
Edited by Roger van Gompel

Visual Word Recognition
Volume 1

Models and methods, orthography, and phonology

Edited by
James S. Adelman

Psychology Press
Taylor & Francis Group

LONDON AND NEW YORK

Educ
LB
1050.44
.V57
2012
v. 1

First edition published 2012
27 Church Road, Hove, East Sussex, BN3 2FA

Simultaneously published in the USA and Canada
by Psychology Press
711 Third Avenue, New York, NY 10017

Psychology Press is an imprint of the Taylor & Francis Group, an informa business

British Library Cataloguing in Publication Data
A catalogue record for this book is available from the British Library

Library of Congress Cataloging-in-Publication Data
Visual word recognition: Models and methods, orthography and phonology /
    Edited by James S. Adelman, University of Warwick.
        pages cm
    Includes bibliographical references and index.
    ISBN 978-1-84872-058-9 (hb)
    1. Word recognition. I. Adelman, James S.
    LB1050.44.V57   2012
    372.46'2—dc23   2012000617

ISBN13: 978-1-84872-058-9 (hbk)
ISBN13: 978-0-20310-701-0 (ebk)

Typeset in Times New Roman
by Cenveo Publisher Services

Printed and bound in Great Britain by
CPI Group (UK) Ltd, Croydon, CR0 4YY

Contents

List of Figures

List of Tables

List of Contributors

James S. Adelman, Department of Psychology, University of Warwick, Gibbet Hill Road, Coventry CV4 7AL, UK

Jane Ashby, Psychology Department, Central Michigan University, Mount Pleasant, MI 48859, USA

David A. Balota, Department of Psychology, Washington University in St. Louis, Campus Box 1125, One Brookings Drive, St. Louis, MO 63130, USA

Marc Brysbaert, Department of Experimental Psychology, Ghent University, Henri Dunantlaan 2, 9000 Gent, Belgium

Qing Cai, Department of Experimental Psychology, Ghent University, Henri Dunantlaan 2, 9000 Gent, Belgium

Max Coltheart, Centre for Cognition and its Disorders and Macquarie Centre for Cognitive Science, Macquarie University, Sydney, NSW 2109, Australia

Michael J. Cortese, Psychology Department, University of Nebraska-Omaha, Omaha, NE 68182, USA

Colin J. Davis, Department of Psychology, Royal Holloway University of London, Egham, TW20 0EX, UK

Stéphane Dufau, Université d'Aix-Marseille, Pôle 3 C, LPC/CNRS/UMR 6146, 3, place Victor Hugo, Bat. 9, Case D, 13331 Marseille Cedex 1, France

Kenneth I. Forster, Department of Psychology, University of Arizona, Tucson, AZ 85721, USA

Pablo Gomez, DePaul University, Department of Psychology, 2219 North Kenmore Avenue, Chicago, IL 60614, USA

Jonathan Grainger, Université d'Aix-Marseille, Pôle 3 C, LPC/CNRS/UMR 6146, 3, place Victor Hugo, Bat. 9, Case D, 13331 Marseille Cedex 1, France

Laura K. Halderman, Learning Research and Development Center, University of Pittsburgh, 3939 O'Hara Street, Pittsburgh, PA 15260, USA

Keith A. Hutchison, Department of Psychology, Montana State University, P.O. Box 173440 Bozeman, MT 59717, USA

Christopher T. Kello, School of Social Sciences, Humanities and Arts, University of California, Merced, 5200 North Lake Road, Merced, CA 95343, USA

Charles A. Perfetti, Learning Research and Development Center, University of Pittsburgh, 3939 O'Hara Street, Pittsburgh, PA 15260, USA

Daragh E. Sibley, Haskins Laboratories, 300 George Street, New Haven, CT 06511, USA

Lise Van der Haegen, Department of Experimental Psychology, Ghent University, Henri Dunantlaan 2, 9000 Gent, Belgium

Melvin J. Yap, Department of Psychology, Faculty of Arts and Social Sciences, National University of Singapore, 9 Arts Link, Singapore 117570, Singapore

Acknowledgments

I thank the contributors for their efforts and Suzanne Marquis for her aid in reminding contributors of their promises. Preparation of this book was supported in part by Economic and Social Research Council (UK) grant RES-062-23-0545.

Figure 1.1 is reproduced with kind permission from Springer Science+Business Media from Figure 1 of Marshall, J.C. and Newcombe, F. (1973). Patterns of paralexia: A psycholinguistic approach. *Journal of Psycholinguistic Research, 2*, 175–199. Psychology Press have detailed of Figure 7.1 Figure 7.4 is reproduced with permission from MIT Press from Hunter, Z.R., Brysbaert, M., and Knecht, S. (2007). Foveal word reading requires interhemispheric communication. *Journal of Cognitive Neuroscience, 19*, 1373–1387. © MIT Press. Figure 8.3 is reproduced from *Trends in Cognitive Sciences, Vol. 12*, Jonathan Grainger, Arnaud Rey, and Stéphane Dufau, "Letter perception: from pixels to pandemonium," pp. 381–387, © 2008, with permission from Elsevier. Figure 8.5 is from Tydgat, I. and Grainger, J. (2009). Serial position effects in the identification of letters, digits and symbols. Reprinted with permission from *Journal of Experimental Psychology: Human Perception and Performance, 35*, 480–498, published by American Psychological Association. Figure 8.6 is from Figure 2.3 of Just, Marcel Adam; Carpenter, Patricia, *Psychology of Reading and Language Comprehension*, 1st Edition, © 1987. Reprinted by permission of Pearson Education, Inc., Upper Saddle River, NJ.

Introduction

James S. Adelman

Words are the building blocks of language, and are the interface between written and spoken language. Recognition of the printed word is both essential to the important skill of reading and among the easiest routes for the experimenter to access higher cognition. In this light, it is little surprise that the identification and pronunciation of written (or more often, printed) words are among the earliest studied (Cattell, 1886) and most studied aspects of cognition.

Visual word recognition is studied both in its own right, in terms of the processes of recognizing a word and the performance of word-based tasks, but also more broadly in context as a link to semantics and concepts, cognitive individual differences, reading prose and learning to read. This volume concentrates on the former, narrower, form of study of visual word recognition, whilst its companion concentrates on the latter, broader form of study.

Chapters 1 through 4 consider the theoretical underpinnings of the study of visual word recognition. In Chapter 1, Coltheart argues that current models of reading aloud all posit two routes, and considers the evidence concerning the nature of these routes. In Chapter 2, Sibley and Kello describe a connectionist recurrent network model of the learning of orthographic representations, and argue that the manner of learning accounts for key properties of behaviour in lexical decision. In Chapter 3, Forster presents a model that incorporates properties of both serial search and network models, arguing that this approach has key advantages in understanding how multiple words can be active in the reading system. In Chapter 4, Gomez surveys the vast array of models of the lexical decision, which, he shows, vary in their emphasis on the lexical and the decision components of the process.

Chapters 5 and 6 are more methodologically focussed. First, Balota and colleagues survey 'mega-studies': large studies involving many words and participants whose data are made available for analysis by the research community, and they consider how these studies have given rise to contributions that complement those from more traditionally sized studies. Then I consider the item selection and statistical analysis issues involved in working with characteristics of words as theoretically important predictors, considering how to control by design known factors affecting visual word recognition, and how to control by statistics unknown factors affecting visual word recognition.

The remaining chapters consider the inputs to the visual word recognition system at various levels. In Chapter 7, Brysbaert and colleagues argue that even in central vision, the left and right halves of an eye's view are initially processed separately, being sent to different halves of the brain, and then must be integrated for effective reading to begin. In Chapter 8, Grainger and Dufau consider the mechanisms of processing letters through into words, arguing that there is specialized processing for letters and that two systems map letters onto words, the systems differing in how they deal with positional information. In Chapter 9, Davis considers this matching process for mapping letters onto words and considers the different forms of stimulus that may be considered 'similar' to a word insofar as it affects processing of that word. Finally, Halderman and colleagues argue that the phonological representation of a word is not merely an outcome of the attempt to visually identify that word, but plays a key role in its identification from a very early stage.

In sum, these chapters cover the key issues involved in understanding the processing of the written word in terms of its written and spoken forms.

Visual word recognition is a constituent process of reading.

References

Cattell, J. M. (1886). The time taken up by cerebral operations. *Mind, 11*, 377–92. Retrieved from http://psychclassics.yorku.ca

1 Dual-route theories of reading aloud

Max Coltheart

At the 1971 meeting of the International Neuropsychology Symposium in Engelberg, Switzerland, John Marshall and Freda Newcombe described six people who had suffered brain damage that had affected their ability to read – six case of acquired dyslexia. These six people fell into three different categories, since the pattern of reading symptoms they showed differed qualitatively as a function of which category they were assigned to. The three categories of acquired dyslexia were named 'deep dyslexia', 'surface dyslexia' and 'visual dyslexia'.

The publication of this work two years later (Marshall & Newcombe, 1973) initiated a major research field – the cognitive neuropsychology of reading. It did this not so much because it emphasized that there are different subtypes of acquired dyslexia – though this was a very important thing to demonstrate – but because the authors offered an explicit information-processing model of reading aloud and suggested how each of the three forms of acquired dyslexia could be understood as generated by three different patterns of impairment of that model.

Their model is shown in Figure 1.1. It is a dual-route model of reading aloud (though Marshall and Newcombe did not use the term 'dual route') because there are two processing routes from print (the stimulus) to speech (the response). One route is via Visual Addresses through Semantic Addresses to articulation. This route can only be used with those letter strings that possess semantic addresses – that is, only with words. The route cannot produce reading-aloud responses for nonwords.

How Marshall and Newcombe conceived of the second route for reading aloud (the A→B→D→T→F route) is not entirely clear from the Figure 1.1 diagram; but it is perfectly clear from their paper: 'If . . . as a consequence of brain damage, the functional pathway bc (Fig. 1) is usually unavailable, the subject will have no option other than attempting to read via putative grapheme-phoneme correspondence rules (pathway bd)' (Marshall & Newcombe, 1973, p. 191).

A processing route that translates print to speech by application of grapheme-phoneme correspondence rules will be able to read letter strings that are not words. However, by definition it will fail for letter strings whose pronunciations differs from the pronunciations generated by the grapheme-phoneme correspondence

STIMULUS

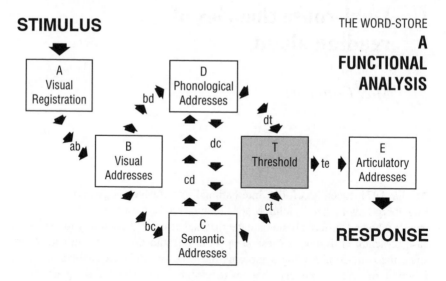

THE WORD-STORE

**A
FUNCTIONAL
ANALYSIS**

RESPONSE

Figure 1.1 The dual-route model of reading proposed by Marshall and Newcombe (1973). With kind permission from Springer Science+Business Media: Figure 1 of Marshall, J.C., & Newcombe, F. (1973). Patterns of paralexia: A psycholinguistic approach. *Journal of Psycholinguistic Research, 2,* 175–199.

rules of the language: the so-called *irregular* or *exception* words[1] of the language. Marshall and Newcombe did not quite make this point about irregular words and the second reading route, but they clearly had it in mind: 'a recent formalism . . . proposes 166 correspondence rules in an analysis of children's reading books. These rules only account for 90% of the data, leaving 10% of quite common words provided with an incorrect pronunciation' (Marshall & Newcombe, 1973, p. 191).

The dual-route model of reading aloud was proposed independently in the same year by Forster and Chambers (1973).

> The pronunciation of a visually-presented word involves assigning to a sequence of letters some kind of acoustic or articulatory coding. There are presumably two alternative ways in which this coding can be assigned. First, the pronunciation could be computed by application of a set of grapheme-phoneme or letter-sound correspondence rules. This coding can be carried out independently of any consideration of the meaning or familiarity of the letter sequence, as in the pronunciation of previously unencountered sequences, such as *flitch, mantiness,* and *streep.* Alternatively, the pronunciation may be determined by searching long-term memory for stored information about how to pronounce familiar letter sequences, obtaining the necessary information

by a direct dictionary look-up, instead of rule-application. Obviously this
procedure would only work for familiar words.

(Forster & Chambers, 1973, p. 627)

These authors did not raise the issue of irregular words (words whose pronunciations disobey grapheme-phoneme rules and so could not be correctly read
aloud using the grapheme-phoneme rule route).

After this dual introduction of the dual-route model of reading aloud, the idea
spread rapidly, for example:

> We can . . . distinguish between an *orthographic* mechanism, which makes
> use of such general and productive relationships between letter patterns and
> sounds as exist, and a *lexical* mechanism, which relies instead upon specific
> knowledge of pronunciations of particular words or morphemes, that is, a
> lexicon of pronunciations (if not meanings as well) . . . It seems that both
> of the mechanisms we have suggested, the orthographic and lexical mecha-
> nisms, are used for pronouncing printed words.

(Baron & Strawson, 1976, pp. 386, 391)

> Naming can be accomplished either by orthographic-phonemic translation,
> or by reference to the internal lexicon.

(Frederiksen & Kroll, 1976, p. 378)

Given the central role played by the concept of irregularity of grapheme-
phoneme correspondence in the dual-route approach, what was clearly needed
next was empirical investigation of the influence of such irregularity on the reading aloud of words. If regular words (those which obey the correspondence rules)
can be read aloud correctly via the rule route and also by the dictionary lookup
route, while irregular words can only be read aloud correctly by the dictionary
lookup route, one might expect this to result in reading-aloud latencies being
shorter for regular words than for irregular words. This was first investigated by
Baron and Strawson (1976), who did indeed find that reading aloud was slower
for irregular words than for regular words.

At this point, it is necessary to say something more, by way of definition, about
the concept of regularity and also about another concept, consistency, which also
became important in reading research from the late 1970s onwards.

The concepts of regularity and consistency

To produce perfectly clear terminology here, we need some definitions. To define
the irregular/regular distinction, we first need to define the term *grapheme*.
Relationships between spellings and pronunciations are often referred to as being
governed by letter–sound rules, but that's incorrect. The word THIGH has five
letters. So if it were literally *letters* that were being translated to sounds
(phonemes), this word would have five phonemes; but it doesn't, it has only two.

So the orthographic units that are being mapped onto phonemes here are not letters: they are orthographic units that are the written representations of phonemes. The definition of 'grapheme' is: the written representation of a phoneme. Thus the graphemes of THIGH are ⟨TH⟩ and ⟨IGH⟩. Hence the correct term for the mappings of spellings to sounds is 'grapheme-phoneme correspondences' (GPCs). And the translation of the letter sequence THIGH to the grapheme sequence ⟨TH⟩ + ⟨IGH⟩ is referred to as 'graphemic parsing'.

For most of the graphemes of English, the grapheme can correspond to different phonemes in different words: consider the grapheme ⟨OO⟩ in BLOOD, GOOD, and FOOD, for example. If there is a set of GPC rules for English, what phoneme is to be associated with the grapheme ⟨OO⟩ in this set of rules? A commonly adopted approach is to choose, as the phoneme for any particular grapheme, the phoneme that is associated with that grapheme in the largest number of words containing that grapheme. For ⟨OO⟩, this is the phoneme /u:/, as in FOOD. So the GPC rule for ⟨OO⟩ is ⟨OO⟩ → /u:/. Alternative approaches are possible. For example, instead of using the type frequency of phonemes to decide what phoneme should be associated with a particular grapheme one could use token frequency. Of the words containing the grapheme ⟨TH⟩, there are more words which have the unvoiced phoneme as in THICK than have the voiced phoneme as in THAT, but the summed frequency of the words which have the unvoiced phoneme is lower than the summed frequency of the words than have the voiced phoneme. So the GPC for the grapheme ⟨TH⟩ would have the unvoiced phoneme if type frequency were used as the criterion, but the voiced phoneme if token frequency were used as the criterion.

Once a set of GPC rules is assembled in this way for all the graphemes of English, one can inspect each word of English to determine whether application of this set of rules generates its pronunciation correctly. When this does occur, the word is classified as regular (e.g. FOOD). When in contrast the rule-generated pronunciation of a word differs from the word's dictionary pronunciation (as in e.g. BLOOD or GOOD), the word is classified as irregular. Note that this means that one cannot speak of nonwords as regular or irregular, since nonwords don't have dictionary pronunciations; so the terms 'regular' and 'irregular' apply only to words. And these terms denote an all-or-none distinction: on this approach, there are not gradations of regularity (unlike consistency, which, as we will see shortly, can be thought of as graded).

Next we need to define the consistent/inconsistent distinction. Here again we need first to define a particular term: the term *body*. The body of a pronounceable monosyllabic letter string is the sequence of letters from the initial vowel to the end of the string. A pronounceable letter string (which may be a word or a nonword) is body-consistent if all the words that contain that body rhyme i.e. have the same pronunciation of that body. If in the set of words containing that body there is more than one pronunciation of the body, any letter-string containing that body is body-inconsistent. The concept of consistency can be applied to orthographic components other than the body (e.g. the orthographic onset), but this has rarely been done. So almost all work on consistency has been work on body-consistency, and so when I use the term 'consistency' I will just be referring to body-consistency, and will not consider other kinds of consistency in this chapter.

One can treat the consistent/inconsistent distinction as all-or-none; or one can think of degrees of consistency, as measured, for example, by the proportion of words containing a particular body that share the same pronunciation of that body.

Glushko's work

The next important event in the history of the dual-route theory of reading was the paper by Glushko (1979). Glushko discussed both of the distinctions that I have just defined: irregular[2] versus regular, and inconsistent versus consistent. He would have liked there to be only three categories here: irregular, regular-inconsistent and regular-consistent. But that would amount to the claim that there are no irregular words that are consistent and as he says (Glushko, 1979, p. 684, footnote 3) this is not the case: he acknowledges, with evident disappointment, that there are irregular words which must be classified as consistent since they have no neighbours which fail to rhyme with them. Examples of such consistent irregular words are WALK, PALM, WEALTH, and LEARN. So there are four categories here, not three: there is a two-by-two classification, regular/irregular versus consistent/inconsistent, not a single continuum.

Experiment 1 of Glushko (1979) reported that reading-aloud reaction times (RTs) were 29 ms slower for inconsistent nonwords such as HEAF than for consistent nonwords such as HEAN, and also that that reading-aloud RTs were 29 ms slower for irregular words such as DEAF than for regular words such as DEAN. Since the nonword effect might have arisen because of the presence of irregular words similar to the nonwords and this might have produced some priming effect, Experiment 2 used only the nonwords from Experiment 1: here inconsistent nonwords were still significantly slower (by 22 ms) than consistent nonwords. Experiment 3 used irregular-inconsistent words such as HAVE paired with regular consistent words such as HAZE, and regular-inconsistent words such as WAVE paired with regular consistent words such as WADE. The effect of irregularity + inconsistency (HAVE versus HAZE) was 21 ms; the effect of inconsistency without irregularity (WAVE versus WADE) was 17 ms.

Glushko's argument was that although the effect he found with words could be explained by dual-route theory, the effect he found with nonwords could not: hence he proposed an alternative theory of reading aloud, one in which there is only a single route from print to speech that is capable of correctly translating both nonwords and irregular words from print to speech:

> Regular and exception words are pronounced using the same kinds of knowledge.

> (Glushko, 1979, p. 687)

These results refute current claims that words are read aloud by retrieving a single pronunciation from memory and that pseudowords are pronounced by using abstract spelling-to-sound rules. Instead, it appears that words and pseudowords are pronounced by using similar kinds of orthographic and phonological knowledge: the pronunciations of words that share ortho-graphic features with them, and specific spelling-to-sound rules for multi-letter spelling patterns.

(Glushko, 1979, p. 674)

The single-route theory of reading aloud

Glushko (1979) said nothing about what the nature of this single route might be; but he did discuss this a little in a subsequent publication (Glushko, 1981). There, after describing the standard dual route theory of reading aloud, he immediately observed: 'Despite its plausibility, however, this two-mechanism theory of read-ing aloud is incorrect . . . I conclude that the two-mechanism structure of reading aloud is based more on ideology than on data.' (1981, p. 62).

Glushko (1981) gave two reasons for concluding that the dual-route theory of reading aloud was false. One was his finding that inconsistent nonwords such as BINT have significantly longer reading-aloud RTs than consistent nonwords such as BINK; he also pointed out here that errors with inconsistent nonwords often took the form of pronouncing them to rhyme with the irregular words from which they were derived: BINT read to rhyme with PINT, or HEAF to rhyme with DEAF. The other reason he gave was his finding that regular inconsistent words such as WAVE have significantly longer reading-aloud RTs than regular consist-ent words such as WADE.

Referring to the work of Marcel (1980), Glushko (1981) comments:

Marcel rejects the standard two-mechanism model of reading and proposes that the two dyslexic syndromes[3] arise as impairments at different points in a unitary reading process. This new model of the dyslexias is roughly equivalent to the activation and synthesis model that I propose for normal adult readers. Marcel and I share the idea that phonological translation is not accomplished by grapheme-phoneme rules, but by lexical activation of more specific phonological knowledge.

(Glushko, 1981, p. 69)

We must distinguish two issues here. The first is whether the one-route theory of reading aloud proposed by Glushko and Marcel is viable. The second is whether Glushko's findings really cannot be explained by the dual-route theory of reading aloud. I will consider the first of these issues now, and the second one later in this chapter.

Unfortunately the one-route (activation and synthesis) model is only very briefly sketched in Glushko's chapter; indeed, Glushko says, referring to his model, 'This characterization of the interactive processes in reading is intentionally vague and evasive, because my data offer few constraints at this end of the spelling-to-sound process.' (1981, p. 71).

The general idea, however, was as follows. A letter string, whether it is a word or a nonword, automatically *activates* those words that are orthographic neighbours of the input string. This in turn leads to the activation of the phonological representations of these words. From this set of phonological representations, the correct pronunciation of the input string (whether it is a word or a nonword) is *synthesized*: 'the eventual response emerges through coordination and synthesis of many partially activated phonological representations' (Glushko, 1981, p. 79).

Glushko said nothing at all about what procedure could possibly achieve this synthesizing. However, Marcel (Marcel, 1980; Kay & Marcel, 1981) did, though in very general terms (when doing so, he used the term 'analogy theory' where Glushko had used the term 'activation and synthesis model': These two terms, as Glushko, 1981, said, are roughly equivalent).

There are some immediately obvious challenges that could be raised to this one-route approach. If the initial orthographic cohort activated by a nonword – the words which are analogous to that nonword – are the orthographic neighbours of that nonword, then three obvious difficulties are:

(a) There are perfectly pronounceable nonwords that have no neighbours, such as URTCH, EETH, AWF and IRVE. These would not activate any words, so there would be no phonology activated and available for synthesis.
(b) There are nonwords whose neighbours all differ from it in the same position: YIGHY, VOON and GATCH, for example. None of the neighbours of GATCH begin with the phoneme /g/; so this essential phoneme could not be generated in the synthesis process.
(c) Glushko himself (1979, p. 684) noted, as a problem for the kind of one-route theory that he favoured, that a nonword whose sole neighbour is a highly irregular word is unlikely to be pronounced to rhyme with that word: for example, he thought it unlikely that MAUGH would be read as rhyming with LAUGH, even though this is what is predicted by the one-route theory.

Marcel (1980) suggested, as a way of dealing with such problems, that a letter string is orthographically segmented not just into head + body, but in all possible ways. However, whether this could possibly succeed as the basis of a procedure for reading aloud nonwords is not an idea that was followed up by anyone.

It is important to note that, as pointed out by Patterson and Morton (1985, p. 354), Marcel was not proposing that these multiple segments were created on-line by a segmentation process as a nonword was being read. Instead, he was proposing that all of the segments are permanently present, stored in the orthographic lexicon. This does not seem plausible. If what Marcel had in mind is that every N-letter sequence that occurs in at least one word of English is stored in the orthographic lexicon, with N varying from 2 to the number of letters in the longest real word in the lexicon, the number of entries in that lexicon would be astronomically large.

What was needed here for a proper evaluation of analogy theory was an explicit – preferably computational – version of the analogy model. Such a model, the PbA (Pronunciation by Analogy) model was subsequently developed by Damper, Marchand and colleagues (see e.g. Damper & Eastmond, 1997). This is a genuinely computational model – i.e. a working computer program – which computes pronunciations from print for nonwords, regular words, and irregular words by a single uniform procedure whose first step is to find words in its orthographic lexicon that match the input string according to some orthographic criterion. This model has largely been developed in an engineering context, to try to improve the performance of automatic text-to-speech systems; but the model has also been offered as an account of how humans read aloud (e.g. by Marchand & Friedman, 2005).

However, there are two reasons why the PbA computational implementation of analogy theory cannot be regarded as a serious model of the human reading system. The first is that the PbA model is decidedly worse than human readers are at translating nonwords from print to speech: 'It appears that PbA – at least as implemented here and based on substring matching – is inadequate as a model of the human process of pronouncing pseudowords' (Damper & Eastmond, 1997, p. 19). An even more serious problem is that one of the trickiest[4] processes in reading aloud – graphemic parsing – is not attempted by the model, but is done in preprocessing by the modeler. The phonological lexicon used by the PbA model comes presegmented, with a segment for each *letter* in the word. Thus the pronunciation for THIGH, which has two phonemes, is not represented in this lexicon as two units, but as five, which are aligned with the word's spelling: the representation is /T * A * */. Similarly EIGHT is represented as /e * * *t/, 'thought' as /T * c * * * t/, 'though' as /D * o * * */, and so on. It is because these segmentations and alignments are not performed by the model but given to it by the modeler that one can't treat the PbA model as a serious competitor for modeling the human reading system.

It would seem, then, that the single-route approach to modeling the reading-aloud system has not succeeded. So a dual-route approach must be needed.

One might challenge this conclusion by pointing to various references in the literature which cite, as an example of a successful single-route model of reading aloud, the model of reading aloud proposed by Seidenberg and McClelland (1989; hereafter SM89), which will be discussed further below. For example, Tressoldi (2000, p. 278) refers to 'the class of single-route models' and cites the SM89 model as an example from that class. Simos, Breier, Wheless, Maggio, Fletcher, Castillo, et al. (2000, p. 2443) refer to 'single-route, connectionist theorists' and again cite the SM89 model as an example of this type of theorizing. Van den Bosch and Daelemans (2004, p. 55) say 'Single-route theory (for example Glushko, 1979; Seidenberg & McClelland, 1989) states that skilled reading aloud is accomplished by a single mechanism'. And Wilson, Leuthold, Moran, Pardo, Lewis, and Georgopoulos (2007, p. 248) refer to the SM89 model as a 'single-mechanism formulation'. There are various other references in the literature to the SM89 model as a 'single-route' or 'one-route' model.

However, such references do not represent challenges to my conclusion that the single-route approach to modelling the reading-aloud system has not succeeded, because they are all mistaken. Despite what these various references in the literature say, the SM89 model was *not* a single-route model; it was a dual-route model. The authors themselves emphasized this: 'Ours is a dual route model', they wrote (Seidenberg & McClelland, 1989, p. 559). This point is clear when one looks in any detail at their model or at the other models which were developed from theirs.

Seidenberg and McClelland (1989) and the triangle models of reading

The SM89 model contains three domains of representation: Orthography (O), Phonology (P), and Semantics (S). Each domain is connected to the other two, producing a triangular configuration: that is why this model, and other models subsequently developed using the same configuration, have come to be referred to as triangle models.

There are indeed two routes from print to speech in the SM89 model (a direct route from O to P, and an indirect route from O through S to P) and that is why the SM89 model is a dual-route model of reading aloud, as its authors stated.

The confusion in the literature about whether the SM89 model was a single-route or a dual-route model arose for two reasons. The first reason is that only one of the two routes, the O→P route, was computationally implemented by Seidenberg and McClelland. The second reason is that it was claimed by Seidenberg and McClelland that this single route was capable of correctly computing phonology from orthography for both irregular words and nonwords, which prompted those authors to conclude that

> our model refutes what Seidenberg (1988) has termed the central dogma linking different versions of the dual route model of naming, namely, that separate processes are required for naming exception words on the one hand and novel items on the other. Our model demonstrates that a single computation that takes spelling patterns into phonological codes is sufficient to account for naming of these types of items and others.
>
> (Seidenberg & McClelland, 1989, p. 558)

So the proponents of the SM89 model were not claiming that the human reading system contains only a single route from print to speech. They were instead claiming, following Glushko (1979), that the human reading system includes a single procedure that can correctly compute phonology from orthography both for irregular words and for nonwords, a claim that previous dual-route theorists had doubted or even rejected. Acceptance of this claim however does not entail rejection of the idea that the human reading system incorporates two routes from print to speech.

The claim made about the direct O→S route made here by Seidenberg and McClelland (1989) was based on the belief that the accuracy of the SM89 model's reading of nonwords was comparable to the accuracy of nonword reading by humans. This turned out not to be so. As noted by Plaut, McClelland, Seidenberg, and Patterson. (1996),

> the SM89 work has a serious empirical limitation that undermines its role in establishing a viable connectionist alternative to dual-route theories of word reading in particular and in providing a satisfactory formulation of the nature of knowledge and processing in quasi-regular domains more generally. Specifically, the implemented model is significantly worse than skilled readers at pronouncing nonwords (Besner, Twilley, McCann, & Seergobin, 1990). This limitation has broad implications for the range of empirical phenomena that can be accounted for by the model (Coltheart et al., 1993). Poor nonword reading is exactly what would be predicted from the dual-route claim that no single system – connectionist or otherwise – can read both exception words and pronounceable nonwords adequately. Under this interpretation, the model had simply approximated a lexical lookup procedure: It could read both regular and exception words but had not separately mastered the sublexical rules necessary to read nonwords.
>
> (1996, p. 57)

Plaut et al. (1996), however, did not accept this interpretation, but instead offered a different one, which was that the difficulties the SM89 model had with nonword reading were not intrinsic to the general triangle-model approach, but instead arose because of the particular choices Seidenberg and McClelland made about how to represent inputs and outputs in the model (each input unit represented a 'Wickelgraph', a randomly-constructed sequence of three letters, and each output unit represented a 'Wickelphone', a randomly-constructed sequence of three phonemes). Plaut and colleagues (1996) therefore created a successor to the SM89 model (this will be called the PSMP model from here onwards) that used new forms of input and output representation: each input unit was a local representation of a particular grapheme[5], and each output unit was a local representation of a particular phoneme.

The key point here was whether this new model's nonword reading behavior was comparable to that of human readers. This point turns out to involve a number of subtleties concerning what should count as correct reading aloud responses to nonwords.

Some remarks on nonword reading

The publisher, writer and editor Charles Ollier wrote to the poet Leigh Hunt on 11 December 1855 to report that his son had found a new way of spelling FISH (/fɪʃ/), namely, GHOTI, explaining that this involved GH as in TOUGH, O as in

WOMEN, and TI as in MENTION[6]. We would not expect our subjects in a reading-aloud experiment to read the nonword GHOTI as /fɪʃ/, and, if any subject did, that response would be scored as an error; to do otherwise would be absurdly liberal. On the other hand, to count as correct responses in nonword reading only those that conform to standard GPC rules is too conservative. The reason why this is too conservative is that it is not at all uncommon for skilled adult readers to produce reading-aloud responses to nonwords which do not conform to GPC rules.

For example, Seidenberg, Plaut, Petersen, McClelland, and McRae (1994) gave 24 subjects 590 nonwords to read. The actual responses produced by the subjects were recorded and analysed. For 206 of these nonwords (e.g. BELF), all 24 subjects produced exactly the same response. For 269 of the nonwords, two different responses occurred (e.g. some subjects read REAST to rhyme with BEAST and the remainder read it to rhyme with BREAST). For 100, three different responses were recorded (e.g. WESE rhyming with THESE, GEESE, or LESS). And for 15 there were four different responses (e.g. BREAT rhyming with TREAT, SWEAT, GREAT, or BRAT). The same multiplicity of response to nonwords was reported by Andrews and Scarratt (1998), who gave 44 subjects 216 nonwords to read. Across this set of nonwords the number of different pronunciations given by the subjects to a particular nonword varied from one (i.e. here the 44 subjects were unanimous) to seven.

Given such results from human nonword reading, how are we to judge whether a particular computational model has correctly read a particular nonword? The GPC-based response to BREAT rhymes it with TREAT, but if a model instead rhymes BREAT with SWEAT, GREAT or BRAT, it does not seem reasonable to count that as a failure of the model, because these are responses that human readers do produce. On the contrary: a model that is meant to offer an account of the human reading system should be expected to say something about this variability. This should be taken into account when evaluating a model's nonword reading performance: see, for example, Zevin and Seidenberg (2006).

Back to the PSMP model

Nonword reading by this model was tested using three sets of nonwords: consistent and inconsistent nonwords from Glushko (1979) and nonwords from McCann and Besner (1987). The model sometimes produced pronunciations which were not those specified by GPC rules, but it was almost always the case that when this happened the pronunciation was one which occurs in some real word which contained the same body as a the nonword, such as reading LOME to rhyme with COME. As we have seen, human readers do that too. Hence it may be that nonword reading by this model matches up in a satisfactory way, both quantitatively and qualitatively, with human nonword reading. To evaluate this rigorously one would need to compare the range of responses human readers make to particular nonwords with the response made to each of these nonwords by the PSMP model.

Computational models of reading are meant to be able to simulate not only read-ing in intact skilled readers but also impairments of reading after brain damage. One of the main lines of evidence for dual-route models is the double dissociation between surface dyslexia (poor reading of irregular words with good nonword reading, which is interpreted as selective damage to the lexical route and simu-lated in that way) and phonological dyslexia (poor reading of nonwords with good irregular-word reading, which is interpreted as selective damage to the nonlexical route and simulated in that way). Plaut and colleagues sought to simu-late surface dyslexia by various forms of lesioning of the implemented O→P route in their model, but this turned out not to be possible for the more severe of the two cases whose data they were simulating: when the O→P route was damaged severely enough for the model's accuracy of reading low-frequency irregular words to match the more-severely affected patient's accuracy, the model's nonword reading was also considerably impaired, whereas this patient's nonword reading was unimpaired.

So in the final simulation reported in their paper, the concept of division of labor between the PSMP model's two reading routes was introduced. Essentially the idea was that learning to read low-frequency irregular words is a very difficult job for the direct O→P route and that input to P from the indirect O→S→P route is needed for low frequency irregular words to be correctly read. The O→S→P route not having been implemented, input from S to P was artificially introduced in such a way that when training was terminated, the O→P pathway was not able to read all irregular words by itself; it needed, especially for low-frequency irregular words, input from the S system. Then damage to this input from the S system caused the model to behave like a patient with surface dyslexia. The difference between the milder patient MP and the more severe patient KT was simulated by assuming that premorbidly KT relied much more than MP did on S input to P for reading. So the network was trained for 2000 epochs to simulate KT but only 400 epochs to simulate MP (the more training, the greater the reli-ance on S for irregular word reading).

What this means is that, for the PSMP model to be able to simulate surface dyslexia, the O→P route of the model has to be imperfect at reading irregular words by itself (even though, when trained to read without any S input, it can become perfect at this task). So the claim that the human reading system contains a processing route that is perfect at reading irregular words and at reading nonwords, a claim that was central in the work of Seidenberg and McClelland (1989), had to be abandoned in order to make simulation of surface dyslexia by the triangle model possible. According to the model of Plaut and colleagues, the O→P route in the intact human reading system is imperfect at reading irregular words (if it were perfect, as was thought by Seidenberg and McClelland (1989), then the model could not explain surface dyslexia). The degree of this imperfec-tion is assumed to vary across individuals.

Other versions of the triangle model were created by Harm and Seidenberg (1999, 2004). At least six versions of the triangle model have been published. They share the overall common architecture of three modules (orthography, semantics, phonology) with pathways of communication from each module to each other module, but differ substantially in architectural detail. For example, orthography is represented via random three-letter sequences in one triangle model but as letters or as graphemes in other triangle models; phonology is represented via random three-phoneme sequences in one triangle model but as individual phonemes or as individual phonetic features in other triangle models. Table 1.1 lists features of each of these six versions of the triangle model.

How might we seek to choose between these various architecturally distinct versions of the class of triangle models? And more generally, how might we go about deciding whether the triangle model description of the nature of the human reading system is to be preferred to alternative models of this system, such as the DRC ('dual-route cascaded') model of Coltheart, Rastle, Perry, Langdon, and Ziegler (2001) or the CDP+ ('connectionist dual-process') model of Perry, Ziegler, and Zorzi (2007)? One way to attempt such adjudication between competing models is by invoking the principle of nested incremental modeling.

Nested incremental modeling

This is a principle for deciding whether or not theoretical progress is being made in modeling. The principle has been stated thus:

> A new model should be related to or include at least its own direct predecessors. The new model should also be tested against the data sets that motivated the construction of the old models before it is tested against new data sets
>
> (Jacobs & Grainger, 1994, pp. 1329–30;
> Perry et al., 2007, p. 273)

This statement of the principle needs some clarification, because of the possibility of tensions arising between the two components of the principle as stated. Suppose we have a model, model A, which does a good job of accounting for a wide range of effects that have been observed in the domain addressed by the model. Then a new effect X in this domain is discovered and it is found that model A cannot explain this effect. Suppose then that new theoretical work is done which culminates in the creation of a new model, model B, which *can* explain the new finding X. Has there been theoretical progress here? That depends on whether model B can also explain all the old effects that model A could explain. If amongst these old effects are ones that model A can explain while model B cannot, then model B cannot be considered as an advance on model A. Only if model B can explain *everything* that model A could explain, plus explaining at least one result that model A cannot explain, can the move from A to B be seen as constituting theoretical progress. That is the point of the principle of nested incremental modeling. Notice that what are nested here are the *sets of effects* that the two models can explain: the set of effects that A can explain is nested inside the set of effects that B can explain.

But in this example do we care about the relationship of model A to model B? In the statement of the principle as given in the previous paragraph, a second and

Table 1.1 Six variants of the triangle model of reading aloud. O = orthography, P = Phonology, S = Semantics

	Input units represent:	Output units represent:	Feedback?	Cleanup units?	Semantic input to phonology?	Lexical decision?	Form of position encoding	Pathways with no hidden units?
Seidenberg and McClelland (1989)	Random three-letter sequences ('Wickelgraphs')	Random three-phoneme sequences ('Wickelphones')	Yes	No	No	Yes	None (implicit in input and output coding schemes)	No
PSMP Simulations 1 and 2 (Plaut et al., 1996)	Graphemes	Phonemes	No	No	No	No	O and P both onset/vowel/coda	No
PSMP Simulation 3 (Plaut et al., 1996)	Graphemes	Phonemes	Yes	For P	No	No	O and P both onset/vowel/coda	No
PSMP Simulation 4 (Plaut et al., 1996; Woollams, Plaut, Lambon Ralph, and Patterson, 2007)	Graphemes	Phonemes	No	No	Yes	No	O and P both onset/vowel/coda	No
Harm and Seidenberg (1999); Zevin and Seidenberg (2006)	Letters	Phonetic features	No	For P	No	No	O and P both vowel-centred	No
Harm and Seidenberg, (2001, 2004)	Letters	Phonetic features	No	For P and for S	Yes	Yes	O and P both vowel-centred	Yes

unrelated conception of nesting is mentioned: the nesting of model A inside model B (B 'should include at least its own direct predecessors'). Suppose that, in the example we are considering, theory A was a theoretical dead end: no elaboration of it into some new model of which it would be a predecessor was able to explain effect X; what was needed was a completely new approach. If model B were entirely unrelated to model A, but could explain everything that model A could explain, plus being able to explain at least one finding that model A could not explain, that surely counts as an instance of theoretical progress? For this reason, I will take the principle of nested incremental modeling as stating that any model B counts as a theoretical advance over some other model A if and only if model B can explain everything that model A can explain plus being able to explain some new thing or things which model A cannot explain. When one sees successful examples of nested modeling in practice, it is common for model B to be an elaboration of model A, but I will not take this as a *requirement* for the replacement of model A by model B to be counted as an example of successful nested incremental modeling.[7]

This modeling principle is explicitly espoused by some groups of computational modelers of reading, such as the DRC modelers and the CDP+ modelers. But it is repudiated by the triangle modelers. For example, consideration of the progression from the 1989 Seidenberg and McClelland model to the 2001/2004 Harm and Seidenberg model (which involves six variants of the triangle model), as documented in Table 1.1, reveals numerous departures from the principle of nested incremental modeling.

Take the nature of the input representations in this sequence of models, for example. The move from Wickelgraphs and Wickelphones (Seiedenberg & McClelland, 1989) to graphemes and phonemes (Plaut et al., 1996) was theoretically motivated: the view was taken that the reason the SM89 model was not adequate at reading nonwords was that the model's input and output schemes did not permit sufficiently general knowledge about spelling–sound relationships to be learned during training, and it was argued that an input scheme using graphemic representations and an output scheme using phonemic representations would enable much better learning of such generalizations by the network – that is, would permit much better acquisition of knowledge that would support the reading of nonwords.

But the move from graphemes and phonemes (Plaut et al., 1996) to letters and phonetic features (Harm & Seidenberg,1999, 2004) was not an attempt to solve any problems caused by the use of graphemic and phonemic representations.

More generally, no systematic attempts have been made to compare one triangle model with another in terms of which effects each model can explain and which it can't. Instead, each model was created to explain some relatively small and circumscribed set of effects, with different models used to explain different sets of effects. Hence as one proceeds through the various triangle models in chronological order, one does not see any systematic increase in the number and scope of the findings each chronologically successive model can explain.

Suppose one asked: according to the triangle model approach, what form of input representation does the human reading system actually use? There is no answer, since some of the triangle models use letters and some use graphemes (and one uses Wickelgraphs). Similarly, the triangle approach is silent on the question of what form of output representation the human reading system uses for reading aloud, and on the question of whether the system includes feedback or not. Yet these are rather fundamental questions, answers to which one might expect any theory of how people read aloud to try to provide. It is because the triangle model approach has not adhered to the principle of nested incremental modeling that such questions are left unanswered.

What principles *have* guided the triangle-model (parallel-distributed process-ing or PDP) approach? This is discussed by Seidenberg and Plaut (2006). The PDP approach, they write,

> is grounded in a set of more completely specified and constrained principles. The emphasis in the PDP approach is not on capturing every empirical data point in a single model but rather on providing a framework for addressing issues that will continue to be the focus of attention for the foreseeable future.
>
> (2006, p. 26)

and they note that that a result of this approach is that

> in the short run, specific PDP models may not match particular empirical findings or account for as much variance in empirical data as approaches for which data fitting[8] is the primary goal
>
> (2006, p. 38)

The contrast between the triangle-model approach and the approach adopted by the DRC and CDP+ modelers (the nested incremental modeling approach) is very clear. The latter groups of modelers see modeling as a matter of getting closer and closer to the true functional architecture of the relevant human cogni-tive system. The triangle approach repudiates this idea:

> Where, then, is the integrative model that puts all the pieces together? The answer is there is none and there is not likely to be one . . . The goal of the en-terprise, as in the rest of science,[9] is the development of a general theory which *abstracts away from* details of the phenomena to reveal general, fundamental principles. Each model serves to explore a part of this theory-in-progress.
>
> (2006, p. 42)

In contrast, the nested incremental modeling approach *focuses in on* details of the phenomena, rather than abstracting away from them. One way in which this is done is by seeking to assemble a list of all the well-attested phenomena in the field and evaluating any model by determining which of these phenomena the model can explain (or simulate, in the case of computational models) and which it cannot: the nesting of the set of phenomena that have been explained by an old model inside the set that a new model can explain must be respected here.

This approach was adopted by Coltheart et al. (2001, p. 251), who listed 27 effects (from the literatures on skilled reading aloud, visual lexical decision, acquired dyslexia and the Stroop effect) that the DRC model reported by Coltheart et al. (2001) could successfully simulate. This was seen as a list of benchmark effects that would assist nested incremental modeling in the sense that if some new version of the DRC model, or some alternative computational model, were to be developed, the principle of nested incremental modeling requires that these new models be able to simulate these benchmark effects, as well as being able to simulate new effects that previously existing models could not.

The same approach was adopted by Perry et al. (2007) in relation to their CDP+ ('connectionist dual-process') computational model of reading aloud. Their table 4 listed 13 benchmark effects (from the literatures on skilled reading aloud and acquired dyslexia) and evaluated three computational models of reading aloud (the DRC model, the CDP+ model, and the triangle model) in terms of how many of these benchmark effects each model could simulate. The triangle model fared least well here, but given that modelers working within this framework reject the nested incremental modeling approach one might expect this to have no influence on their future modeling work. However, a set of four effects from the literature which the CDP+ model could simulate but the DRC model could not have an effect on DRC modeling work, since those doing such work *do* subscribe to the nested incremental modeling approach, and so must seek to meet the challenge represented by these four effects.

The DRC model and the consistency effect

Coltheart et al. (2001) discussed the body-consistency effect reported by Jared (1997, Experiment 4) because any effect genuinely due to the body acting as an orthographic unit will be inconsistent with the DRC model as formulated in Coltheart et al. (2001) (since that model does not use the body as an orthographic unit). Surprisingly, there was a consistency effect in DRC's RTs with the materials from this experiment. Coltheart and colleagues were able to show that in the materials used in that experiment there were confoundings of consistency with regularity and with the whammy effect (Rastle & Coltheart, 1998). Hence the results of Jared (1997) turned out not to be problematic for the DRC model.

However, in subsequent work Jared (2002), using very well-matched materials that avoided these confoundings, obtained a consistency effect, and she also showed that the DRC model did not produce this effect with her items even though her human readers did. This effect was one of the four in the benchmark list offered by Perry et al. (2007) which the CDP+ model could simulate but the DRC model could not.

The full list of these effects was:

(a) As mentioned above, Jared (2002), using a particularly well-controlled stimulus set, showed that regular words were read with longer RTs when they were inconsistent than when they were consistent provided that the summed frequency of their orthographic enemies was higher than the summed frequency of their orthographic friends.

(b) In nonword reading, subjects do not always make the response that is prescribed by GPC rules (Andrews & Scarratt, 1998).

(c) Reading accuracy for irregular words by the surface dyslexic patient MP is influenced by the degree of consistency of these words (Patterson & Behrmann, 1997.)

(d) Words with many body neighbors are read with faster RTs than words with few body neighbors (Ziegler Perry, Jacobs, and Braun, 2001).

These four DRC failures to simulate may have a single cause: they all suggest, in one way or another, that the current DRC model[10] is insufficiently sensitive to orthographic bodies. It is therefore conceivable that a single alteration to the model – an alteration that makes the model more sensitive to bodies – might allow all four effects to be simulated by such a modified version of the model. If that turns out to be true, then these four failures to simulate will not be devastating for the general enterprise of DRC modeling.[11]

In what way might the current DRC model be modified that might enable it to simulate these four effects? Coltheart (1985) suggested three ways in which the standard dual-route theory might be revised so as to make it more sensitive to orthographic bodies, if this should prove necessary. All three are implementable in the DRC computational version of dual-route theory. The three ways considered by Coltheart (1985) were as follows:

(a) Adding body-rime rules to the nonlexical reading route, as suggested by Patterson and Morton (1985). If there were such rules, then the phoneme activations generated by the body-rime rules would agree with those generated by the GPC rules for consistent words or nonwords, whereas there would be conflict for inconsistent words or nonwords. Such conflict might produce a consistency effect in the DRC model's reading of regular words and nonwords. Only implementation and then simulation will tell us whether this move will allow reconciliation between the DRC model and the effects of consistency.

(b) A less radical possibility is to introduce variable GPC rule strengths into the DRC model. The grapheme ⟨EE⟩ is pronounced /i:/ in all (at least monosyllabic) words, whereas the grapheme OO has three different pronunciations in words that contain it. This corresponds to the fact that the regular word MEET is consistent whereas the regular word MOOD is inconsistent. So one can conceive of the GPC rule ⟨EE⟩ → /i:/ as being stronger – producing more rapidly rising activations in its phoneme unit – than the GPC rule ⟨OO⟩ → /u:/. That might produce faster responding by DRC to MEET than to MOOD. Rosson (1985) reported results from experiments on reading aloud words and nonwords that she interpreted as supporting the concept of variable GPC rule strengths. I refer to this possibility as 'less radical' because it does not involve any architectural change to the DRC model (whereas adding body-rime rules does). In the present version of the DRC model, all of the GPC rules have strengths of 1: that could very easily be modified once one has decided on how GPC rule strength should be measured (there are various possible ways of doing this).

(c) Even less radical is the third possibility considered by Coltheart (1985): that the inconsistency of a nonword such as YEAD hurts its reading because nonwords activate their orthographic neighbors, and YEAD has the neighbor HEAD whose vowel pronunciation conflicts with the pronunciation specified by the GPC rules. This is an even less radical possibility because it requires just a change in a single parameter of the DRC model: letter→word inhibition. The lower the value of this parameter, the more strongly an input string will activate words in the orthographic lexicon that are orthographically similar to it. In the current version of DRC, this parameter is set very high because if it is not there are lexical influences on nonword pronunciation, that is, nonwords are not always read as the GPC rules dictate. But it was a mistake to do this, because human readers don't always read nonwords as the GPC rules dictate.

All three of these ways of modifying the DRC model so that it might be able to simulate the four body effects identified by Perry et al. (2007) are currently being investigated. If a solution is found – a modification of the model which allows it to simulate all four effects – the principle of nested incremental modeling demands that there then be an investigation of whether the new version of the DRC model can still simulate all the effects that the previous version did.

The CDP+ model

Comparisons between the DRC and CDP+ model focus on the nonlexical routes of these models because the CDP+ lexical route has been imported from the DRC model, whereas the CDP+ nonlexical route is quite different from that of DRC. The CDP+ nonlexical route is not based on a set of explicit GPC rules, but consists of a connectionist network trained on a set of spelling–sound correspondences using a connectionist learning algorithm, the Delta rule.

So an important issue is to consider how good a job the CDP+ model does of simulating human nonword reading. A detailed evaluation of this remains to be done, but two potentially problematic points can be identified already.

The first point concerns the whammy effect (Rastle & Coltheart, 1998). The nonlexical route of the DRC model operates left-to-right, letter by letter, translating print to phonology. Consider the nonword PHAL. When the nonlexical route begins to analyse this nonword, it initially processes just the first letter, and so via the grapheme-phoneme correspondence rule ⟨P⟩→/p/ activates the phoneme /p/ in the first-position set of phoneme units. Some time later the nonlexical route moves on to the second letter so now is analysing the two-letter sequence ⟨PH⟩. Via the grapheme-phoneme correspondence rule ⟨PH⟩→/f/ the phoneme /f/ in the first-position set of phoneme units will be activated. But in this set of units a different phoneme, /p/, will already have been activated. There is lateral inhibition within each set of phoneme units. Hence activation of the correct phoneme /f/ will be slowed by inhibition from the incorrect preactivated phoneme /p/. That will slow the reading aloud response to PHAL, compared to a nonword such as PRAL which will not excite competing phonemes within any phoneme set. This effect predicted by the DRC model was confirmed by Rastle and Coltheart (1998), who called it the 'whammy effect', and Coltheart et al. (2001) successfully simulated the effect with the DRC model.

This effect is important for computational models of reading. Firstly, models that have no serial processing component (such as the connectionist triangle model of reading) will not be able to simulate it, since serial processing is critical for the effect to occur. But even a model which does include serial processing, the CDP+ model, does not simulate this effect (see Perry et al., 2007, pp. 294–295). So at present the only computational model in existence that can simulate the whammy effect is the DRC model.

The second point concerns nonword reading in general. CDP+ often produces responses to nonwords which differ from the response that is dictated by GPC rules but, as mentioned above, this is true of human readers too: so that in itself is not a problem. However, some of CDP+'s nonword reading responses seem to be responses that no human reader would ever produce. Table 1.2 provides some examples (the responses are coded using the phonetic symbols from Perry et al., 2007).

At present, we only have our intuitions to tell us whether these particular responses to these particular nonwords would ever be made by any human reader; but these results do suggest that a detailed comparison between CDP+'s nonword reading and human reading of the same nonwords needs to be carried out.[12]

Table 1.2 Some readings of nonwords by the CDP+ model which seem unlikely ever to be produced by any human skilled reader

Stimulus	CDP+ response	Error type
STRAST	str#t (rhymes with 'bat')	S missing
DECH	dE (short vowel E as in 'bet')	CH missing
DIFTS	drIfts ('drifts')	/r/ inserted
FYXE	f2kst (vowel as in 'die')	Final /t/ added
FALG	f{l (rhymes with 'pal')	G missing
HOLK	h5 ('ho')	LK missing
WAUST	w9t ('wart')	S missing
BANTCH	b{n ('ban')	TCH missing
STRUTCH	strVJs ('strutch' followed by 's')	Final /s/ added
FITHE	f2 ('fie')	TH missing
STYGS	strIgz (rhymes with 'pigs')	/r/ inserted
FLOYT	fl4ts (rhymes with 'quoits')	Final /s/ added
NEWKS	njEkst (rhymes with 'next')	Final /t/ added
SPROND	sprEnd (rhymes with 'spend')	Incorrect vowel

Conclusion

All current theories of reading aloud are dual-route theories; there was once a single-route theory but it has not survived. Woollams et al. (2007) used the word 'consensus' here, by which they meant that

> Current computational models of normal and disordered reading aloud differ in their architectural, representational, and processing assumptions. There is, however, general agreement that there are at least two procedures involved in the translation of orthography to phonology (O→P), one restricted to whole-word information and the other including or specializing in subword information.
>
> (2007, p. 316)

Current theories and computational models of reading aloud certainly differ in very many details, but when one defines the dual-route conception generically, in a way that abstracts away from these details, all of these theories/models contain two routes – let's call them route X and route Y – with unanimous agreement on the following general characterizations of the two routes:

ROUTE X: this route correctly translates print to speech for any word known to the reader (regardless of whether it is regular or irregular), but cannot perform this task correctly for any nonword.

ROUTE Y: this route is required if a nonword is to be read correctly, and it performs perfectly also for regular words. However, it has difficulty with irregular words. The various models disagree on the severity of this difficulty, but all agree that there is a route in the reading system that is imperfect at reading irregular words aloud while being perfect at reading regular words aloud.

Hence there is now a consensus that, broadly speaking, Marshall and Newcombe (1973) and Forster and Chambers (1973) were right. It seems highly unlikely that the future will see any disturbance to this consensus about the functional architecture of the human reading system.

Acknowledgments

I thank Ken Forster for an extremely valuable critique of an earlier version of this chapter, and Stephen Pritchard for many useful comments.

- How do people read aloud? According to the dual-route theory of reading aloud, skilled readers have acquired two different procedures for doing this: one based on rules that map letters to sounds, and the other involving looking up a mental dictionary of the spellings and pronunciations of words.

- This theory, first proposed by two independent groups in 1973, was for a time challenged by the theory that there is only a single procedure by which reading aloud is achieved, but that single-route theory failed to explain much that became known about reading, and so has not succeeded. Thus the dual-route theory of reading aloud is currently universally accepted by reading theorists.
- But there are currently various different forms of dual-route theory, and much theoretical and empirical work is currently being devoted to evaluating the relative merits of these different forms of dual-route theory.
- Some of these theories are developed using connectionist learning algorithms to build their structures. Other theorists do not consider that such algorithms are psychologically realistic and so 'hard-wire' the structure of their models.
- Some theorists in this area adhere to the principle of 'nested incremental modeling', according to which, if scientific progress is to occur, any new model must be able to explain all the facts that the model it is replacing can explain, plus some new ones. Other reading theorists do not concern themselves with this as a criterion for scientific progress.
- There are two distinctions that are critical in research on reading. One is the distinction between regular and irregular words: regular words are those which obey the standard letter–sound rules of English (e.g. SAVE) and irregular words are those which disobey these rules (e.g. HAVE). The other is the distinction between consistent and inconsistent letter-strings. A consistent letter string is one whose orthographic body is pronounced in the same way in all the words in which it occurs: REED and ZEED are examples, their orthographic bodies being –EED. A consistent letter string is one whose orthographic body is pronounced in more than one way in the words in which it occurs: RAVE and ZAVE are examples, their orthographic bodies being –AVE, which has different pronunciations in the words HAVE and SAVE. Human reading is affected by both regularity and consistency, so any theory or model of reading has to explain both of these facts if it is to be considered adequate.

Notes

1 These terms are synonymous. I will use the term 'irregular' throughout this chapter.
2 He sometimes used the synonym 'exception' for 'irregular'.
3 Deep and surface dyslexia.
4 'Segmentation of printed character strings into pronunciations is a significant impediment to nonlexical print-to-sound translation' (Berndt, Reggia, and Mitchum, 1994, p. 987).

5 Note therefore that, as with the PbA model described earlier, this model does not have to cope with the difficult task of parsing letters into graphemes: that is done in precoding by the modelers.

6 This is often (wrongly) attributed to George Bernard Shaw.

7 As such, what is described here as 'nested incremental modeling' does not necessarily involve 'nested models' in the statistical sense – *JSA*.

8 These authors are using 'data fitting' as a synonym for the activity of seeking to 'match particular empirical findings', which seems an odd use of the term 'data fitting'.

9 Do the theories in other sciences – physics, microbiology, astronomy – really abstract away from the details of data in this way? I don't think so.

10 The current version of the DRC model is DRC 1.2.1 (used by, for example, Mousikou, Coltheart, Saunders, and Yen, 2010, and referred to there as DRC beta6), and is downloadable from http://www.maccs.mq.edu.au/~ssaunder/DRC/2009/10/drc-1-2-1/. It can simulate some effects that the original DRC model could not, but it still does not simulate effects of consistency.

11 Perry et al. (2007) also note that the correlations across individual words between human and model naming latencies are lower for DRC than for CDP+. It will be important therefore to see whether any modification to the DRC model that enables it to simulate consistency effects also improves these correlations.

12 This has now been done (Pritchard et al., 2012, in press). This work shows that the nonword reading responses produced by the DRC model correspond much more closely to the responses produced by human readers than do the nonword reading responses of the CDP+ model.

References

Andrews, S. & Scarratt, D. R. (1998). Rule and analogy mechanisms in reading nonwords: Hough Dou Peapel Rede Gnew Wirds? *Journal of Experimental Psychology: Human Perception and Performance, 24*, 1052–1086.

Baron, J. & Strawson, C. (1976). Use of orthographic and word-specific knowledge in reading words aloud. *Journal of Experimental Psychology: Human Perception and Performance, 2*, 386–393.

Berndt, R. S., D'Autrechy, C. L., & Reggia, J. A. (1994). Functional pronunciation units in English words. *Journal of Experimental Psychology: Learning, Memory and Cognition, 20*, 977–991.

Coltheart, M. (1985). In defence of dual-route models of reading. *Behavioral and Brain Sciences, 8*, 709–710.

Coltheart, M., Rastle, K., Perry, C., Langdon, R., & Ziegler, J. C. (2001). DRC: A computational model of visual word recognition and reading aloud. *Psychological Review, 108*, 204–256.

Damper, R. I. & Eastmond, J. F. G. (1997). Pronunciation by analogy: Impact of implementational choices on performance. *Language and Speech, 40*, 1–23.

Forster, K. I. & Chambers, S. M. (1973). Lexical access and naming time. *Journal of Verbal Learning and Verbal Behavior, 12*, 627–635.

Frederiksen, J. R. & Kroll, J. F. (1976). Spelling and sound: Approaches to the internal lexicon. *Journal of Experimental Psychology: Human Perception and Performance, 2*, 361–379.

Glushko, R. J. (1979). The organization and activation of orthographic knowledge in reading aloud. *Journal of Experimental Psychology: Human Perception & Performance, 5*, 674–691.

Glushko, R. J. (1981). Principles for pronouncing print: The psychology of phonography. In A. M. Lesgold & C. A. Perfetti (Eds.), *Interactive processes in reading* (pp. 61–84). Hillsdale, NJ: Lawrence Erlbaum Associates.

Harm, M. W. & Seidenberg, M. S. (1999). Phonology, reading acquisition, and dyslexia: Insights from connectionist models. *Psychological Review, 106,* 491–528.

Harm, M. W. & Seidenberg, M. S. (2004). Computing the meanings of words in reading: Cooperative division of labor between visual and phonological processes. *Psychological Review, 111,* 662–720.

Jacobs, A. M. & Grainger, J. (1994). Models of visual word recognition: Sampling the state of the art. *Journal of Experimental Psychology: Human Perception and Performance, 20,* 1311–1334.

Jared, D. (1997). Spelling-sound consistency affects the naming of high-frequency words. *Journal of Memory and Language, 36,* 505–529.

Jared, D. (2002). Spelling-sound consistency and regularity effects in word naming. *Journal of Memory and Language, 46,* 723–750.

Kay, J. & Marcel, A. (1981). One process, not two, in reading aloud: Lexical analogies do the work of non-lexical rules. *Quarterly Journal of Experimental Psychology Section A: Human Experimental Psychology, 33,* 397–413.

McCann, R., & Besner, D. (1987). Reading pseudohomophones: Implications for models of pronunciation assembly and the locus of word frequency effects in naming. *Journal of Experimental Psychology: Human Perception and Performance, 13,* 14–24.

Marcel, T. (1980). Surface dyslexia and the beginning reader: A revised hypothesis of the pronunciation of print and its impairments. In M. Coltheart, K. Patterson, & J. C. Marshall (Eds.), *Deep Dyslexia.* London: Routledge & Kegan Paul.

Marchand, Y. & Friedman, R. (2005). Impaired oral reading in two atypical dyslexics: A comparison with a computational lexical-analogy model. *Brain and Language, 93,* 255–266.

Marshall, J. C. & Newcombe, F. (1973). Patterns of paralexia: A psycholinguistic approach. *Journal of Psycholinguistic Research, 2,* 175–199.

Mousikou, P., Coltheart, M., Saunders, S., & Yen, L. (2010). Is the orthographic/phonological onset a single unit in reading aloud? *Journal of Experimental Psychology: Human Perception and Performance, 36,* 175–194.

Patterson, K. & Behrmann, M. (1997). Frequency and consistency effects in a pure surface dyslexic patient. *Journal of Experimental Psychology: Human Perception and Performance, 23,* 1217–1231.

Patterson, K. E. & Morton, J. (1985). From orthography to phonology: An attempt at an old interpretation. In K. E. Patterson, J. C. Marshall, & M. Coltheart (Eds.), *Surface Dyslexia.* Hillsdale, NJ: Lawrence Erlbaum Associates.

Perry, C., Ziegler, J. C., & Zorzi, M. (2007). Nested incremental modeling in the development of computational theories: The CDP+ model of reading aloud. *Psychological Review, 114,* 273–315.

Plaut, D. C., McClelland, J. L., Seidenberg, M. S., & Patterson, K. (1996). Understanding normal and impaired word reading: Computational principles in quasi-regular domains. *Psychological Review, 103,* 56–115.

Pritchard, S., Coltheart, M., and Castles, A. (2012). Nonword reading: Comparing Dual-Route Cascaded and Connectionist Dual-Process models with human data. *Journal of Experimental Psychology, Human Perception and Performance* (in press).

Rastle, K. & Coltheart, M. (1998). Whammies and double whammies: The effect of length on nonword reading. *Psychonomic Bulletin & Review, 5,* 277–282.

Rosson, M. B. (1985) The interaction of pronunciation rules and lexical representations in reading aloud. *Memory & Cognition, 13*, 90–99.

Seidenberg, M. S. & McClelland, J. L. (1989). A distributed, developmental model of word recognition and naming. *Psychological Review, 96*, 523–568.

Seidenberg, M. S. & Plaut, D. C. (2006). Progress in understanding word reading: Data fitting versus theory building. In S. Andrews (Ed.), *From Inkmarks to Ideas: Current Issues in Lexical Processing*. Hove, UK: Psychology Press.

Seidenberg, M. S., Plaut, D. C., Petersen, A. S., McClelland, J. L., & McRae, K. (1994). Nonword pronunciation and models of word recognition. *Journal of Experimental Psychology: Human Perception and Performance, 20*, 1177–1196.

Simos, P. G., Breier, J. I., Wheless, J. W., Maggio, W. W., Fletcher, J. M., Castillo, E. M., & Papanicolaou, A. C. (2000). Brain mechanisms for reading: the role of the superior temporal gyrus in word and pseudoword naming. *NeuroReport, 11*, 2443–2447.

Tressoldi, P. E. (2000). Treatment of specific developmental reading disorders, derived from single- and dual-route models. *Journal of Learning Disabilities 33*, 278–285.

Van den Bosch, A. & Daelemans, W. (2004). A distributed, yet symbolic, model for text-to-speech processing. In Broeder, P., and Murre, J. (Eds.), *Models of Language Acquisition*. Oxford: Oxford University Press.

Wilson, T. W., Leuthold, A. C., Moran, J. E., Pardo, P. J., Lewis, S. M., & Georgopoulos, A. P. (2007). Reading in a deep orthography: Neuromagnetic evidence for dual-mechanisms. *Experimental Brain Research, 180*, 247–262.

Woollams, A. M., Plaut, D. C., Lambon Ralph, M. A., & Patterson, K. (2007). SD-squared: On the association between semantic dementia and surface dyslexia. *Psychological Review, 114*, 316–339.

Zevin, J. D. & Seidenberg, M. S. (2006). Simulating consistency effects and individual differences in nonword naming: A comparison of current models. *Journal of Memory and Language, 54*, 145–160.

Ziegler, J. C., Perry, C., Jacobs, A. M., & Braun, M. (2001). Identical words are read differently in different languages. *Psychological Science, 12*, 379–384.

2 Learned orthographic representations facilitates large-scale modeling of word recognition

Daragh E. Sibley and Christopher T. Kello

Computational models are valuable tools for theory building, particularly for exploring whether cognitive processes are sufficient to account for a pattern of behavioral data. This is apparent in the lexical processing literature, where progress over the last three decades is marked by the development and refinement of computational models (e.g., Morton, 1970; McClelland & Rumelhart, 1981; Seidenberg & McClelland, 1989; Plaut, McClelland, Seidenberg, & Patterson, 1996; Grainger & Jacobs, 1996; Harm & Seidenberg, 1999; Davis, 1999; Coltheart, Rastle, Perry, Langdon, & Ziegler, 2001; Kello, 2006; Perry, Ziegler, & Zorzi, 2007; Sibley, Kello, & Seidenberg, 2010). These models constrain theorizing about the representations and mechanisms involved in word recognition behaviors.

A productive line of modeling has examined how domain general learning processes might support the acquisition of skilled reading behaviors (e.g., Seidenberg & McClelland, 1989; Plaut et al., 1996; Harm & Seidenberg, 2004; Sibley et al., 2010). These models show how a system that learns orthographic (i.e., spelling) to sound or meaning correspondences can simulate many behavioral phenomena displayed by typical and dyslexic readers. To focus on this process, modelers stipulated orthographic representations that could support the recognition of some English words. While this strategy has yielded numerous theoretically informative models, it does not inform how orthographic representations are learned.

Orthographic representations are more than just the visual form of a word, because they must be invariant to a stimulus' particular visual properties (e.g., position on the retina, font, or case; Dehaene, Le Clec'H, Poline, Le Bihan, & Cohen, 2002, Dehaene, Jobert, Naccache, Ciuciu, Poline, Le Bihan, et al., 2004). Moreover, children acquire orthographic representations in the context of a given writing system and so orthography is considered the first language-specific representation used during reading (Grainger, 2008). There is an active field examining the neural circuits that support orthographic learning (Vinckier, Dehaene, Jobert, Dubus, Sigman, & Cohen, 2007; Price & Devlin, 2003). These studies have identified cortical sites involved in orthographic representation, most notably the putative Visual Word Form Area (Warrington & Shallice, 1980), where activation changes as a function of reading skill (Shaywitz, Shaywitz, Pugh, Mencl, Fulbright, Skudlarski, et al., 2002). Anomalies in this region's activation have been repeatedly implicated in delayed and disordered reading acquisition (e.g.,

Cohen, Martinaud, Lemer, Lehericy, Samson, Obadia, et al., 2003) and change as a function of reading intervention (Shaywitz et al., 2004). Collectively, these behavioral and neurobiological studies indicate that activation in cortical regions engaged by orthographic processes changes over reading development and indicates the critical role that learning plays in the formation of orthographic representations.

The orthographic representations used in a model will critically impact its performance because they are the inputs that drive subsequent processing. The orthographic representations stipulated for most models limit them to processing monosyllabic words or words of a restricted length. The English Lexicon Project (ELP; Balota, Cortese, Hutchison, Neely, Nelson, Simpson, et al., 2002) contains lexical decision latencies for more than 40,000 different English words, most of which are multisyllabic. Extant models cannot process these multisyllabic words and so cannot inform theories of multisyllabic word recognition. More generally, a model that is fundamentally incapable of processing the majority of words in an adult's vocabulary has a limited capacity to inform theories of adult word recognition behaviors.

In this chapter, we demonstrate how one might scale up models of visual word recognition using a system that learns orthographic representations, termed a sequence encoder. We show that learned distributed representations of orthography can be used to access a simple lexical system. The resulting network accounts for variance associated with many stimulus characteristics that influence word recognition behaviors. We conclude that this demonstrates the utility of integrating systems that learn orthographic representations into existing frameworks.

Existing models of orthographic representation

One of the original simulations of word recognition, the Interactive Activation model, utilizes a slot-based scheme of orthographic representation (McClelland & Rumelhart, 1981). This scheme uses four slots that correspond to the four positions in a four-letter word. Each slot codes information independently, and so each letter is represented independently in each of the four slots. As a result, this system cannot support the recognition of any similarity between words that share letters in different positions. To illustrate, the letter sequences FLOW and WOLF are no more similar than FLOW and ZZZZ.

The orthographic layer in the Interactive Activation model is connected to a lexical layer, where a separate node represents each known word. The orthographic layer's four slots have independent connections to each node in the lexical layer. Activation propagates through these connections in both directions: orthographic nodes send activation to lexical nodes, and active lexical nodes propagate activity back to orthographic nodes. So activation of the four letters C, A, R, and T (in slots corresponding to this order) would induce activation in the lexical node that represents the word CART. This orthographic representation would partially activate any lexical nodes representing a word that share letters in the same slots (e.g., CARS and to a lesser extent BARD). The CART and CARS nodes would both reinforce activation of the letters nodes C, A, and R, in their respective slots. In this way, an orthographic input that was similar to multiple lexical items could receive additional activation. However, in response to the orthographic input C, A, R, and T the CARS node may also moderately activate the letter S in the fourth slot. This activation would diminish during a settling process, where activation repeatedly flowed between the orthographic and lexical layers of representations. Through this process of Interactive Activation, orthographically similar words could influence each other's processing. These types of words have become known as orthographic neighbors and there are myriad demonstrations that a word's orthographic neighborhood effects how it is processed (for a review, see Andrews, 1997).

The Interactive Activation model is a seminal contribution to the field of word recognition, but it has substantial limitations that stem from its orthographic representations. Because orthography was coded using four slots, the Interactive Activation model could only process four-letter stimuli. As a part of the Dual Route Cascaded model, Coltheart et al. (2001) adapted the Interactive Activation framework to allow for words with one to eight letters. This model utilized eight slots, where empty slots at the end of a word were filled with a 'null character'. Although a step forward, maintaining slot-based representations means that each letter in each position is still coded independently. These models cannot treat two words as orthographically similar if they share the same letters in different positions. In a slot code, the palindromes DRAWER and REWARD are not represented as more similar than DRAWER and the letter string XXXXXX.

The problem associated with slot codes is exacerbated when representing words of variable length, where it is unclear how to define positions (see Plaut et al., 1996; Davis, 1999; and Sibley, Kello, Plaut, & Elman, 2008). Again, taking the DRC model as an example, Coltheart et al. (2001) aligned letters to slots using the front of a word and so could conceivably recognize that JUMP and JUMPS are orthographically similar. However, a front alignment scheme cannot capture any similarity between the strings BACK and ABACK. More generally, when dealing with words of different lengths, a front alignment scheme cannot generalize information about word final regularities (e.g., -ING) and a back alignment scheme will not generalize learning about word initial dependencies (e.g., UN-). In sum, any system that utilizes slot codes will have difficulty recognizing orthographic similarities between many words, particularly when they are of different lengths.

These issues are exacerbated when considering a set of words with a variety of number of syllables. For instance, consider the CDP++ model that reads mono- and disyllabic words (Perry, Ziegler, & Zorzi, 2010). Here, letters are parsed into graphemes that are assigned to slots, which are defined by position within a syllable and this syllable's position in a word. This orthographic representation requires a procedure for optimally aligning words into syllabic slots. This algorithm, which is external to the model, must align each monosyllabic word to either the first or second syllabic slot, prior to any processing. As a result, any learning that is achieved on a grapheme in a given syllable cannot be generalized to the same grapheme in a different syllable. To illustrate, learning about the pronunciation of BALL, in BALLER and JUMPBALL is independent. The problems associated with these syllabic slots would be further exacerbated in models that attempt to read words with 1, 2, 3, 4, or 5 syllables. This stands in stark contrast to an adult's ability to read words.

Orthographic representational schemes have been designed to avoid positionally-defined slots. Wickelgren (1969) and later Seidenberg and McClelland (1989) adopted this approach when they coded each letter in a word with respect to the adjacent letters. In effect, this scheme represents a word's orthography as a set of unordered trigrams or letter triples. Some positional information is imbedded in these representations, because a word is considered to be flanked by delimiting characters. To illustrate, the orthographic representation for CAT would be composed of the triples #CA, CAT, and AT#. This scheme can similarly represent words of different lengths (e.g., relative to CAT, consider AT-#AT and AT#), but only if letters occur in the same relative order; WAS and SAW are composed of totally different trigrams. Ultimately, this form of orthographic representation was shown to limit the Seidenberg and McClelland (1989) model of reading. Plaut et al. (1996) replaced these representations with a vowel-centered slot-based code (among other changes) and showed it improved the models ability to simulate word reading behaviors. However, the scheme utilized by Plaut et al. (1996) limits the model to processing only monosyllabic words and inherited the previously discussed problems with slot codes.

Mozer (1987) and Whitney (2001) extended the approach of Wickelgren by coding letters with respect to the adjacent and non-adjacent letters in a word. These open bigram or trigram codes provide additional information that helps disambiguate between words and allows the system to extract dependencies between non-adjacent letters. Grossberg (1978) and later Davis (1999) adopted a different approach, termed *spatial coding*, which does not use slots or explicitly code letters with respect to the surrounding letters. Davis's (1999) spatial coding represents orthography as a vector with 26 dimensions, where each dimension corresponds to a particular English letter. Activation along a given dimension indicates the presence of a particular letter in a word. Information about the order of letters is conveyed by the relative level of activation of each dimension. The dimension corresponding to the first letter is the most activated and dimensions for subsequent letters receive a monotonically decreasing amount of activation. The advantage of this representational scheme, relative to a slot code, is that letters occurring in different positions of a word are coded similarly. However, Grainger, Granier, Farioli, Van Assche, and van Heuven (2006) have questioned whether these representations have sufficient sensitivity to the relative order of letters.

The extant schemes for representing orthography all have strengths and weaknesses. These are a function of the purpose for which they were designed. For instance, the Interactive Activation model used a slot code because it was simple and sufficient to demonstrate some properties of systems with interacting levels of representation. Similarly, Grainger and van Heuven (2003) have created representations based on open-bigrams that address a substantial body of data regarding transposition letter effects and repetition priming. However, to our knowledge these representational systems have not been implemented in large-scale simulations of the lexical decision task. So there is an open question regarding how they will perform on a large scale, and whether they can simulate phenomena that only exist in multisyllabic words. Further, these schemes do not address our primary concern in this chapter, which is how orthographic representations might be learned.

Learning orthographic representations

The representational schemes discussed above do not address the process that acquires information about the statistical dependencies between letters in a writing system. For example, studies have shown that infants and adults have a remarkable capacity to learn about the statistical dependencies in linguistic sequences (Aslin, Saffran, & Newport, 1999; Jusczyk, Luce, & Charles-Luce, 1994; Saffran, 2001). At only 8 months of age, infants are acquiring knowledge about the probability of some sounds following other sounds (Saffran, Aslin & Newport, 1996). Infants also learn about the backwards transitional probabilities between sounds (Pelucchi, Hay, & Saffran, 2009). There is even evidence of early learning of statistical dependencies between non-adjacent elements (Gomez, 2002; Newport & Aslin, 2004). The learning of these dependencies is thought to support the segmentation of discrete words out of a continuous acoustic stream (Saffran et al., 1996), early word labeling (Graf-Estes et al., 2007), and learning about the grammatical and semantic properties of words based on their distributional properties (Lany & Saffran, 2010).

The effect of learned orthographic dependencies is evident in many lexical tasks. For instance, participants can identify single letters more rapidly when they are embedded within words relative to random sequences of letters (Reicher, 1969; Bergman, Hudson, & Eling, 1988; Frisch, Large, Zawaydeh, & Pisoni, 2001; Grainger, Bouttevin, Truc, Bastien, & Ziegler, 2003; Maris, 2002; Wheeler, 1970). This effect does not occur exclusively at the lexical level; single letters are identified faster in nonwords that conform to the statistical dependences between letters in a language's writing system (Aderman & Smith, 1971; Baron & Thurston, 1973).

Sensitivity to learned orthographic dependencies is evident when participants explicitly distinguish between sequences that do and do not conform to the regularities of a language. Bailey and Hahn (2001) showed that subject's judgments of a nonword's legality could be predicted in part by the nonword's conformity to transitional probabilities in English words. This predictive power was largely independent of the nonword's similarity to particular English words, with measures of the nonword's lexical neighborhood accounting for a largely independent portion of variance in the subjects' judgments. This suggests that the locus of this statistical learning is at least partially at the orthographic level.

In light of these issues, Sibley, Kello, Plaut, and Elman, (2008, 2009) created the sequence encoder, a connectionist architecture that learns orthographic and phonological representations for nearly 75,000 mono- and multisyllabic

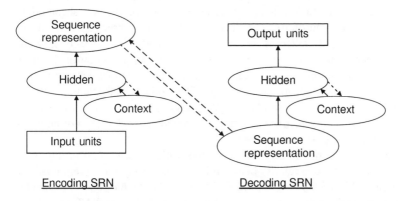

Figure 2.1 General sequence encoder architecture. The letters of a word are presented
sequentially to the Encoding SRN (simple recurrent network), where they are
integrated into a learned orthographic representation. This representation is
then copied to the Decoding SRN and used to regenerate the original sequence
of letters.

English words. These representations are sensitive to the statistical regularities
among elements of its corpus, even when the corpus contained strings that vary
substantially in length. As a result, representations created by the sequence
encoder capture a graded level of similarity when words include similar letters in
similar positions, and even when pairs of words vary substantially in length.
Furthermore, these models can predict individual's ratings of nonwords'
conformity to dependencies in English orthography (Sibley et al., 2008).

A sequence encoder (Sibley et al., 2008, 2009) learns to create representations
sensitive to the structure in English wordforms under pressure of an imitation task,
i.e., the reproduction of input sequences as output sequences. This auto-encoding
task drives a connectionist network to discover a means of re-representation that
exploits structure in the learned domain (Bishop, 1995). The sequence encoder
(Figure 2.1), is created by concatenating two Simple Recurrent Networks (SRN;
Jordan, 1986; Elman, 1990). The first SRN, called the encoding SRN, receives a
sequence of inputs and encodes them into a single distributed representation. The
second SRN, called the decoding SRN, decodes this representation into a
sequence of outputs. The orthographic representations created by this model are
the activation values that are copied between the encoding and decoding SRNs.
For the model to achieve the auto-encoding of a word, this single distributed
representation must contain sufficient information to reproduce the letter
sequence.

Analyses in Sibley et al. (2008, 2009) showed that when a sequence encoder
learns a corpus of sequences without dependences between its elements, each of
the representations is a linear combination of the distributed representations
for its constituent letters with respect to their absolute and relative positions.

To illustrate, the representation for CAT# is a linear combination of the representation for: C in the first position of a three-letter wordform, A in the second position of a three-letter wordform, T in the third position of a three-letter wordform, and the end-of-word 'letter' # occurring at the end of a three-letter word. However, representations created by a sequence encoder do not suffer from the same problem as slot codes, because distributed representations for constitution elements are more similar to the extent that they code similar letters, in similar positions, of wordforms of similar lengths. Also, over the course of learning, the network becomes sensitive to statistical dependencies that are not bound to absolute or relative positions in words.

This property extends to sequence encoders which process real orthographic sequences. The graded similarity between letters occurring in different positions is apparent in the types of errors produced by an orthographic sequence encoder. In particular, anticipation errors (e.g., anticipating the T is SPAT to produce STAT) and perseveration errors (e.g., perseverating the P in SPAT to produce SAP) suggest that letters are represented similarly across positions. Sibley et al. (2009) reported that 76% of an orthographic sequence encoder's errors on words and pseudowords involved an anticipation or perseveration of a letter, often across many intervening positions.

A sequence encoder learns to exploit statistical structure in English orthography to facilitate performance of the auto-encoding task. For instance, the model will become sensitive to the concurrence of the letters I, N, and G at the end of English words. Unlike a slot-based code that aligns words by their first letter a sequence encoder will generalize this regularity across words of different lengths. The networks use of statistical dependencies is evident when it has more success auto-encoding letter strings that conform to English Bigram frequencies, than letter strings that violate common dependencies. This was demonstrated in Sibley et al. (2008), where a sequence encoder had more success auto-encoding nonwords that conform to English orthographic dependencies (76% correct), relative to the same nonwords, but with scrambled letter orders (23% correct). This orthographic sequence encoder was also shown to predict subjects' ratings of nonwords' legality.

A sequence encoder learns orthographic representations by auto-encoding sequences of letters. However, sequence encoders can also learn correspondences between different input and output sequences. Sibley et al. (2010) explored this capacity in a model that mapped sequence of letters onto sequences of phonemes. This simulation was able to read 13,191 mono- and bisyllabic words. This model accounted for 16.6% of the variance in item-level naming latencies compiled in the ELP. This increased to 25.2% of the variance when considering only monomorphemic words. Further, the model exhibited sensitivity to many variables that impact behavioral latencies. This demonstrated that a system that learns correspondences between sequences of letters and phonemes is sufficient to simulate many phenomena in single word naming.

Bowers and Davis (2009) raised two concerns regarding the sequence encoder. First, they suggest that sequence encoder representations suffer from the same flaw as slot-based codes, because a sequence encoder does not represent letter information independent of position. Sibley et al. (2009) argued that complete positional independence is not desirable, as there are positional dependencies in English orthography. Instead, a sequence encoder represents similarity in a graded fashion, where representations for words will be more similar when they have letters in more similar positions and contexts. The second criticism raised by Bowers and Davis was that orthographic representations did not distinguish words from nonwords. Sibley et al. responded that a system for learning ortho-graphic representations should distinguish between letter strings on the basis of graphotactics, not lexicality. Here we present a model that distinguishes known from novel items, by integrating a sequence encoder with a lexical system.

Integrating learned orthographic representations into a model of word recognition

The present work seeks to demonstrate the utility of using learned orthographic representations in computational models of word recognition. To this end, we present a new model of single word recognition that processes 60,000 mono- and multisyllabic English words. This model was created by integrating a sequence encoder that learned orthographic representations for 60,000 English words, with a bank of 60,000 lexical nodes.

As demonstrated by the Interactive Activation model, a lexical level of repre-sentation permits discriminating known from novel orthographic sequences. This approach has been adopted in many subsequent models, notably the Multiple Read-Out Model (Grainger & Jacobs, 1996), SOLAR (Davis, 1999), Dual-Route Cascaded (Coltheart et al., 2001), and Connectionist Dual Process + (Perry et al., 2007; Perry, Ziegler, & Zorzi, 2010). All of these models achieved word recogni-tion through the use of lexicons that conform to Barlow's (1972) definition of localist coding, where increased activation on a particular node corresponds to an increasing probability that a particular word was encountered.

We adopted the lexical representation scheme because our goal is to demon-strate the feasibility and utility of integrating learned orthographic representa-tions into existing modeling frameworks. There is an active debate about whether localist lexical representations are theoretically tenable (Plaut, 1997; Rastle & Coltheart, 2006; Bowers, 2009; Plaut & McClelland, 2010; Bowers, 2010). However, alternatives to lexical representations have not been developed and demonstrated as viable at large scale. As a result, we have utilized the lexical system that enables our primary goal. If a viable alternative to lexical representa-tions is developed, then we suggest that learned orthographic representations should also be integrated into that framework.

In the present work, we implemented a localist lexicon where each lexical node was instantiated as a radial basis function. Effectively, each node behaved like a receptive field centered on a particular word. A node became active when an input fell within its receptive field, producing an increased response when the input was closer to its center. Closeness was determined by vector similarities computed among sequence encoder representations. As we will see, this approach yielded a capacity to distinguish words from pseudowords. But further, we show that this simple system exhibits sensitivity to many variables that have been shown to impact lexical decision latencies for large volumes of mono- and multisyllabic words.

Training corpora

Orthographic wordforms were selected from the set used in Sibley et al. (2008). This corpus was an intersection of the Wall Street Journal corpus (Marcus, Santorini, & Marcinkiewicz, 1993) and the CMU Pronunciation Dictionary (http://speech.cs.cmu.edu/cgi-bin/cmudict). After removing homographs and words with more than 11 letters, the remaining list was intersected with the ELP database to yield 28,032 words with associated behavioral data. To demonstrate scalability we included 31,968 words from the Sibley et al. (2008) corpus that did not appear in the ELP. The ELP also contains a volume of behavioral data regarding lexical decisions to nonwords, 27,881 of which were randomly selected to match the number of words.

Learning orthographic representation

Orthographic input representations were learned by a sequence encoder trained for the current work. This sequence encoder was similar to the model described as Simulation 2 in Sibley et al. (2008). It had two banks of analogous input and output units. One bank consisted of 26 letter units plus one word-delimiting unit and the other bank consisted of two units that identified whether a given letter was a consonant or vowel ('Y' was considered a vowel). A given letter was coded by activating a single unit from each bank, at a moment in time.

There were two differences between the new orthographic sequence encoder and Simulation 2 in Sibley et al. (2008). First, the sequence element previously representing end-of-wordform was activated at both the beginning and end of each sequence, which meant that letters could appear before or after this sequence element. Second, the new sequence encoder reached asymptotic training after 400,000 epochs, while Simulation 2 in Sibley et al. (2008) was trained for 250,000 epochs. The new sequence encoder correctly auto-encoded every letter and consonant/vowel unit for 90.17% of the 60,000 words. Figure 2.2 depicts that errors tended to occur on longer words. The large majority of mistakenly decoded words contained only one incorrect letter (i.e., 85.49%).

Architecture

A set of 60,000 nodes were attached to the layer that interfaces between encoding and decoding SRNs in a sequence encoder. Each of these 60,000 nodes locally coded for a word in the model's training corpus. Each node was instantiated as a radial basis function, whose centroid was the orthographic representation of a particular word, produced by the sequence encoder. Effectively, each node acted

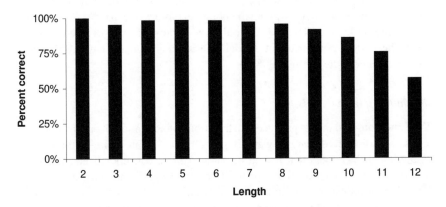

Figure 2.2 Orthographic sequence encoder performance, by length. A word was decoded correctly if every letter, or end-of-wordform output unit was activated in the correct sequence.

as a receptive field centered on a particular word. A node became active when an input fell within its receptive field, producing an increased response when the input was closer to its center. These receptive fields were tuned so that multiple nodes could be partially activated in response to most word-like English stimuli.

Receptive fields were created by setting connection weights between the sequence encoder's wordform layer and each word node. Each weight was set to the activation of the corresponding node in the distributed orthographic representation, when this layer is processing the word corresponding to the lexical node. Prescribing weights in this way does not model reading acquisition, but some learning algorithms (Grossberg, 1980; Rumelhart et al., 1995) for localist representations could be used for this purpose. Each lexical node's net input was calculated as

$$I_j = \sum_i (a_i - w_{ij})^2, \tag{2.1}$$

which is the squared difference between incoming connection weights and the activation on the orthographic wordform layer. The dot product activation function used in the sequence encoder was not used here because it generates larger net inputs as a result of more binary activations. For radial basis functions, net inputs should increase as inputs move closer to a centroid. Output activation of each node in the lexicon was calculated as,

$$a_j = f_j e^{-\gamma * I_j}, \tag{2.2}$$

where f_j was the $\log_{10}$ of the WSJ frequency for word j and γ is input gain, a multiplicative term that modulated the size of each node's receptive field. Input gain was set to 0.035 which was large enough that most nodes did not become active for every input, but it was small enough that nonwords produced activation throughout the lexicon. This was the only free parameter that governed processing in the lexical portion of the model (the sequence encoder used other free parameters; see Sibley et al., 2008).

Simulating a lexical decision

Word and nonword inputs produced distributions of activation over sets of lexical nodes, and lexical decisions were based on these distributions. Balota and Chumbley (1984) noted that lexical decisions can be conceptualized as a signal detection process, where a participant differentiates word and nonword distributions along a dimension of familiarity. Familiarity can be related to two aspects of lexical node activation distributions, i.e., heights of their peaks and spreads of their 'valleys', so to speak. More familiar inputs correspond to higher peaks because word inputs activate their corresponding lexical node far more than any other input. A similar effect may occur for nonword inputs – a nonword may be very orthographically similar to a known word (e.g., CABAPULT), or may be very distinct (e.g., JXYLRPS). But nonwords can also seem familiar if they are in a neighborhood of words, and the extent of this neighborhood can be measured by the spread of activation around the peak. The peak and spread dimensions of familiarity can be combined as,

$$fam(w) = a_1 + SD_k,$$

(2.3)

where the first term is the activation of the most excited node in the lexicon and the second term is the standard deviation of the activations for the second through 50th most excited nodes. The second term stopped at the 50th node for the sake of computational simplicity. Figure 2.3 depicts word and nonword distributions, plotted along the axis of familiarity. Within this conceptualization, a lexical decision can be simulated using a decision boundary placed along the continuum of familiarity. The average lexical decision accuracy for words and nonwords in the ELP were 87.94% and 87.97%. For this simulation, a boundary parameter was fit (i.e., it was a free parameter) to the value of 2.5, so that 91.44% of words and 90.51% of nonwords were correctly classified (we did not assess whether adjustments to the decision boundary could simulate word recognition performance without time pressure). This competency alone demonstrates the utility of learned orthographic representations, in so far as the model recognizes nearly an order of magnitude more words than models utilizing stipulated orthographic representations.

Despite its size, this is a simple, working model of lexical decision that takes advantage of both localist (lexical) and learned distributed (orthographic) representations. Models like the Dual Route Cascaded and Connectionist Dual Process+, models instantiate distinct orthographic and phonological lexicons to better simulate behavioral data (Coltheart et al., 2001; Perry et al., 2007, 2010),

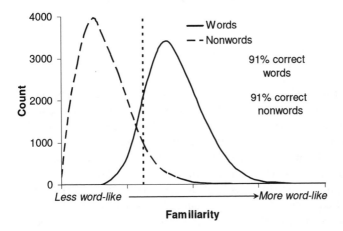

Figure 2.3 Word and nonword distributions. Distributions of 28,032 words and 27,881 nonwords are shown along a continuum of familiarity defined by Equation 2.3.

and lexical decisions are certainly influenced by semantic associations with orthographic inputs (Plaut, 1997). The current model does not incorporate these and various other mechanisms and factors.

The model was tested in terms of its ability to simulate lexical decision latencies and account for a wide range of lexical factors known to affect lexical decision performance. Lexical decisions were operationalized as being more difficult as familiarity approached the boundary between words and nonwords. Thus lexical decision reaction times were a function of distance between the familiarity of an orthographic input and a decision boundary (Balota & Chumbley, 1984), i.e.,

$$RT(w) = -|fam(w) - bound|, \tag{2.4}$$

where *fam(w)* is the stimuli's familiarity calculated according to Equation 2.3, *bound* is the previously discussed decision boundary between word and nonword distributions.

Relative to mean *z*-scored recognition latencies in the English Lexicon Project, the current network accounted for 40.51% of the variance in reaction times for 27,881 words. We utilized the *z*-scored ELP latency metric, because every participant did not provide a response to every stimulus and so these *z*-scores are more stable estimates of item latencies (see Yap & Balota, 2009). This metric was generated exclusively from activation on lexical nodes, which does not incorporate information about the serial process that activates the lexicon. Thus it does not approximate how stimuli with more letters tend to take longer to visually input. This effect can be approximated by adding a second term to Equation 2.4 to create,

$$RT2(w) = -\left| fam(w) - crit \right| + l(w) * \alpha,$$

(2.5)

where *l(w)* is the orthographic length of word *w*, and α was a free parameter set to 0.25 to fit the data. Incorporating this length term is a proxy for the inclusion of orthographic processing time that could be derived from the sequence encoder (Sibley et al., 2008). Adding length allows the model to account for 44.76% of the item-variance in ELP lexical decision latencies. However, it is informative to examine how this model accounts for item variance. First, consider that a word's frequency and length account for 46.4% of the variance in the ELP latencies. If linear effects of frequency are residualized out of ELP and simulated latencies, then the two measures share 12.39% of item-level variance. If the effect of letter length is removed from ELP and simulated latencies then the two measures share 31.81% of variance. However, if both frequency and length effects are removed, then the model predicts only 1.06% of the variance in behavioral latencies. Although this is still a statistically significant relationship ($p < 0.001$), it is clear that the vast majority of the ability to simulate item latency is a function of the model's sensitivity to frequency and length effects. However, it is unclear whether this reflects a shortcoming in the model or this approach to assessing models, because most of the systematic variance in item latencies is associated with length and frequency effects.

Next, we examined the simulation's sensitivity to additional stimuli characteristics that affect recognition behaviors. We utilized a technique developed by Yap and Balota (2009) where the relative effect sizes and directions of theoretically important variables in human and simulated latencies are examined. Comparing effect sizes provides a means of assessing the networks sensitivity to a variable, relative to behavioral data. In these analyses, we utilized behavioral data and stimuli variables from the English Lexicon Project.

Before proceeding, we should note that there is substantial multicolliniarity in the variables that impact behavioral latencies. In some cases, variables measure different aspects of similar word characteristics. For instance, the number of letters and syllables in a word are obviously related. In other cases, multicoliniarity results from word characteristics being confounded in English. As a result, we examine the relationship between each lexical variable and ELP or simulated latencies, before and after variance associated with frequency and length have been removed. Table 2.1 displays R^2 of word characteristics predicting lexical decision latencies. All of the effects displayed in these tables are in the same direction for human and simulated latencies, and statistically significant ($p < 0.05$).

One of the most robust findings in the study of lexical behaviors is that words which are encountered more often tend to be read and recognized faster (Forster & Chambers, 1973). The logarithm of a word's frequency is one of the most common and strongest predictors of its naming and lexical decision latencies,

Table 2.1 R^2 (%) from lexical variables predicting ELP or simulated latencies. All of the relationships were statistically significant ($p < 0.05$) and in the same direction in ELP and simulation

	ELP	ELP Frequency and length removed	Simulation	Simulation Frequency and length removed
Frequency	39.19	NA	66.10	NA
Length	19.71	NA	54.91	NA
Syllabic length	21.53	2.89	33.29	0.07
Morpheme length	6.00	0.44	22.85	0.03
Coltheart's N	10.56	0.02	30.58	3.65
Levenshtein orthographic distance	24.70	1.21	48.16	0.61

whether the word is monosyllabic (Balota, Cortese, Sergent-Marshall, Spieler, & Yap, 2004) or multisyllabic (Yap, 2007). As a result, frequency has played a substantial role in theorizing about the lexical system. For instance, Forster and Chambers (1973) argued that lexical access involves a serial search through a list ordered from the most to least frequent word and Morton (1969) proposed that frequency multiplicatively scaled a threshold on word detectors. Akin to the suggestion of Morton, the current simulation exhibits a frequency effect because of a multiplicative term placed on the activation functions of lexical nodes. This is very similar to how the Dual Route Cascaded (Coltheart et al., 2001) and Connectionist Dual Process+ (Perry et al., 2007) models produce a frequency effect. However, future work can explore the use of orthographic representations that are learned by a process that is sensitive to the frequency with which children encounter different orthographic forms.

It has been repeatedly reported that the time needed to recognize a word is influenced by the stimuli's length (Weekes, 1997; Ziegler, Perry, Jacobs, & Braun, 2001; Yap & Balota, 2009). This became a theoretically important phenomenon when Coltheart et al. (2001) proposed that length effects indicate a serial processes involvement in reading. It has been argued that this would contradict systems that recognize and read words via parallel distributed processing, such as the Triangle model of reading. Kawamoto, Kello, and colleagues (Kawamoto & Kello, 1999; Kawamoto, Kello, Jones, & Bame, 1998; Kawamoto, Kello, Higareda, & Vu, 1999) argued that seriality in speech articulation can account for Coltheart et al.'s results and their own findings of initial phoneme duration effects in word naming data. The current model does not implement cascaded processing from input to output. Nor does it include seriality in an output process, because it is simulating lexical decision rather than naming. As a result, it cannot directly simulate the theoretical principle espoused by Kawamoto et al. (1998). Nonetheless, this model exhibits sensitivity to elements in a word, across multiple grain sizes. Table 2.1 shows that ELP participants and this model are sensitive to the number of letters, syllables, and morphemes in a word. It is unsurprising that the model exhibits a sensitivity to letter length, as the number of letters in a word was literally added into the latency measure (see Equation 2.5). However, even when variance that is linearly associated with frequency and letter length is removed, the ELP and simulated word recognition latencies both exhibit effects of syllabic and morphological length.

Words with more syllables take longer to recognize, before and after the variance associated with frequency and letter length are removed. This result is consistent with prior behavioral reports of syllabic length effects (Jared & Seidenberg, 1990; New, Ferrand, Pallier, & Brysbaert, 2006; Yap & Balota, 2009). These effects were interpreted by Álvarez, Carreiras, & Taft (2001) and New et al. (2006) as implying a functional role of syllables in the cognitive system. As a result, it is notable that the present model exhibits an effect of syllabic length, even though it does not explicitly represent or employ syllables. Rather, the sequence encoder's learning process created orthographic representations that were sensitive to some statistical dependencies related to syllables.

Word recognition latencies are related to the number of morphemes in a word (Yap, Balota, Sibley, & Ratcliff, 2012). Words with more morphemes are typically recognized slower, however, the direction of this effect reverses after the linear effects of letter length are removed. To illustrate, the word RUN tends to be recognized faster than REMODELED. However, REMODELED tends to be recognized faster than RAVISHING or REMINISCE, because it has the same number of letters but more morphemes (i.e., RE-MODEL-ED). This effect of morphological length and its reversal are evident in ELP and simulated latencies (see Table 2.1). This pattern suggests that more morphemes delay ELP and simulated reaction times because words with more morphemes tend to include more letters. However, in words of a given length, more morphemes are related to faster recognition in ELP and simulated latencies. The sequence encoder's learning process appears to generate orthographic representation that are sensitive to repeatedly encountered letter sequences, which sometimes form morphemes (e.g., UN- or -ED). This demonstrates that an orthographic learning process coupled to a lexical system is sufficient to simulate some effects of morphological structure. Additional work is needed to understand whether this system is sufficient to simulate related effects like morphological priming, or if these effects arise from the systematicity that morphology builds into the orthographic-semantic mapping (see Rastle & Davis, 2008, and Rueckl & Raveh, 1999 for contrasting views on this issue).

Numerous behavioral experiments have explored how lexical processing is affected by similarly spelled words (Coltheart et al., 1977; Glushko, 1979; Ziegler et al., 2001). One way to explain this effect is with orthographic neighborhood size, which reflects the density of words within regions of orthographic space. Although the effect of orthographic neighborhood is complex, and not yet fully understood, it appears that large numbers of orthographic neighbors generally facilitate naming and lexical decision to words (for a review, see Andrews, 1997). The most utilized measure of neighborhood size is Coltheart's N, which for a given word denotes how many other English words can be created by substituting a single letter. Notice that this measure implicitly conceptualizes words as using a slot-based representation of orthography. As a result, Coltheart's N operates well for monosyllabic words where orthographic neighbors are often of the same length. However, longer words, which seem orthographically similar, are often of different lengths (e.g., BASEBALL and BASEBALLS cannot be recognized as neighbors by a scheme that restricts similarity to within a given word length). Another option is to define a word's neighbors by letter substitutions, additions, and deletions. Yarkoni, Balota, & Yap (2008) proposed such a metric called Levenshtein orthographic distance, which is computed as the average of the minimum number of letters that must be added, removed, or substituted to transform a word into its nearest 20 orthographic neighbors. ELP participants exhibit sensitivity to this measure of orthographic neighborhood (Yap, 2007; Yap & Balota, 2009). The current simulation exhibits statistically significant effects of Coltheart's N and Levenshtein orthographic distance, before and after linear frequency and length effects have been partialled out of the model.

General discussion

In this chapter we showed the feasibility and utility of integrating learned orthographic representations into a simulation of word recognition. A sequence encoder was trained on orthographic representations for 60,000 mono- and multisyllabic words. These representations were mapped onto 60,000 lexical nodes. The resulting model distinguished words from nonwords at a rate similar to adult readers in a speeded lexical decision task. Lexical decision latencies were simulated as the distance between a word's familiarity (computed as the peak and spread of activation across the lexical nodes) and a decision boundary. These simulated latencies predicted a substantial amount of the item-variance in ELP word recognition latencies, mostly by virtue of the shared sensitivity to frequency and length effects. Also, several stimulus characteristics similarly impacted behavioral and simulated latencies.

The orthographic representations learnt by a sequence encoder have several desirable properties (see Sibley et al., 2008, 2009). Unlike a slot-coding scheme, letters were not represented with respect to an absolute position. As a result, pairs of words were more similarly if they shared similar constituents, even if they were in different positions, or if the words varied substantially in length. As a result, recognition of longer words was impacted by orthographically similar, though prominent (e.g., high frequency) monosyllabic words. This capacity is crucial to scaling up models, because the majority of English words are multisyllabic. Achieving this large scale will increase models' fidelity to the adult reading system that is the target of these simulations.

This work explored a system that learns orthographic representations that are sensitive to statistical dependencies across several grain sizes (again see Sibley et al., 2008, 2009, 2010 for more discussion of this point). This system utilized domain general learning processes identical to numerous prior models of single word reading (e.g., Seidenberg & McClelland, 1989; Plaut et al., 1996; Harm & Seidenberg, 1999, 2004). As a result, this system for learning about orthography could be integrated into related frameworks while preserving parsimony (see Sibley et al., 2010 for a related model of word reading).

Limitations and future work

There are a variety of perspectives about the goals and utility of computational modeling (see Seidenberg & Plaut, 2006; and Rastle & Coltheart, 2006 for contrasting positions). We believe that computational models are useful for testing when a set of mechanisms are sufficient to produce a pattern of behavioral data. As a result we do not interpret this model as an instantiated theory of lexical decision, but rather as a tool for developing theories. Our goal was to demonstrate that learned orthographic representations can be integrated into existing frameworks, to produce large-scale simulations of lexical processing. The utility of learned orthographic representations becomes apparent when considering the need to address phenomena relevant to multisyllabic words.

Several properties of our model were utilized for the sake of expediency, rather than as theoretical commitments. Foremost, we utilized localist representations of words. There is an active debate about the biological and psychological plausibility of this representational form (Rastle & Coltheart, 2006; Bowers, 2009; Plaut & McClelland, 2010; Bowers, 2010). Localist representations were used here because they offer a simple means of simulating lexical decisions, i.e., known inputs have nodes whereas novel inputs do not. This architectural distinction between known and novel inputs is used by many models of lexical processing (e.g., the Dual Route Cascaded, Connectionist Dual Process+, and Self-Organising Lexical Acquisition and Recognition (SOLAR) models). Although localist representations were currently necessary to account for lexical decision performance on a large scale, it remains to be seen whether they are a useful simplification, or if they provide deep insights into skilled word-recognition behaviors.

Alternatives to localist representations propose that semantic processing can provide a basis for simulating lexical decisions. The rationale is that only known words have associated meanings. Plaut (1997) demonstrated this approach in a computational model for which words and nonwords were distinguished by the information content, or entropy, of distributed semantic representations. However, we are unaware of a demonstration that this approach can be scaled up to support lexical decision to tens of thousands of words. Nonetheless, a number of semantic variables impact word reading and recognition, such as imageability (Cortese & Fugett, 2004), number of semantic associates (Toglia & Battig, 1978), number of semantic senses (Miller, 1990), and semantic priming (Plaut & Booth, 2000). So semantic information clearly constrain the lexical decision behavior, though it is unclear exactly how this operates.

Finally, because of its simplicity there are many phenomena that our model does not address. For instance, the current work says little about reading acquisition (e.g., Cunningham & Stanovich, 1991; Saffran et al., 1996; Dufva, Niemi, &

Voeten, 2001; Ziegler & Goswami, 2005; Goswami & Ziegler, 2006), reading disabilities (e.g., Pugh, Sandak, Frost, Moore, & Mencl, 2005; Pugh, 2006; Preston, Frost, Mencl, Fulbright, Landi, Grigorenko, et al., 2010; Shankweiler, Mencl, Braze, Tabor, Pugh, & Fulbright, 2008), individual differences (e.g., Yap et al., 2012; Frost, Landi, Mencl, Sandak, Fulbright, Tejada, et al., 2009), the neural basis of orthographic representation (e.g., Dehaene et al., 2002, 2004; Vinckier et al., 2007), morphological priming (e.g., Rastle & Brysbaert, 2006; Feldman & Soltano, 1999), or lexical decision phenomena to nonwords (e.g., Coltheart et al., 1977, 2001). These phenomena merit further examination within this and other frameworks.

- Children must learn to represent a word's orthography as they acquire the ability to read. There is an active field examining the neural circuits that support this orthographic learning. Yet the orthographic representations in most current models are specified by the modeler, and so do not address the critical process of orthographic learning.
- Despite notable progress, most computational models of lexical decision only process monosyllabic words or words of a restricted length. This limitation stems from how current models represent a word's orthographic (i.e., written) form.
- We present a system designed to learn orthographic representations, and show it can be integrated into a model of word recognition.
- Our model simulates lexical decision on the scale of adult, skilled reading, and in doing so, is sensitive to several stimulus characteristics that influence lexical decision latencies.

References

Aderman, D. & Smith, E. E. (1971). Expectancy as a determinant of functional units in perceptual recognition. *Cognitive Psychology*, *2*, 117–129.

Álvarez, C. J., Carreiras, M., & Taft, M. (2001). Syllables and morphemes: Contrasting frequency effects in Spanish. *Journal of Experimental Psychology: Learning, Memory, and Cognition*, *28*, 545–555.

Andrews, S. (1997). The effect of orthographic similarity on lexical retrieval: Resolving neighborhood conflicts. *Psychonomic Bulletin & Review*, *4*, 439–461.

Aslin, R. N., Saffran, J. R., & Newport, E. L. (1999). Statistical learning in linguistic and nonlinguistic domains. In B. MacWhinney (Ed.), *Emergence of language.* (pp. 359–380). Mahwah, NJ: Lawrence Erlbaum.

Bailey, T. M. & Hahn, U. (2001). Determinants of wordlikeness: Phonotactic or lexical neighborhoods? *Journal of Memory and Language*, *44*, 568–591.

Balota, D. A. & Chumbley, J. I. (1984). Are lexical decisions a good measure of lexical access? The role of word frequency in the neglected decision stage. *Journal of Experimental Psychology: Human Perception & Performance*, *10*, 340–357.

Balota, A. A., Cortese, M. J., Hutchison, K. A., Neely, J. H., Nelson, D., Simpson, G. B., et al. (2002). *The English lexicon project: A web-based repository of descriptive and behavioral measures for 40,481 English words and nonwords*. http://elexicon.wustl. edu, Washington University.

Balota, D. A., Cortese, M. J., Sergent-Marshall, S. D., Spieler, D. H., & Yap, M. (2004). Visual word recognition of single-syllable words. *Journal of Experimental Psychology: General, 133*, 283–316.

Barlow, H. (1972). Single units and sensation: A neuron doctrine for perceptual psychology. *Perception, 1*, 371–394.

Baron, J. & Thurston, I. (1973). An analysis of the word-superiority effect. *Cognitive Psychology, 4*, 207–228.

Balota, D. A., Yap, M. J., Cortese, M. J., Hutchison, K. A., Kessler, B., Loftis, B., Neely, J. H., Nelson, D. L., Simpson, G. B., & Treiman, R. (2007). The English Lexicon Project. *Behavior Research Methods, 39*, 445–59.

Bergman, M. W., Hudson, P. T., & Eling, P. A. (1988). How simple complex words can be: Morphological processing and word representations. *Quarterly Journal of Experimental Psychology: Human Experimental Psychology, 40*, 41–72.

Bishop, C. M. (1995). *Neural networks for pattern recognition*. Oxford: Oxford University Press.

Bowers, J. S. (2009). On the biological plausibility of grandmother cells: Implications for neural network theories in psychology and neuroscience. *Psychological Review, 116*, 220–251.

Bowers, J. S. (2010). More on grandmother cells and the biological implausibility of PDP models of cognition: A reply to Plaut and McClelland (2010) and Quian Quiroga and Kreiman (2010). *Psychological Review, 117*, 300–306.

Bowers, J. & Davis, C. (2009). Learning representations of wordforms with recurrent networks: Comment on Sibley, Kello, Plaut, and Elman. *Cognitive Science, 33*, 1183–1186.

Cohen, L., Martinaud, O., Lemer, C., Lehericy, S., Samson, Y., Obadia, M., Slachevsky, A., & Dehaene, S. (2003). Visual word recognition in the left and right hemispheres: anatomical and functional correlates of peripheral alexias. *Cerebral Cortex, 13*, 1313–1333.

Coltheart, M. (1978). Lexical access in simple reading tasks. In G. Underwood (Ed.), *Strategies of information processing* (pp. 151–216). London: Academic Press.

Coltheart, M., Jonassaon, J. T., Davelaar, E., and Besner, D. (1977). Access to the internal lexicon. In S. Dornic (Ed.), *Attention and performance VI*. New York: Academic Press.

Coltheart, M., Rastle, K., Perry, C., Langdon, R., & Ziegler, J. (2001). DRC: A dual route cascaded model of visual word recognition and reading aloud. *Psychological Review, 108*, 204–256.

Cortese, M. J. & Fugett, A. (2004). Imageability ratings for 3,000 monosyllabic words. *Behavior Research Methods, Instruments & Computers, 36*, 384–387.

Cunninghan, A. E. & Stanovich, K. E. (1991). Tracking the unique effects of print exposure in children: Associations with vocabulary, general knowledge and spelling. *Journal of Educational Psychology, 83*, 264–274.

Davis, C. J. (1999). *The self-organizing lexical acquisition and recognition (SOLAR) model of visual word recognition*. Unpublished doctoral dissertation. University of New South Wales, Australia.

Dehaene, S., Le Clec'H, G., Poline, J. B., Le Bihan, D., & Cohen, L. (2002). The visual word-form area: A prelexical representation of visual words in the fusiform gyrus. *Neuroreport, 13*, 321–325.

Dehaene, S., Jobert, A., Naccache, L., Ciuciu, P., Poline, J. B., Le Bihan, D., & Cohen, L. (2004). Letter binding and invariant recognition of masked words. *Psychological Science*, *15*, 307–313.

Dufva, M., Niemi, P., & Voeten, M. (2001). The role of phonological memory, decoding, and comprehension skills in reading development: From preschool to grade 2. *Reading and Writing: An Interdisciplinary Journal*, *14*, 91–117.

Elman, J. L. (1990). Finding structure in time. *Cognitive Science*, *14*, 179–211.

Feldman, L. B. & Soltano, E. G. (1999). Morphological priming: The role of prime duration, semantic transparency, and affix position. *Brain & Language*, *68*, 33–39.

Forster, K. I. & Chambers, S. M. (1973). Lexical access and naming time. *Journal of Verbal Learning and Verbal Behavior*, *12*, 627–635.

Frisch, S. A., Large, N. R., Zawaydeh, B., & Pisoni, D. B. (2001). Emergent phonotactic generalizations in English and Arabic. In J. Bybee & P. Hopper (Eds), *Frequency and the emergence of linguistic structure* (pp. 159–179). Amsterdam: John Benjamins.

Frost, S. J., Landi, N., Mencl, W. E., Sandak, R., Fulbright, R. K., Tejada, E., Jacobsen, L., Grigorenko, E. L., Constable, R. T., & Pugh, K. R. (2009). Phonological awareness predicts activation patterns for print and speech. *Annals of Dyslexia*, *58*, 78–97.

Glushko, R. J. (1979). The organization and activation of orthographic knowledge in reading aloud. *Journal of Experimental Psychology: Human Perception and Performance*, *5*, 674–691.

Gomez, R. (2002). Variability and Detection of Invariant Structure. *Psychological Science*, *135*, 431–6.

Goswami, U. & Ziegler, J. C. (2006). A developmental perspective on the neural code for written words. *Trends in Cognitive Sciences*, *10*, 142–143.

Graf Estes, K., Evans, J. L., Alibali, M. W., & Saffran, J. R. (2007). Can infants map meaning to newly segmented words? Statistical segmentation and word learning. *Psychological Science*, *18*, 254–60.

Grainger, J. (2008). Cracking the orthographic code: An introduction? *Language and Cognitive Processes*, *23*, 1–35.

Grainger, J. & Jacobs, A. M. (1996). Orthographic processing in visual word recognition: A multiple read-out model. *Psychological Review*, *103*, 518–565.

Grainger, J. & van Heuven, W. (2003). Modeling letter position coding in printed word perception. In P. Bonin (Ed.), *The mental lexicon* (pp. 1–23). New York: Nova Science.

Grainger, J., Bouttevin, S., Truc, C., Bastien, M., & Ziegler, J. (2003). Word superiority, pseudoword superiority, and learning to read: A comparison of dyslexic and normal readers. *Brain & Language*, *87*, 432–440.

Grainger, J., Granier, J. P., Farioli, F., Van Assche, E., & van Heuven, W. (2006). Letter position information and printed word perception: The relative-position priming constraint. *Journal of Experimental Psychology: Human Perception and Performance*, *32*, 865–884.

Grossberg, S. (1978). A theory of human memory: Self-organization and performance of sensory-motor codes, maps, and plans. In R. Rosen & F. Snell (Eds.), *Progress in theoretical biology* (pp. 233–374). New York: Academic Press.

Grossberg, S. (1980). How does a brain build a cognitive code? *Psychological Review*, *87*, 1–51.

Harm, M. W. & Seidenberg, M. S. (1999). Phonology, reading acquisition, and dyslexia: Insights from connectionist models. *Psychological Review*, *106*, 491–528.

Harm, M. W. & Seidenberg, M. S. (2004). Computing the meanings of words in reading: Cooperative division of labor between visual and phonological processes. *Psychological Review*, *111*, 662–720.

Jared, D. & Seidenberg, M. S. (1990). Naming multisyllabic words. *Journal of Experimental Psychology: Human Perception and Performance*, *16*, 92–105.

Jordan, M. I. (1986). *Serial order: A parallel distributed processing approach* (No. 8604 ICS Technical Report): University of California at San Diego, La Jolla, CA.

Jusczyk, P. W., Luce, P. A., & Charles-Luce, J. (1994). Infants' sensitivity to phonotactic patterns in the native language. *Journal of Memory & Language*, *33*, 630–645.

Kawamoto, A. H. & Kello, C. T. (1999). Effect of onset cluster complexity in speeded naming: A test of rule-based approaches. *Journal of Experimental Psychology: Human Perception & Performance*, *25*, 361–375.

Kawamoto, A. H., Kello, C. T., Jones, R., & Bame, K. (1998). Initial phoneme versus whole-word criterion to initiate pronunciation: Evidence based on response latency and initial phoneme duration. *Journal of Experimental Psychology: Learning, Memory, & Cognition*, *24*, 862–885.

Kawamoto, A. H., Kello, C. T., Higareda, I., & Vu, J. V. Q. (1999). Parallel processing and initial phoneme criterion in naming words: Evidence from frequency effects on onset and rime duration. *Journal of Experimental Psychology: Learning, Memory, & Cognition*, *25*, 362–381.

Kello, C. T. (2006). Considering the junction model of lexical processing. In S. Andrews (Ed.), *From inkmarks to ideas: Current issues in lexical processing*. Sydney: Psychology Press.

Lany, J. & Saffran, J.R. (2010). From statistics to meaning. *Psychological Science*, published online 8 January 2010. doi:10.1177/0956797609358570.

McClelland, J. L. & Rumelhart, D. E. (1981). An interactive activation model of context effects in letter perception, Part 1: An account of basic findings. *Psychological Review*, *88*, 375–405.

Marcus, M., Santorini, B., & Marcinkiewicz, M. A. (1993). Building a large annotated corpus of English: The Penn Treebank. *Computational Linguistics*, *19*, 313–330.

Maris, E. (2002). The role of orthographic and phonological codes in the word and the pseudoword superiority effect: An analysis by means of multinomial processing tree models. *Journal of Experimental Psychology: Human Perception & Performance*, *28*, 1409–1431.

Miller, G. A. (1990). WordNet: An on-line lexical database. *International Journal of Lexiography*, *3*, 235–312.

Morton, J. (1969). Interaction of information in word recognition. *Psychological Review*, *76*, 165–178.

Morton, J. (1970). A functional model for memory. In D. A. Norman (Ed.), *Models of human memory* (pp. 203–254). New York: Academic Press.

Mozer, M. C. (1987). Early parallel processing in reading: A connectionist approach. In M. Coltheart (Ed.), *Attention and Performance XII: The Psychology of Reading* (pp. 83–104). Hove, UK: Lawrence Erlbaum Associates Ltd.

New, B., Ferrand, L., Pallier, C., & Brysbaert, M. (2006). Re-examining word length effects in visual word recognition: New evidence from the English Lexicon Project. *Psychonomic Bulletin & Review*, *13*, 45–52.

Newport, E. L. & Aslin, R. N. (2004). Learning at a distance: I. Statistical learning of non-adjacent dependencies. *Cognitive Psychology*, *48*, 127–162.

Pelucchi, B., Hay, J. F., & Saffran, J. R. (2009). Statistical learning in a natural language by 8-month-old infants. *Child Development, 80*, 674–685.

Perry, C., Ziegler, J. C., & Zorzi, M. (2007). Nested incremental modeling in the development of computational theories: The CDP+ Model of reading aloud. *Psychological Review, 114*, 273–315.

Perry, C., Ziegler, J. C., & Zorzi, M. (2010). Beyond single syllables: Large-scale modeling of reading aloud with the Connectionist Dual Process (CDP++) model. *Cognitive Psychology, 61*, 106–151.

Plaut, D. C. (1997). Structure and function in the lexical system: Insights from distributed models of word reading and lexical decision. *Language and Cognitive Processes, 12*, 767–808.

Plaut, D. C. & Booth, J. R. (2000). Individual and developmental differences in semantic priming: Empirical and computational support for a single-mechanism account of lexical processing. *Psychological Review, 107*, 786–823.

Plaut, D. C. & McClelland, J. L. (2010). Locating object knowledge in the brain: A critique of Bowers's (2009) attempt to revive the grandmother cell hypothesis. *Psychological Review, 117*, 284–290.

Plaut, D. C., McClelland, J. L., Seidenberg, M. S., & Patterson, K. (1996). Understanding normal and impaired word reading: Computational principles in quasi-regular domains. *Psychological Review, 103*, 56–115.

Preston, J. L., Frost, S. J., Mencl, W. E., Fulbright, R. K., Landi, N., Grigorenko, E., Jacobsen, L., & Pugh, K. R. (2010). Early and late talkers: School-age language, literacy and neurolinguistic differences. *Brain, 133*, 2185–2195.

Price, C. J. & Devlin, J. T. (2003). The myth of the visual word form area. *NeuroImage, 19*, 473–481.

Pugh, K. R. (2006). A neurocognitive overview of reading acquisition and dyslexia across languages. *Developmental Science, 9*, 448–450.

Pugh, K. R., Sandak, R., Frost, S. J., Moore, D., & Mencl, W. E. (2005). Examining reading development and reading disability in English language learners: Potential contributions from functional neuroimaging. *Learning Disabilities Research & Practice, 20*, 24–30.

Rastle, K. & Brysbaert, M. (2006). Masked phonological priming effects in English: Are they real? Do they matter? *Cognitive Psychology, 53*, 97–145.

Rastle, K. & Coltheart, M. (2006). Is there serial processing in the reading system; and are there local representations? In Andrews, S. (Ed). *All about words: Current issues in lexical processing*. Hove: Psychology Press.

Rastle, K. & Davis, M. H. (2008). Morphological decomposition based on the analysis of orthography. *Language and Cognitive Process, 23*, 942–971.

Reicher, G. M. (1969). Perceptual recognition as a function of meaningfulness of stimulus material. *Journal of Experimental Psychology, 81*, 275–280.

Rueckl, J. G. & Raveh, M. (1999). The influence of morphological regularities on the dynamics of a connectionist network. *Brain & Language, 68*, 110–117.

Rumelhart, D. E., Durbin, R., Golden, R., & Chauvin, Y. (1995). Backpropagation: The basic theory. In Y. Chauvin & D. E. Rumelhart (Eds), *Backpropagation: Theory, architectures, and applications. Developments in connectionist theory* (pp. 1–34). Hillsdale, NJ: Erlbaum.

Saffran, J. R. (2001). Words in a sea of sounds: The output of infant statistical learning. *Cognition, 81*, 149–169.

Saffran, J. R., Aslin, R. N., & Newport, E. L. (1996). Statistical learning by 8-month old infants. *Science, 274,* 1926–1928.

Seidenberg, M. & McClelland, J. (1989). A distributed developmental model of word recognition and naming. *Psychological Review, 96,* 523–568.

Seidenberg, M. S. & Plaut, D. C. (2006). Progress in understanding word reading: Data fitting versus theory building. In S. Andrews (Ed.), *From inkmarks to ideas: Current issues in lexical processing.* Psychology Press: Hove, UK.

Shankweiler, D. P., Mencl, W. E., Braze, D., Tabor, W., Pugh, K. R., & Fulbright, R. K. (2008). Reading differences and brain: Cortical integration of speech and print in sentence processing varies with reader skill. *Developmental Neuropsychology, 33,* 745–776.

Shaywitz, B. A., Shaywitz, S. E., Blachman, B. A., Pugh, K. R., Fulbright, R. K., Skudlarski, P., Mencl, W. E., Constable, R. T., Holahan, J. M., Marchione, K. E., Fletcher, J. M., Lyon, G. R. & Gore, J. C. (2004). Development of left occipito-temporal systems for skilled reading in children after a phonologically-based intervention. *Biological Psychiatry, 55,* 926–933.

Shaywitz, B. A., Shaywitz, S. E., Pugh, K. R., Mencl, W. E., Fulbright, R. K., Skudlarski, P., Constable, R. T., Marchione, K. E., Fletcher, J. M., Lyon, G. R., & Gore, J. C. (2002). Disruption of posterior brain systems for reading in children with developmental dyslexia. *Biological Psychiatry, 52,* 101–110.

Sibley, D. E., Kello, C. T., Plaut, D. C., & Elman, J. L. (2008). Large-scale modeling of wordform learning and representations. *Cognitive Science, 32,* 741–754.

Sibley, D. E., Kello, C. T., Plaut, D. C., & Elman, J. L. (2009). Sequence encoders enable large-scale lexical modeling: Reply to Bowers and Davis (2009). *Cognitive Science, 33,* 1187–1191.

Sibley, D. E., Kello, C. T., & Seidenberg, M. S. (2010). Learning orthographic and phonological representations in models of monosyllabic and bisyllabic naming. *European Journal of Cognitive Psychology, 22,* 650–668.

Toglia, M. P. & Battig, W. F. (1978). *Handbook of semantic word norms.* Hillsdale, NJ: Erlbaum.

Vinckier, F., Dehaene, S., Jobert, A., Dubus, J. P., Sigman, M., & Cohen, L. (2007). Hierarchical coding of letter strings in the ventral stream: Dissecting the inner organization of the visual word-form system, *Neuron, 55,* 143–156.

Warrington, E. K. & Shallice, T. (1980). Word form dyslexia. *Brain, 103,* 99–112.

Weekes, B. S. (1997). Differential effects of number of letters on word and nonword naming latency. *Quarterly Journal of Experimental Psychology: Human Experimental Psychology, 50A,* 439–456.

Wheeler, D. D. (1970). Processes in word recognition. *Cognitive Psychology, 1,* 59–86.

Whitney, C. (2001). How the brain encodes the order of letters in a printed word: The SERIOL model and selective literature review. *Psychonomic Bulletin and Review, 8,* 221–243.

Wickelgren, W. A. (1969). Context-sensitive coding, associative memory, and serial order in (speech) behavior. *Psychological Review, 76,* 1–15.

Yap, M. (2007). *Visual word recognition: Explorations of megastudies, multisyllabic words, and individual differences.* Unpublished PhD thesis, Washington University.

Yap, M. J. & Balota, D. A. (2009). Visual word recognition of multisyllabic words. *Journal of Memory and Language, 60,* 502–529.

Yap, M. J., Balota, D. A., Sibley, D. E., & Ratcliff, R. (2012). Individual differences in visual word recognition: insights from the ELP. *Journal of Experimental Psychology: Human Perception and Performance, 38,* 53–79.

Yarkoni, T., Balota, D. A., & Yap, M. J. (2008). Beyond Coltheart's *N*: A new measure of orthographic similarity. *Psychonomic Bulletin & Review 15*, 971–979.

Ziegler, J. C. & Goswami, U. (2005). Reading acquisition, developmental dyslexia, and skilled reading across languages: a psycholinguistic grain size theory. *Psychological Bulletin, 131*, 3–29.

Ziegler, J. C., Perry, C., Jacobs, A. M., & Braun, M. (2001). Identical words are read differently in different languages. *Psychological Science, 12*, 379–384.

3 A parallel activation model with a sequential twist

Kenneth I. Forster

Recognizing a word involves finding a match between a coded version of the input stimulus and an internalized lexical representation. A central issue in the investigation of this process concerns the mechanism by which a match is found. On the one hand, parallel activation models based on the Interactive Activation model (McClelland & Rumelhart, 1981) involve a system in which each letter increases the activation level of every word unit that contains that letter in the correct position, and decreases the activation level of every word unit that does not contain that letter in that position. The word unit that receives the most activation is the correct word unit. This approach essentially assumes that the input letter string is compared with every lexical representation in the lexicon simultaneously. The dominant examples of this approach are the Dual Route Cascaded Model (DRC) developed by Coltheart, Rastle, Perry, Langdon, and Ziegler (2001) and the Multi-Level Readout Model (MROM) developed by Grainger and Jacobs (1996). At the opposite extreme, search models assume that the comparison with the input is carried out one word at a time in a sequential fashion (Forster, 1976). In what follows, we will consider a third type of model that occupies a position intermediate between these two extremes, one that incorporates both parallel and sequential features.

We begin with a simple question. In an activation-based model, how important is the assumption that each letter unit is capable of activating every word that the reader knows simultaneously? Is there no limit to the number of words that can be accessed simultaneously, even for readers who know several languages? Obviously, there must be some limit (it cannot be infinite), and so the question is really whether that limit is bigger or smaller than the size of the lexicon. If it is smaller, then a sequential component to access is introduced, and lexical access will necessarily involve multiple activation cycles. Of course, there is no direct evidence about the number of word units that could be activated simultaneously, but nevertheless, theorists must make a decision about whether that number is larger or smaller than the number of lexical items that have to be accessed. In this chapter, we will explore the consequences of assuming that the number is substantially smaller than the number of lexical items. This assumption has implications in three areas: masked priming, frequency effects, and content-addressable access to the lexicon.

Modeling masked priming

In a typical masked priming experiment (e.g., Forster & Davis, 1984), the prime is presented very briefly (usually 50 ms), preceded by a forward mask and followed immediately by the target. Under these conditions, the prime cannot be identified (and for most individuals, is quite invisible), yet it has a marked effect on responses to the following target. In tasks that require lexical access, responses to word targets are faster when the prime is related to the target. The strongest effect is obtained when the prime is the same word as the target (e.g., contrast-CONTRAST), but a clear effect is also obtained when the prime closely resembles the target (e.g., bontrast-CONTRAST). Similar effects are generally not obtained when the target is not a word (for a review, see Kinoshita & Lupker, 2003). In activation-based models, priming is assumed to occur because the prime activates the word unit for the target, so that when the target is presented, its word unit is already in an active state. The extent of this pre-activation depends on the duration of the prime, and the degree of orthographic overlap with the target. In general, the results correspond fairly well with this approach (see Davis, this volume).

The issue of central concern here is what happens to the prime when it is replaced by the target. As argued by Davis and Lupker (2006), activation models give a better account of the data if the activation in the letter units produced by the prime is switched off immediately. This means that the prime no longer contributes any activation to the target, or to its competitors, and that any activation produced by the prime will then decay. When the target is orthographically related to the prime, the activation produced by the target is combined with the activation produced by the prime, which means that the target word unit reaches threshold faster. This approach works well when the relationship between the prime and target is one of form, but problems arise when the relationship involves semantic overlap. The clearest example of this type of priming is cross-language translation priming (Grainger & Frenck-Mestre, 1998; Duñabeitia, Perea, & Carreiras, 2010; Gollan, Forster, & Frost, 1997; Jiang & Forster, 2001; Finkbeiner, Forster, Nicol, & Nakamura, 2004; Wang & Forster, 2010), where the prime is a translation equivalent of the target (e.g., cheval-HORSE). The problem is that for priming to occur, the meaning of the prime must be activated, and it seems unlikely that 50 ms would be long enough for the network to settle on the precise meaning of the prime. For one thing, it is estimated that it takes at least 20–30 ms for the information on the retina to arrive at striate cortex (Maunsell & Gibson, 1992), leaving very little time for lexical activation. Further, evidence from EEG studies indicates that the semantic properties of words are not generated until about 160 ms after stimulus onset (e.g., Hauk, Davis, Ford, Pulvermüller, & Marslen-Wilson, 2006; Segalowitz & Zheng, 2009; Sereno, Rayner, & Posner, 1998). The implication of these results is very clear – somehow the processing of the prime must continue after it has been replaced by the target, and this processing must be carried out while the target is being processed.

Obviously, this multiplexing feature would be difficult to implement in a traditional activation model such as DRC or MROM. Somehow the letter information from the prime must be preserved, and somehow both the prime and the target must activate the same set of word units independently at the same time. One way to model this would be to suggest that processing of the target is delayed until processing of the prime is completed – a kind of 'spillover' effect, analogous to similar effects in eye-tracking studies of sentence processing. However, this would imply that the response to a target word would be much slower when the prime is an unrelated word or nonword compared to when the prime is a non-linguistic visual pattern, such as '$&$&$&', or characters in an unfamiliar script, which would not require extensive lexical processing. Unpublished data from our laboratory suggests that this is almost certainly not the case. Another method would be to postulate two identical networks, so that the prime could activate one network and the target could activate the other. This is not a particularly parsimonious solution, especially since such a capacity would be relevant only for processing extremely rapid visual inputs, such as in a masked priming experiment. It would also fail to explain how repetition priming could occur since the prime would not activate the same word unit as the target.

One way in which overlapping processing could be arranged is to design the system so that the input does not activate the entire set of word units at one time, but rather does so piece-by-piece (thereby allowing for the possibility that only a limited subset of word units could be activated at any one time). In this design, the lexicon would be divided into a series of non-overlapping partitions, which are activated one at a time in a fixed sequence. Thus when the prime is presented, it activates all the word units in the first partition in parallel, then the next, and so forth until all partitions have been activated. When the target is presented, it will go through the same sequence of operations, but will lag behind the prime. Thus the prime could begin a search by activating the first partition, then moving on to the next partition, allowing the target to activate the first partition. In this way, the prime is recognized when a word unit that is a match for the prime is activated, and the time taken will be a function of the number of partitions that had to be activated. Recognition of the target will occur in the same way, except for the fact that if the prime and target are related, the search for the prime will have already activated the word unit for the target, which leads to faster recognition. How this might be implemented will be discussed in the next section.

A brief overview of the model

The model is a parallel-serial hybrid model, hence referred to as PSM, and combines features of a standard parallel activation model with those of the entry-opening model of masked priming (Forster, 1999, 2009). The parallel activation component of PSM is based on a standard interactive-activation model, as described in McClelland and Rumelhart (1981). The input letter string activates word units by the usual mechanism – a letter in a given position sends activation to all word units that have that letter in the same position.[1] The critical element in the design of the system is a device suggested by Sloman and Rumelhart

(1992), namely a *gatekeeper*. This is a system that has excitatory and inhibitory connections to the actual connections between letter units and word units. This gives it the capacity to enable one set of connections between a letter unit and a subset of word units, while disabling all other connections between that letter unit and the remaining word units. The original purpose of a gatekeeper was to avoid the problem of catastrophic interference, in which forming new connections during the learning of new words interfered with the connections for already learned words. Applied to our current problem, the gatekeeper is responsible for partitioning the lexicon. It is designed so that initially, the only letter-to-word connections that are enabled are those for the word units in the first partition. After activation of that partition is completed, the gatekeeper disables those connections (allowing the activation levels in the word units to decay), and enables the connections for the second partition. This procedure is repeated until all partitions have been activated.

The other component of PSM is based on the entry-opening model of masked priming (Forster, 1999, 2009). To link the two models, we need to distinguish between a word unit, and the lexical entry that is associated with it. The word unit plays a role in the operation of the parallel activation component, which is solely concerned with finding the word unit that best matches the input. The lexical entry is where information about the word is stored, and this is the site at which priming takes place, not the word unit itself. After each partition is activated, activation levels in all word units in that partition return to zero. However, if a given word unit reaches threshold, a process is triggered that 'opens' the lexical entry associated with that word unit, so that information can be retrieved from it. This is a mandatory procedure, and takes approximately 30 ms. Once an entry is in the open state, further processing is enabled. When a target word that is related in form to the prime is presented, processing of the target is facilitated because the prime has already initiated the opening process for that entry, which means that information can be extracted from it immediately (a kind of 'read-out' effect). To see how this works, consider a case in which the prime is a close match for the target. When the partition containing the target word unit is activated by the prime, activation in the target word unit reaches threshold, and entry-opening is triggered. After 30 ms has elapsed, the lexical entry corresponding to the target word unit will be in an open state, although the activation level in the word unit will have returned to zero. When the subsequent search for the target activates the same partition, the activation level in the target word unit will reach threshold once again, triggering entry-opening. However, because the prime has already initiated this process, it will be completed sooner, producing a savings effect. Thus priming is determined not by activation levels in word units, but whether the lexical entry has been opened by the prime (this distinction becomes important when we consider the effect of an intervening stimulus).

This kind of priming is assumed to take place at the level of form. However, priming due to semantic overlap involves words that differ in form, so a different kind of entry-opening must be involved. In PSM, lexical access can be seen as a two-stage process. The first stage is purely form-driven, and involves isolating the word unit that matches the input. The second stage involves using the information provided by that unit to retrieve the semantic and syntactic properties of that word, which involves an entirely separate network. The function of the first network is essentially to provide a more efficient input to the second network, an input which is far more effective than an actual letter string, where there is a great deal of form overlap between words that nevertheless have totally different semantic properties. Rather than attempting to map directly from letter strings to meanings, an intermediate mapping operation is introduced which recodes the letter string into what we can think of as an 'address' in an associative network (see Forster & Taft, 1994, for a similar idea). The second network can then retrieve the stored properties of word units associated with these addresses in a more efficient manner. Now, if the prime and the target are related semantically, then we can assume that some of the information that is retrieved for the interpretation of the prime is also required for the interpretation of the target, and hence there is again the possibility of a savings effect.

In a perfect system, the gatekeeper responsible for supervising lexical searches would keep the processes associated with the prime and the target quite separate (especially when the prime is a different word to the target), but under extreme time pressure, this is not possible, and the processing of the prime cannot be completed before the target is presented. The consequence of this is that the processing of the prime and target become merged. The result of this processing error is the masked priming effect.

As argued earlier, the fact that semantic properties take much longer to activate than the typical time interval between the onset of a masked prime and the target implies that processing of the prime must somehow continue after target onset, which means that in some sense, the system must remember what the prime was, and continue to activate the appropriate word units. This is evident from eye-tracking experiments in which the target word is erased 60 ms after it has been fixated, but reading still proceeds at a normal rate (Rayner, Liversedge, & White, 2006). As these authors note, this does not mean that the processing of the target word is completed within 60 ms, only that this was long enough to initiate lexical processing. One way to model this might be to propose two banks of letter units, each connected to the same set of word units. The prime activates the first bank, and the letter information is clamped, so that activation is transmitted to the word units whether the prime is present or not. When the target is presented, it is assigned to the second bank of word units if processing of the prime has not been completed. The gatekeeper is then required to control the activation sequences for each bank.

An unattractive feature of this proposal is that the letter-to-word connections have to be duplicated, which is a bit like having two entirely separate networks. A better (but perhaps more complicated) solution might be to assume that while the prime is physically present, activation of successive partitions proceeds normally, but once the target is presented, the letters of the prime are shifted to working memory and are replaced by the letters of the target, allowing the target to activate the first partition (which is no longer being activated by the prime). After one or two cycles of activation, the target letters are shifted to working memory, and the prime letters are returned, so that the next step in the processing of the prime can be completed. Once again, the gatekeeper would have to keep track of which partition should be activated for each search.

One might object that this shuttling mechanism seems very far-fetched, but it is hard to see how else two searches could be carried out simultaneously. It must be emphasized that the evidence for overlapped processing of multiple inputs does not come solely from masked priming. There must also be a mechanism to explain preview effects in eye-tracking experiments. In these experiments, the movement of the eyes is monitored during normal reading, and it can be shown that the reader is able to pick up information not only about the word currently being fixated, but also about the next word (e.g., see Rayner, 1998). Such a capacity also appears to be required in order to explain the existence of parafoveal-on-foveal effects in reading. For example, Kennedy, Pynte, and Ducrot (2002) showed that when a list of words had to be scanned in order to find a word with a particular semantic property, gaze duration on a foveal word was influenced by the frequency of the unfixated parafoveal word. If these effects are genuine (this is contested, see Schotter and Rayner, accompanying volume, Chapter 4), then it is hard to interpret these effects without assuming that both words were being processed simultaneously.

Given the far-reaching implications of this argument, it is only sensible to ask whether there is any alternative way to account for the results. For example, translation priming with a masked 50-ms prime might be explained by assuming that the lexicons for the two languages are entirely separate, each having its own bank of letter/character units. This arrangement seems inevitable in languages that have different scripts, for instance, Chinese and English. This would eliminate the problem of shuttling the letters of the prime and target back and forth within a single bank of letter/character units, but would still require that processing of the prime continues long enough to activate semantic properties. This argument works well for the case of translation priming between languages with different scripts (priming would occur at the second, semantic stage), but not for languages with the same script, nor for cases where priming occurs between semantically or morphologically related words within one language. For example, Frenck-Mestre and Bueno (1999) obtained strong masked priming between words referring to objects with similar physical properties (e.g., PUMPKIN-SQUASH, WHALE-DOLPHIN), and similar effects have been reported for associatively related pairs, provided that a relatively long prime duration is used (e.g., Perea & Gotor, 1997; Rastle, Davis, Marslen-Wilson, & Tyler, 2000). Perhaps the clearest evidence for semantic interpretation of a masked prime comes from response congruence experiments, where slower categorization times for the target are obtained if the prime belongs to a different semantic category to the target (Dehaene, Shaywitz, Pugh, Menc, Fulbright, Skudlarski, et al., 1998; Quinn & Kinoshita, 2008; Van den Bussche, Van den Noortgate, & Reynvoet, 2009). Thus it seems we have no choice but to assume that somehow the visual word recognition system can interpret the prime and the target simultaneously. In effect we have parallel streams of word recognition.

Finally, it might be argued that a system with multiple partitions would be very slow compared to existing models, which typically take 30–40 cycles to recognize a word. However, there is no particular reason why so many cycles are necessary. In fact, a single cycle is quite sufficient to activate the correct word unit to threshold if the letter-to-word activation parameter is set sufficiently high. Obviously, there is a strong motivation in PSM to keep the number of activation cycles for each partition to an absolute minimum. If a search must cover the entire lexicon, then it needs to be very rapid. So we assume that each partition is activated for just one cycle.

Modeling the frequency effect

Words that occur frequently (e.g., HOME) are recognized faster than words that occur infrequently (e.g., EAGLE), despite the fact that both types of words may be perfectly familiar. This variable is by far the most important in terms of the percentage of variance accounted for (e.g., Balota, Cortese, Sergent-Marshall, Spieler, & Yap, 2004). In completely parallel activation models such as DRC and MROM, the frequency effect is explained by assuming that the word units corresponding to high-frequency words have higher resting levels of activation than the word units for low-frequency words. However, as pointed out by Norris (2006), there is nothing about these models that explains why this should be the case, nor is there any particular reason why low-frequency words should not be recognized just as rapidly as high-frequency words. The system would work perfectly well in either case, and there is no particular advantage in just giving high-frequency words a head start. This makes the explanation somewhat ad hoc.

There are ways to improve the parallel account. For example, the connections between letter units and word units could be stronger for high-frequency words, so that activation builds up in those word units more rapidly. This is the approach taken in the SOLAR model (Davis, 2010). But there is a further aspect of the frequency effect that needs to be considered, and that is the nature of the mathematical function relating frequency to lexical access time, as indexed by lexical decision time. This is typically assumed to be logarithmic, which helps to explain why large changes in frequency at the high end result in very small changes in decision time, and very small changes in frequency at the low end produce large changes in decision time. But beyond this, there is no account of why the function should have this shape.

In contrast, a search model explains this effect by assuming that the search is optimized, so that the entries for frequently occurring words are compared with the input before the entries for low-frequency words (e.g., Forster, 1976). A similar assumption could be made in a model with a partitioned lexicon. The partitions would be activated in a fixed order, and the first partition to be activated would contain the highest-frequency words, and the last partition to be activated would contain the lowest-frequency words. So access would involve a wave of activation across the lexicon.

Whereas the resting-level explanation of the frequency effect seems ad hoc, in a search model it is inevitable that low-frequency words will take longer to access than high-frequency words, provided that the search process is designed in the most efficient manner, i.e., that words are assigned to partitions in terms of their frequency. If words were assigned to partitions at random, then the search would be less efficient, and there would be no frequency effect. An additional advantage of this approach is that a frequency-ordered search model specifies the form of the frequency effect. In such a model, access time is not a function of the frequency itself, but instead it is a function of *relative* frequency. Specifically, access time should be a function of the rank of a word in a frequency-ordered list. As shown by Murray and Forster (2004), this rank model provides a surprisingly accurate account of the function relating frequency and lexical decision time, and explains why the frequency effect is roughly logarithmic. Murray and Forster claimed that the rank account is in fact slightly superior to a logarithmic function, which tends to underestimate the time required for low-frequency words, and to overestimate the time required for high-frequency words. Whether the rank function provides a better fit to the data than a power function is a matter of some dispute, but there can be no doubt that it provides a very close approximation (but see Adelman & Brown, 2008, who argue that the rank function is not an adequate fit). For now, suffice it to say that a parallel model with partitions will produce a rank frequency effect, without any special assumptions. In fact, access time will be a function of which partition a word is assigned to. The difference in access time between words in partitions no. 1 and no. 2 will be the same as the difference between words in partitions no. 2 and no. 3, but the average frequency differences will be far greater for no. 1 and no. 2 than for no. 2 and no. 3. This argument is exactly the same as the argument used by Murray and Forster.

Content-addressable access

A third problem area where the concept of a partitioned lexicon is helpful concerns the hash coding feature of the original 'bin' model of lexical access (Forster, 1976). The problem arises in the following way. The most obvious objection to a serial search model is that in order to classify the input as a nonword, a search of the entire lexicon would be necessary, which would be far too slow. Typically, decisions for nonwords are about 50–100 ms slower than the decision time for the average word, and in this time it would be necessary to scan many thousands of entries. In order to minimize this problem, it was proposed that the input letter string is first fed to a hash coder, an algorithm designed to convert an alphabetic array into an address in memory. If this was a unique address (i.e., every word has a different address), then full content-addressability would be achieved. However, in practice this is impossible to achieve, and the hash coder assigns the same address to many different words, which essentially divides the lexicon into a number of bins. Each bin contains the lexical entries of words that are assigned the same address by the hash coder. Lexical access involves first establishing which bin should contain the input (if it is a word), and then searching through the members of the bin according to their frequency of occurrence. If the input is a word, a matching entry will be found. If it is not a word, no matching entry will be found. Thus, only the contents of a single bin need to searched in order to establish the lexical status of the input.

At a purely theoretical level, this solution to the size of the search set sounds promising, but in practice there are serious problems to overcome. For example, it is well known that in a lexical decision task, nonwords derived from a word by changing one letter (e.g., BONTRAST) take longer to reject than nonwords that do not closely resemble a word (e.g., Coltheart, Davelaar, Jonasson, & Besner, 1977). A search model can explain this by assuming that the function that assesses the degree of match between the input string and a lexical entry is noisy (perhaps because it operates so rapidly), and hence any lexical entry that closely matches the input must be flagged as a potential match. If no perfect match is discovered, any close-match candidates must be evaluated before a 'No' decision can be made. This evaluation is carried out by a subsequent verification process, which executes a slower and more precise comparison between the candidate and the input. The assumption is that this arrangement is more efficient than one in which the initial comparison is a relatively slow, but accurate process. Thus, if the search for BONTRAST encounters the entry for CONTRAST, then the entry for CONTRAST will be flagged as a potential match, which will then trigger a verification process, which delays the decision relative to a nonword that does not closely resemble any word (e.g., BENCROST). However, in order for the search to encounter the entry for CONTRAST, it must be the case that the hash coder assigns the same bin number to both BONTRAST and CONTRAST. This seems quite straightforward until one realizes that other nonwords derived from the same base word (e.g., CANTRAST, COPTRAST, and CONTREST) would also show longer decision times, indicating that they are all assigned the same hash code. How to design a hash function that assigns the same bin number to all of these stimuli is not at all clear. A similar problem arises in masked form-priming (Forster, Davis, Schoknecht, & Carter, 1987). Lexical decision times to words are faster when they are preceded by a masked prime that differs by one letter. So, if LAUGHTER primes DAUGHTER, then the search for LAUGHTER must have encountered the entry for DAUGHTER, and therefore they must be in the same bin. However, Peressotti and Grainger (1999) found strong priming for the French word BALCON when primed with the letters blcn. Perea and Lupker (2004) found strong priming for pairs such as caniso-CASINO, where two non-adjacent letters have been transposed. Guererra and Forster (2008) reported robust priming when all letters but two had been transposed (e.g., sdiwelak-SIDEWALK). Further, there is evidence that adding letters does not disrupt priming (Van Assche & Grainger, 2006). In each of these cases, we would have to assume that the prime was assigned the same bin number as the target, otherwise there would be no priming. Clearly, the hash function would have to take letter position into account, yet the evidence indicates that considerable latitude is possible as far as the number of matching letters and their positions are concerned. As Grainger noted, the task of cracking the orthographic code is formidable (Grainger, 2008).

This problem is minimized if we abandon the constraint that the prime and target have to be assigned the same bin number in order for form-priming to occur.

Thus, CANISO might be assigned a different bin number from CASINO, but if the search for CANISO was allowed to spread across multiple bins, contact with the entry for CASINO might eventually be established. But this simply exchanges one problem for another, since all bins would still have to be searched in order to establish that CANISO is not a word. What this argument suggests is that an exhaustive search of the lexicon will always be required to classify nonwords. In a traditional parallel activation model this is not a problem, since all word units are compared with the input simultaneously. In a model with a partitioned lexicon, this is not the case, but if the processing of each partition is rapid enough, then an exhaustive search of the lexicon is more plausible.

How many searches can be active at once?

An interesting question is whether more than two searches can be active at the same time. The 'shuttle' mechanism discussed earlier could theoretically cope with a larger number of searches, provided that there is enough working memory capacity to store the various inputs while they wait their turn, and provided that the gatekeeper can keep track of more than two searches. Under normal circumstances, the capacity to run two searches at the same time would be sufficient to cope with even the most rapid reading rate. But what about a task such as RSVP where the successive words of a sentence are presented at a rapid rate? If we assume that 150 ms is required to process each word, then a presentation rate of 75 ms per word (150/2) would be the fastest rate that a two-search system could cope with. This conclusion fits well with the finding that subjects are unable to accurately report short sentences with a presentation rate of 16 words per second, i.e., 62.5 ms per word (Forster, 1970).

Another method of investigating this issue is to use two masked primes, rather than just one (Forster, 2009). Whether both primes are adequately processed is assessed by seeing whether they are capable of generating a normal priming effect. In these 'intervenor' experiments, the first prime is related to the target (either an identity prime, or a one-letter-different form prime), but the second prime is a completely unrelated word, and functions purely as an intervenor. Both primes are presented for 50 ms, and the second prime is followed immediately by the target. These conditions should force the system to attempt a third search, because the second prime arrives before processing of the first is completed, and the target arrives before either of these searches has been completed, so a third search would be required for the target. Under these conditions, it was found that form priming was eliminated altogether, although identity priming survived in a reduced form (Forster, 2009, Experiments 3–4). This result indicates that the addition of a third search did in fact exceed the capacity of the system. However, when the order of the primes was reversed, so that the related prime was adjacent to the target, perfectly normal priming effects were obtained, indicating that it was the search for the first prime, not the second, that was most severely affected. It should be noted that a simple decay mechanism could not explain these results. When the duration of the second (unrelated) prime was increased to 500 ms (which should have produced an even stronger decay), normal form priming effects were observed (Forster, 2009, Experiments 1–2). This is consistent with the two-search argument, since the long duration of the second prime would enable the search for the first prime to be completed before the target was presented, and hence no more than two simultaneous searches would be required.

How do the partitions develop?

It may be that the beginning reader begins with just a single network, and as new words are learned they are added to the network until the capacity of the network is exceeded. This triggers the creation of a second network, and the connections necessary to recognize any new words are formed in the second network, while the first network is essentially frozen. This approach suggests that the members of a partition are determined by the order in which they are acquired, which predicts that access time should be a function of age of acquisition (AoA), not frequency of occurrence. However, because high-frequency words are learned first, frequency is highly correlated with AoA, and hence frequency would still be highly correlated with access time. Or, more precisely, access time will be highly correlated with the rank of a word in a list ordered according to AoA, which in turn will be highly correlated with the rank of a word in a frequency-ordered list.

But there is one empirical result that raises problems for the PSM approach. Gardner, Rothkopf, Lapan, and Lafferty (1987) found that lexical decision latencies were influenced by occupational background. Nurses were faster than engineering students to recognize familiar words relevant to medicine, while engineering students were faster to recognize words relevant to engineering. This indicates that changes in the relative frequencies of words encountered in adult life have an impact on access time (which is not consistent with the AoA account). To explain this within PSM, some mechanism would have to be found that enabled words to move forward to a higher-frequency partition. However, achieving this is not at all straightforward, and there seems to be no independent motivation for such a mechanism.

One solution might be to investigate more carefully whether this occupational effect really reflects faster access time at the level of form. In considering this issue, recall that access is seen as a two-stage process. The first stage is purely form-driven, and is designed to find the internal representation that matches the input at the level of form. The second stage involves using that representation to retrieve the semantic and syntactic properties of the word, and it is possible that these functions involve completely different operations, so that changes in the relative frequencies of words in adult life affect the second semantic stage, but not the first. Thus there would be two components to the frequency effect. One would be the form effect, which is determined by age of acquisition, and is unmodifiable. The other would be the semantic component, which would be modifiable by recent experience in adult life. Viewed this way, the occupational effect would be located in the semantic stage, not the form stage. Given this approach, it is encouraging that some researchers find that both frequency of occurrence and age of acquisition have independent effects on measures of access time (e.g., Brysbaert, Lange, & Wijnendaele, 2000). More importantly, it appears that age of acquisition may be more closely associated with naming time than with lexical decision, when frequency is controlled (e.g., Morrison & Ellis, 1995). This makes sense if retrieval time at the second (semantic) stage is more relevant for lexical decision than naming.

This two-stage approach may also provide a way of modeling other effects. There is steadily mounting evidence that lexical access time is also a function of semantic variables such as imageability (Balota et al., 2004; Balota and colleagues, Chapter 5, this volume), number of semantic neighbors (Buchanan, Westbury, & Burgess, 2001), or semantic 'richness' (Pexman, Hargreaves, Siakaluk, Bodner, & Pope, 2008; Pexman, accompanying volume, Chapter 2). Explaining such effects in terms of differences in resting activation levels would amount to little more than a redescription of the facts. Also, there is no obvious way to explain such effects in a frequency-ordered search system. But if the second stage of retrieval has quite different properties, these effects can perhaps be accommodated.

Is there any evidence to support this two-stage approach? Recent work in masked priming is suggestive. The evidence comes from the intervenor experiments mentioned earlier that were designed to determine whether priming effects could survive across an intervening word (Forster, 2009). According to the entry-opening model, once the intervening word has been identified, all open entries would be closed down in preparation for the upcoming word, and hence there should be no priming. Activation models also make a similar prediction, since the activation levels in all word units would be reset once the intervenor has been identified. However, priming did survive, but in a reduced form. The critical result was that the intervenor affected identity priming and form priming in different ways. When the intervenor was visible (500 ms duration), identity priming was substantially reduced but form priming was relatively unaffected, the result being that there was no longer any difference between them. But as discussed earlier, when the intervenor was masked, identity priming survived in a reduced form, but form priming was eliminated altogether. These effects can be understood if we assume that identity priming consists of two components – an effect which occurs at the level of form, and an additional effect which occurs at a semantic level. When the intervenor is visible, the semantic component is affected, but when the intervenor is masked, the form component is affected. This dissociation between the two forms of priming is at least consistent with a two-stage model of access.

There is also another source of evidence that may be relevant. In the eye-tracking literature, it is argued that the preview benefit derived from processing a word in the parafovea is restricted to words of similar form. There is apparently no benefit at all from words that overlap semantically with the currently fixated word (Rayner, Balota, & Pollatsek, 1986, also Schotter and Rayner, accompanying volume). The implication is that processing at the level of form does not automatically lead to activation of semantic properties.

Implications of PSM

Adopting an approach such as PSM has a number of consequences, some good, some perhaps not so good. One good consequence is that it is no longer necessary to assume that word units have different resting activation levels in order to explain frequency effects. It also means that there is no longer any problem explaining how a very low-frequency word can be recognized when it has a very high-frequency competitor, that is, the BLIGHT-BRIGHT problem outlined in Forster (1976). In a standard activation model, the input BLIGHT activates the word unit for BRIGHT as well as BLIGHT, but BRIGHT has an advantage because of its higher resting level. The problem is how to make sure that this advantage does not permit the higher-frequency competitor to reach threshold first. In PSM, which word unit reaches threshold first is purely a function of the number of matching and mismatching letters. Although the input BLIGHT would initially open the entry for BRIGHT as a close match candidate, the system would eventually register BLIGHT as a perfect match, and discard BRIGHT as a candidate.

What might be seen as a less attractive consequence of adopting a PSM approach is that some of the interactive flavor of a parallel system may be lost. For example, there is no role for competition between word units. Basically, the competitive process is a device whereby a network can arrive at a decision about which word unit is the best match to the input without any executive control. In PSM, this decision is left up to a post-activation verification process that evaluates whether each of the candidates produced by the activation process actually matches the input, and therefore there is no need for competition. Also, the procedure that allows two inputs to activate word units independently requires that activation levels in word units return to zero after each partition has been activated. Note that persisting activation in word units is not required to explain priming, since priming occurs at the lexical entry associated with the word unit through the mechanism of entry-opening.

Defending this departure from standard assumptions will not be easy, since there is evidence from masked priming that word primes can have an inhibitory effect on recognition of form-related words (Davis & Lupker, 2006). However, it is not clear that the inhibitory effect is an automatic consequence of using a word prime, since this depends on other factors such as the length of the target, and the nature of the nonword targets. If the nonword targets are designed so that they do not closely resemble any particular word, then word primes are just as effective as nonword primes (Forster & Vereš, 1998).

There is another positive feature to the PSM approach, namely that it has the potential to explain how masked priming effects can survive across a visible word that intervenes between the prime and the target word (Forster, 2009). This fact presents a problem for standard activation models, because once the intervening word has been recognized, activation levels in all word units would have to be reset, which would wipe out any influence of the preceding masked prime. But in PSM, priming is mediated by the state of the lexical entry for the target, not the activation level in its word unit. The state of a lexical entry (open or closed) is independent of the activation pattern across the word units. The lexical entry for the target word can remain in an open state while another word is being processed. However, the activation level in the target word unit cannot remain at the same level while another word is being processed.

Another consequence of adopting a PSM approach is that word recognition is no longer seen in terms of a gradual accumulation of evidence. This assumption is required in parallel-activation models in order to account for variation in lexical decision times, but in PSM, the time taken to reach threshold is constant for all words. Instead, variation in recognition time is explained in terms of the number of partitions that have to be activated. A further consequence is that there is a limited role for feedback mechanisms. Recall that in order to keep the number of activation cycles comparable to existing parallel models, activation to threshold was assumed to occur within a single cycle. Under these conditions, there is simply no opportunity for feedback (or competition) to develop. Whether existing research findings can be satisfactorily explained without recourse to feedback mechanisms or competition remains to be seen.

We started out this research program asking what was the minimal modification that would have to be made to an interactive activation model so that it could explain why lexical decision time is related to the rank of a word in a frequency-ordered list. Introducing a sequential activation system achieved this goal, but it soon became apparent that there were other far more important advantages of this approach. The most important of these was the capacity to process more than one word at the same time, which appears to be essential to explain masked priming effects. Another advantage was the ability to explain how masked priming effects could survive across an intervening word. These results represent genuine advances, but the question is whether they are cost-free. Committing to a system that explains variation in access time in terms of search time, rather than a slow, gradual accumulation of activation might well rob some models of their ability to explain other phenomena, and it may be necessary to find other explanations for them. Finally, it will no doubt be objected that PSM is not a computational model, and therefore we cannot be sure what it predicts and what it does not predict. This is a valid point if one is dealing with a highly interactive system, but PSM is not a highly interactive system. Actually, in its infancy, PSM started out as a computational model, and the exercise of being forced to specify the detailed design of the system was extremely instructive. Hopefully this has had a beneficial effect on this version of the theory.

- Most contemporary models of visual word recognition are based on interactive-activation or similar frameworks that propose that the input is compared with all words in the vocabulary simultaneously.
- An alternative parallel-serial model (PSM) proposes that at any given time, only a subset of words is under consideration, these subsets being considered in a sequential fashion, the sequence being linked to frequency of occurrence (or a correlated variable). Access to these subsets of word units is controlled by a gatekeeper mechanism.
- Masked cross-language translation priming occurs with a prime-target SOA of 50 ms, yet electrophysiological evidence suggests that semantic interpretation of a word requires at least 150 ms. This implies that the prime continues to be processed after it has been replaced by the target. This is difficult (if not impossible) to implement in a standard interactive activation model, but is readily explained in PSM.
- It is proposed that priming occurs at two sites. Form priming occurs in word units, but there is an additional semantic component that occurs at the lexical entry associated with the word unit.
- Key advantages of this approach are:

  o An explanation of how multiple words can be active to process phrases and sentences.
  o A principled account of the functional form of frequency effects.
  o An explanation of 'intervenor' effects, which are difficult to reconcile with activation accounts.
  o Providing a mechanism to explain mounting evidence that semantic variables affect access time.

Note

1 Recent work on transposed-letter priming shows that this approach cannot be correct (see Grainger, 2008, for a review). Instead there is some flexibility about letter position. However, this issue is not critical for the current discussion.

References

Adelman, J. S. & Brown, G. D. A. (2008). Modeling lexical decision: The form of frequency and diversity effects. *Psychological Review, 115*, 214–227.

Balota, D. A., Cortese, M. J., Sergent-Marshall, S. D., Spieler, D. H., & Yap, M. (2004). Visual word recognition of single-syllable words. *Journal of Experimental Psychology: General, 133*, 283–316.

Brysbaert, M., Lange, M., & Wijnendaele, I. V. (2000). The effects of age-of-acquisition and frequency-of-occurrence in visual word recognition: Further evidence from the Dutch language. *European Journal of Cognitive Psychology, 12*, 65–85.

Buchanan, L., Westbury, C., & Burgess, C. (2001). Characterizing semantic space: Neighborhood effects in word recognition. *Psychonomic Bulletin & Review*, *8*, 531–544.

Coltheart, M., Davelaar, E., Jonasson, J. T., & Besner, D. (1977). Access to the internal lexicon. In S. Dornic (Ed.), *Attention and performance VI* (pp. 535–555). Hillsdale, NJ: Erlbaum.

Coltheart, M., Rastle, K., Perry, C., Langdon, R., & Ziegler, J. (2001). DRC: A dual route cascaded model of visual word recognition and reading aloud. *Psychological Review*, *108*, 204–256.

Davis, C. J. (2010). The spatial coding model of visual word identification. *Psychological Review*, *117*, 713–758.

Davis, C. J. & Lupker, S. J. (2006). Masked inhibitory priming in English: Evidence for lexical inhibition. *Journal of Experimental Psychology: Human Perception and Performance*, *32*, 668–687.

Dehaene, S., Naccache, L., Le Clec'H, G., Koechlin, E., Mueller, M., Dehaene-Lambertz, G., van de Moortele, P. F., & Le Bihan, D. (1998). Imaging unconscious semantic priming. *Nature*, *395*, 597–600.

Duñabeitia, J., Perea, M., & Carreiras, M. (2010). Masked translation priming effects with highly proficient simultaneous bilinguals. *Experimental Psychology*, *57*, 98–107.

Finkbeiner, M., Forster, K., Nicol, J., & Nakamura, K. (2004). The role of polysemy in masked semantic and translation priming. *Journal of Memory & Language*, *51*, 1–22.

Forster, K. I. (1970). Visual perception of rapidly presented word sequences of varying complexity. *Perception & Psychophysics*, *8*, 215–221.

Forster, K. I. (1976). Accessing the mental lexicon. In R. J. Wales & E. Walker (Eds), *Approaches to Language Mechanisms* (pp. 257–287). Amsterdam: North-Holland.

Forster, K. I. (1999). The microgenesis of priming effects in lexical access. *Brain & Language*, *68*, 5–15.

Forster, K. I. (2009). The intervenor effect in masked priming: How does masked priming survive across an intervening word? *Journal of Memory and Language*, *60*, 36–49.

Forster, K. I. & Davis, C. (1984). Repetition priming and frequency attenuation in lexical access. *Journal of Experimental Psychology: Learning, Memory, and Cognition*, *10*, 680–698.

Forster, K. I. & Taft, M. (1994). Bodies, antibodies, and neighborhood-density effects in masked form priming. *Journal of Experimental Psychology: Learning, Memory, and Cognition*, *20*, 844–863.

Forster, K. I. & Vereš, C. (1998). The prime lexicality effect: Form-priming as a function of prime awareness, lexical status, and discrimination difficulty. *Journal of Experimental Psychology: Learning, Memory, & Cognition*, *24*, 498–514.

Forster, K. I., Davis, C., Schoknecht, C., & Carter, R. (1987). Masked priming with graph-emically related forms: Repetition or partial activation? *Quarterly Journal of Experimental Psychology: Human Experimental Psychology*, *39A*, 211–251.

Frenck-Mestre, C. & Bueno, S. (1999). Semantic traits and semantic categories: Differences in rapid activation of the lexicon. *Brain & Language Special Issue: Mental lexicon*, *68(1–2)*, 199–204.

Gardner, M. K., Rothkopf, E. Z., Lapan, R., & Lafferty, T. (1987). The word frequency effect in lexical decision: Finding a frequency-based component. *Memory & Cognition*, *15*, 24–28.

Gollan, T. H., Forster, K. I., & Frost, R. (1997). Translation priming with different scripts: Masked priming with cognates and noncognates in Hebrew-English bilinguals.

Journal of Experimental Psychology: Learning, Memory, and Cognition, 23, 1122–1139.

Grainger, J. (2008). Cracking the orthographic code: An introduction. *Language and Cognitive Processes, 23,* 1–35.

Grainger, J. & Frenck-Mestre, C. (1998). Masked priming by translation equivalents in proficient bilinguals. *Language & Cognitive Processes, 13,* 601–623.

Grainger, J. & Jacobs, A. M. (1996). Orthographic processing in visual word recognition: A multiple read-out model. *Psychological Review, 103,* 518–565.

Guerrera, C. & Forster, K. I. (2008). Masked form priming with extreme transposition. *Language and Cognitive Processes, 23,* 117–142.

Hauk, O., Davis, M. H., Ford, M., Pulvermüller, F., & Marslen-Wilson, W. D. (2006). The time course of visual word recognition as revealed by linear regression analysis of ERP data. *Neuroimage, 30,* 1383–1400.

Jiang, N. & Forster, K. I. (2001). Cross-language priming asymmetries in lexical decision and episodic recognition. *Journal of Memory and Language, 44,* 32–51.

Kennedy, A., Pynte, J. L., & Ducrot, S. P. (2002). Parafoveal-on-foveal interactions in word recognition. *The Quarterly Journal of Experimental Psychology A: Human Experimental Psychology, 55A,* 1307–1337.

Kinoshita, S. & Lupker, S. L. (Eds) (2003). *Masked priming: State of the art.* Hove, UK: Psychology Press.

McClelland, J. L. & Rumelhart, D. E. (1981). An interactive activation model of context effects in letter perception: I. An account of basic findings. *Psychological Review, 88,* 375–407.

Maunsell, J. H. & Gibson, J. R. (1992). Visual response latencies in striate cortex of the macaque monkey. *Journal of Neurophysiology, 68,* 1332–1344.

Morrison, C. M. & Ellis, A. W. (1995). Roles of word frequency and age of acquisition in word naming and lexical decision. *Journal of Experimental Psychology: Learning, Memory, and Cognition, 21,* 116–133.

Murray, W. S. & Forster, K. I. (2004). Serial mechanisms in lexical access: The Rank Hypothesis. *Psychological Review, 111,* 721–756.

Norris, D. (2006). The Bayesian Reader: Explaining word recognition as an optimal Bayesian decision process. *Psychological Review, 113,* 327–357.

Perea, M. & Gotor, A. (1997). Associative and semantic priming effects occur at very short stimulus-onset asynchronies in lexical decision and naming. *Cognition, 62,* 223–240.

Perea, M. & Lupker, S. J. (2004). Can CANISO activate CASINO? Transposed-letter similarity effects with nonadjacent letter positions. *Journal of Memory and Language, 51,* 231–246.

Peressotti, F. & Grainger, J. (1999). The role of letter identity and letter position in orthographic priming. *Perception & Psychophysics, 61,* 691–706.

Pexman, P. M., Hargreaves, I. S., Siakaluk, P. D., Bodner, G. E., & Pope, J. (2008). *Psychonomic Bulletin & Review, 15,* 161–167.

Quinn, W. & Kinoshita, S. (2008). Congruence effect in semantic categorization with masked primes with narrow and broad categories. *Journal of Memory and Language, 58,* 286–306.

Rastle, K., Davis, M. H., Marslen-Wilson, W. D., & Tyler, L. K. (2000). Morphological and semantic effects in visual word recognition: A time-course study. *Language and Cognitive Processes, 15,* 507–537.

Rayner, K. (1998). Eye movements in reading and information processing: 20 years of research. *Psychological Bulletin, 124*, 372–422.

Rayner, K., Balota, D. A., & Pollatsek, A. (1986). Against parafoveal semantic preprocessing during eye fixations in reading. *Canadian Journal of Psychology, 40*, 473–483.

Rayner, K., Liversedge, S. P., & White, S. J. (2006). Eye movements when reading disappearing text: The importance of the word to the right of fixation. *Vision Research, 46*, 310–323.

Segalowitz, S. J. & Zheng, X. (2009). An ERP study of category priming: Evidence of early lexical semantic access. *Biological Psychology, 80*, 122–129.

Sereno, S. C., Rayner, K., & Posner, M. I. (1998). Establishing a time-line of word recognition: evidence from eye movements and event-related potentials. *Neuroreport, 9*, 2195–2200.

Sloman, S. A. & Rumelhart, D. E. (1992). Reducing interference in distributed memories through episodic gating. In A. F. Healy & S. M. Kosslyn (Eds), *Essays in honor of William K. Estes, Vol. 1: From learning theory to connectionist theory; Vol. 2: From learning processes to cognitive processes.* (pp. 227–248). Hillsdale, NJ: Erlbaum.

Van Assche, E. & Grainger, J. (2006). A study of relative-position priming with superset primes. *Journal of Experimental Psychology: Learning, Memory and Cognition, 32*, 399–415.

Van den Bussche, E., Van den Noortgate, W., & Reynvoet, B. (2009). Mechanisms of masked priming: A meta-analysis. *Psychological Bulletin, 135*, 452–77.

Wang, X. & Forster, K. I. (2010). Masked translation priming with semantic categorization: Testing the Sense model. *Bilingualism: Language and Cognition, 13*, 327–340.

4 Mathematical models of the lexical decision task

Pablo Gomez

Visual word recognition tasks have been used by researchers since the 1950s. It wasn't until 40 years ago that Meyer and Schvaneveldt (1971) coined the term *lexical decision task* (LDT) which has been used ever since. There has been a wide range of theoretical and empirical aims in studies using the LDT; hence, there has been some variability in the methodology used in the task (e.g., presentation and response modalities, priming, masked vs unmasked presentation). In spite of these variations, the defining aspect of the task is a binary classification of a stimulus as a 'word' or as a 'nonword'. This chapter is concerned with mathematical models of the LDT. Most of these models have focused on visual presentation of the stimuli and manual responses (key presses); hence, I will consider only this version of the task.

Why model?

Thousands of articles that feature the LDT have been published over the last 40 years; given the prevalence and reach of the task, there has been considerable interest in understanding the task itself (or *LDTology*, to borrow from Steve Luck's, 2005, description of the study of evoked related potentials or ERPs). LDTology has been of critical importance in spite of the task's apparent simplicity because the LDT's data is necessarily affected by factors intrinsic to the task itself (e.g., decisional biases), and it is not a pure measurement of the process of interest to the researcher (e.g., lexical access or availability of a word in memory).

Mathematical modeling has been an important tool for progress in LDTology. Just like in other domains within the study of cognition, there are some important advantages to formal modeling over verbal descriptions of theories (for a general introduction to modeling in cognitive science, see Busemeyer & Diederich, 2010, or Hunt, 2007). One of these advantages is that verbal descriptions are often hard to falsify and hard to distinguish from other verbal descriptions because of their inherent ambiguities (see Massaro, 1992); mathematical models, on the other hand, have forced researchers to make their assumptions explicit. A second advantage of modeling is that models have generated quantitative predictions that have been tested and sometimes falsified. Often, this process of generating predictions, testing through empirical work, and refining of theories has been an important path for advancement in cognitive science.

The types of mathematical models that discussed here are derived from assumptions about cognitive processing. Note that there are other types of formal models (e.g., regression models) that do not emerge from assumptions about cognitive processes; even if such models can be applied to lexical decision data, they are silent about the cognitive processes involved in the task. It is important to point out that, as it will become apparent in this chapter, the level of detail in the different models' explanation of all components of the LDT varies considerably, and some models are more concerned with the *lexical* aspects, while others care more about the *decision* aspects of the LDT. In addition, not all models of word reading or visual word recognition include a formal account of the LDT (see Jacobs & Grainger, 1994). This chapter focuses only on models of the LDT.

Early ideas

Even if some of the early accounts of the LDT were only verbal theories that were not implemented in mathematical models, they were the springboard for some of the later formal models. One of the early debates in the field was between so-called serial search models and parallel processing models. The serial search models (e.g., Rubenstein, Lewis, & Rubenstein, 1971) assume that words are ordered in the lexicon by frequency. When a letter string is presented, it is compared to each entry in the lexicon, starting with the highest-frequency words and proceeding through to the low-frequency words until a match is found. The serial search hypothesis was later refined by Forster's (1976) model, which assumes that the orthographic representations of words are ordered in a peripheral access file that provides the address of a lexical entry in a master file. Similar ideas were later espoused in models like the Activation-Verification model (Paap & Johansen, 1994; Paap, Newsome, McDonald, & Schvaneveldt, 1982; Paap, McDonald, Schvaneveldt, & Noel, 1987). Recently, Murray and Forster (2004, and Murray & Forster, 2008) revisited this idea and generated predictions regarding the relationship of frequency rank and RT (which will be discussed later in this chapter).

The parallel search models that competed with the serial matching mechanism were inspired by Morton's (1969, 1979) logogen model. According to Morton's formulation, lexical entries are represented as *logogens* (i.e., detectors for each word in the lexicon). When a string of letters is presented, the counters for all of the logogens that contain the features extracted from the stimulus letter string are incremented in parallel. Word identification occurs when evidence from the input reaches a threshold amount in a word's logogen. The threshold level for identification is a function of frequency: less information is needed to identify a more frequent word than a less frequent word.

Although the parallel vs serial debate lost steam across many areas of cognitive science (see Townsend, 1972), there are still echoes of these early ideas in current mathematical models, particularly in the focus of the modeling efforts. Contemporary accumulation of evidence models (see section below) share with the logogen model the assumption of accumulation of evidence over time, while other contemporary models like the MROM share with both models the notion that a response in the LDT could be generated from precise identification of a string as one word in the lexicon.

After a decade of LDT research, it became clear that a fundamental issue in *LDTology* would be the identification of the effects that emerge from the decisional or task-specific processes, versus the effects that emerge from the components of word identification (e.g., lexical, orthographic or semantic). Balota and Chumbley (1984, 1990) emphasized this issue in their *familiarity-recheck* model. They argued that word frequency effects in the LDT are, to a large extent, a by-product of the decisional processes in the task and might not be as informative about the organization of the mental lexicon as previously thought. They proposed a signal-detection theory interpretation of the LDT according to which the familiarity values of words and nonwords are distributed normally, with higher frequency words having higher familiarity than lower frequency words. The model assumes that there are two decision criteria (as opposed to one, like in standard signal detection). If the familiarity value of a string of letters is higher than the upper criterion, a positive response is initiated. If it is below the lower criterion, a negative response is initiated. The recheck component is an extra process triggered by some strings if their familiarity value is between the two decision thresholds. This model qualitatively accounts for the effect of familiarity (word frequency) on the latencies in the LDT, but does not generate quantitative predictions. In spite of this limitation, Balota and Chumbley made a very important observation: LDT data is not a pure measurement of lexical processes. This idea became a central theme in LDTology, as we will see in the next sections of this chapter.

Connectionist models

Within the connectionist tradition, there have been two approaches to modeling: the localist and the distributed representation (see, for example, Grainger & Jacobs, 1996; Jacobs, Rey, Ziegler, & Grainger, 1998). The implications and advantages of each of these two approaches have been discussed extensively elsewhere. In this chapter I will only discuss the contributions of these two approaches to the modeling of the LDT.

Localist representation: The Interactive Activation Model and its heirs

One cannot understand the development of the study of visual word recognition without the two articles by McClelland and Rumelhart (1981; Rumelhart & McClelland, 1982) on an *Interactive Activation Model* (IAM) of letter and word perception. Although the IAM was not a model of lexical decision per se, it has been so influential that many subsequent models have used its architecture, and it is probably one of the most visible connectionist models. In the IAM there is a localist representation of words, letters and visual features. These three types of units correspond to three levels of processing. When a string of letters is inputted to the system, visual features are activated and this activation spreads into the letter units that contain such visual features. Similarly, activation of letters in the specific letter position in the string feeds activation into the word nodes, so that representations of all words orthographically similar to the input are activated. The IAM includes a lateral inhibition mechanism among words, which means that word recognition is also influenced by inhibitory connections within the word unit level. This lateral inhibition among words that share features causes them to inhibit each other until the strongest one beats down its competitors.

Although the original formulation of the IAM had as a primary concern the word superiority effects, two different groups of researchers have used its principles as a starting point for full models of the LDT and other word recognition tasks. One of them is the Dual Route Cascaded (DRC) model, discussed in Chapter 1 of this volume. The other one is the multiple readout model (MROM; Grainger & Jacobs, 1996; Jacobs, Rey, Ziegler, & Grainger, 1998a). The MROM, along with its extensions, has been one of the most influential models in LDTology, and for good reasons.

One of Grainger & Jacobs (1996) strengths is that they followed a very principled approach to model development. They proposed that models of visual word recognition should follow three stratagems:

1. *Modeling functional overlap*, which refers to a process via which the task-specific and the task-independent processes are separated. For example, many tasks (e.g., LDT, naming, perceptual identification) share a visual word recognition component (a core component), but vary in the task-specific components.
2. *Canonical modeling* (Stone & van Orden, 1994), which refers to the principle that states theory development is a process that begins with the simplest model, and is then refined into more complex formulations only after the simpler ones fail to account for a phenomenon.
3. *Nested modeling*, which is the idea that a new model should either include the old one as a special case or dismiss it only after falsification of the core assumptions of the old model. The multiple-read-out model 'represents the most general case of connectionist models' (Grainger & Jacobs, 1996, p. 519) like the IAM (McClelland & Rumelhart, 1981; Rumelhart & McClelland, 1982), and it is nested within the semistochastic interactive activation model (SIAM: Jacobs & Grainger, 1992) and the dual read-out model (Grainger & Jacobs, 1994). It is worth noting that this type of nested modeling implies that the nested models are 'special cases' of more general models.

Following these three principles, Grainger and Jacobs developed a model in which 'word' decisions in the LDT are based on two sources of information (both fed from IAM activation across cycles of processing): (1) global activity, which is the summed activation (σ) of all the words in the lexicon; and (2) local activity, which includes the activation values of individual words (μ). A 'word' response is made when either σ or μ exceed criterial values (Σ and M respectively). The criterial values vary across trials, and the mean of the global activity criterion can be adjusted by the participant as a consequence of strategy, instructions, or other aspects in the experimental context like the proportion of words and nonwords in the experiment. 'Nonword' responses are based on a time deadline (T) which varies across trials with its mean being adjustable in the same way as the word criteria. If global activity is small, the deadline is set to a short value and nonword responses are fast. According to the model, errors occur because of variability in the criteria across trials.

To summarize, in the LDT, if either the M or the Σ criterion is reached before the time exceeds the T criterion, a stimulus is classified as a word; otherwise, it is classified as a nonword. In the original formulation of the model, the M criterion is assumed to be fixed across trials, while both the T and the Σ criteria are assumed to vary as a function of the global activation (σ) generated by the stimulus in early cycles and as a function of task-specific strategies. In a later extension of the model, however, Perea, Carreiras, and Grainger (2004) suggested that the M criterion could be adjusted within a trial by the early strength of the most activated word unit at a given point in processing.

In addition to the authors' principled approach to modeling, the MROM has other strengths. It is the first model to explicitly account not only for mean latencies in the LDT, but also for error rates and RT distributions. In addition, thanks to its IAM core, it makes specific predictions not only about lexical variables such as neighborhood and word frequency effects, but also about LDT-specific effects, like list composition and other manipulations which affect strategic factors in the task.

For the most part, the model fared very well in a variety of empirical tests (e.g., Carreiras, Perea, & Grainger, 1997; DeMoor, Verguts, & Brysbaert, 2005; Dijkstra, Grainger, & van Heuven, 1999; Jacobs et al., 1998); and, in general, the idea of a multiple-response criterion for multiple types of information was very well received. However, Ratcliff, Gomez, and McKoon (2004a), Wagenmakers, Ratcliff, Gomez, and McKoon (2008) and Perea, Gomez, and Fraga (2010) have presented strong evidence against the decisional mechanism of the MROM; these articles are critical of the temporal deadline used in the MROM to produce nonword responses. The problem with the temporal deadline mechanism is that it cannot account for two features of the LDT data: (1) there can be shorter RTs for error responses than correct responses, which happens if the experimental context predisposes participants to make the incorrect response (e.g., in a word trial within a block in which most items are nonwords), and also happens in easy conditions; and (2) RT distributions for correct responses to nonwords are just as skewed to the right as the RT distributions for correct responses to words.

The temporal deadline hypothesis for nonword responses has been strongly rebutted by the data; as a matter of fact, Grainger and his colleagues have recently embarked on adjusting the MROM by adopting a new decision mechanism (Grainger, Dufau, & Ziegler, 2009) using the same representational and lexical assumptions of the MROM. We will have to see if these efforts represent a new chapter in the illustrious history of the IA model and its heirs.

Distributed neural networks

In the IA model, words are represented by single units. This, however, is not the only way to implement lexical representations within the neural networks framework; words can also be represented by patterns of activation across the network units (i.e., a distributed connectionist model). Although distributed connectionist models have not been extended to LDT performance to the same degree as the IA model with the MROM, they can provide us with important intuitions about the LDT. Notably, Seidenberg and McClelland's (1989) model is made up of an input layer of orthographic nodes, a hidden layer, and an output layer of phonological nodes. Given that there are no predefined lexical units that correspond to specific words, the network needs to first develop a representation of the lexicon. During word learning, for each word used as input to the system, a pattern of activation is entered into the input nodes. Activation flows from the input orthographic nodes through the hidden nodes and then to the phonological nodes and back to the orthographic nodes. The output activation patterns at the orthographic and phonological layers are compared with target patterns, and the differences between them are used to adjust the weights of the connections among all the nodes using the back-propagation algorithm. High-frequency words are presented to the system more frequently during training, which leads to better learning. During test trials, activation from an input string of letters flows from the orthographic units to the phonological units and back to the orthographic units. The degree of match between the input and the internally-generated output drives the decision process. If the match value is above a criterion, a 'word' response is produced, and if not, a 'nonword' response is produced.

Although Seidenberg and McClelland (1989) suggested that in a LDT when the nonwords are pseudowords, phonological as well as orthographic output could be assessed, this idea was not implemented in the model (see the critique by Besner, Twilley, McCann, & Seergobin, 1990, and the reply by Seidenberg & McClelland, 1990). Error responses come from high-match values when nonwords are presented, and from low-match values when words are presented. The model does not have an explicit mechanism to produce RTs, although Seidenberg and McClelland (1989) suggested that the degree of match might map onto a rate of accumulation of evidence in a manner similar to Ratcliff's (1978) diffusion model. With such an output process, correct and error responses and their distributions could be predicted.

Plaut (1997) expanded on this model by adding a layer of semantic nodes to the layers of orthographic and phonological nodes. He proposed that a measure of semantic stress based only on activity in the semantic nodes could be used as the basis for lexical decisions, with the value of semantic stress driving a stochastic decision process that would generate accuracy and response times predictions. Further extensions of this distributed neural network approach include an account for individual and developmental differences (Plaut & Booth, 2000), but there has been no explicit LDT modeling published to date. In fact,

Plaut (1997) says: 'We assume that LD responses are actually generated by a stochastic decision process.' The types of models that Plaut refers to are examined below.

Evidence accumulation models

Besides the MROM, the other influential approach in LTDology in the last decade is the stochastic evidence accumulation framework. Although this framework evolved independently from the visual word recognition tradition (Laming, 1968; Link, 1975; Link & Heath, 1975; Stone, 1960; Ratcliff, 1978), some of the early verbal models of the LDT share some of its assumptions. The logogen model, for example, assumes that evidence accumulates over time towards response thresholds of individual words, with the values of these thresholds being related to word frequency (e.g., Ratcliff & McKoon, 1997). Gordon's (1983) resonance model shares with the logogen model the assumption that the internal representations of all words are activated when a string of letters is presented to the system. In Gordon's model, presentation of a letter string causes the internal representations of the words to resonate as a function of the degree to which they match the test string. The strength of the resonance drives the rate of accumulation of evidence in a single boundary decision process. Stone and van Orden (1993) applied Gordon's resonance idea to a qualitative analysis of the LDT within a random walk model using the principle of canonical modeling explained earlier. Although no fits to data were provided, Stone and Van Orden argued that the nature of responses in the LDT are produced via an accumulation-of-evidence process.

Diffusion model

Although a number of researchers had suggested that evidence accumulator models could be used to describe the LDT, it was important to actually provide a full account of the quantitative data from the LDT. Ratcliff, Gomez, and McKoon (2004) applied the full Ratcliff (1978) diffusion model to a number of lexical decision manipulations and showed that the model provides an excellent quantitative account of the data.

The diffusion model is a sequential sampling model for two-choice RT tasks. Over the last decade, it has been applied to most of the dual-choice tasks in use by cognitive psychologists (e.g., Ratcliff, 1978, 1981; Ratcliff & Rouder, 2000; Voss, Rothermund, & Voss, 2004; see Wagenmakers, 2009, for a recent review).

According to the diffusion model, binary decisions are the product of a process in which the information relevant to the discrimination task is accumulated over time toward one of two decision boundaries (e.g., whether the string of letters is a word or a nonword). The accumulation of evidence is noisy, meaning that within a trial the rate of accumulation of evidence varies around a mean value (a parameter called the *drift rate*: v) and the variation of sample paths around the mean values in the accumulation process is described by the diffusion coefficient s^2 (within-trial variability). This variability is at the heart of how the model accounts for the natural variability in RTs and the production of errors (the process arrives at the incorrect boundary due to the variability in the path). In addition to the within-trial variability s^2, the model also assumes that the drift rate varies across trials (e.g., we would not expect all 'high-frequency' words to have the same drift rate); hence, the model's parameter η is the standard deviation of the drift rate across trials.

The distance from the starting point to the decision boundaries represents the amount of evidence needed to make a decision. In the model, this is implemented assuming that the bottom boundary (the 'nonword' boundary in Ratcliff et al., 2004a) has value of 0, while the starting point of the diffusion process is the z parameter, and the upper boundary (the 'word' boundary in Ratcliff et al., 2004a) is parameter a. The model assumes that the starting point might vary from trial to trial, and the parameter s_z is the range of such variability.

Besides the decision process, the response time in a LDT trial includes other components of processing, such as encoding and response execution. These nondecisional components of the RT are summarized in the diffusion model into the parameters T_{er}, which is the mean duration of these nondecisional processes, and s_t, which is their range.

One of the reasons why the diffusion model is very appealing is that the different parameters have a connection to hypothesized cognitive processes. When one examines the diffusion model literature, it becomes apparent that this has led to two different types of applications of the model. I will refer to the first one as *diffusion model accounts*, and to the second one as *empirical validations*. Although sometimes researchers do a little of both even within a single experiment, the logic behind the two applications is slightly different.

Diffusion model account

In the diffusion model account, there is an empirical phenomenon of interest, and the diffusion model is used to try to find out what aspects of the decision process might have changed due to an experimental manipulation. For example, we might want to know if aging affects drift rate, non-decisional components, or decision boundaries.

Empirical validation

In the empirical validation, there is an empirical manipulation that researchers believe should affect certain parameters of the model but not others. For example, instructions that emphasize speed vs accuracy should not affect the drift rate, but should affect the decision boundaries. An experiment is run, the model is fitted to the data, and the researcher assesses whether the parameters behaved in the expected ways.

The Ratcliff et al. (2004a) article is, as its title indicates, an account of the LDT and, in particular, of the effects of word frequency, repetition priming, and type of foil. The most important conclusion of that article is that all of these effects can be accounted for by variations in the drift rate, which can be thought of as a measurement of discriminability because it is assumed to reflect the quality of the signal necessary to make the decision. The drift rate is higher for higher- than lower-frequency words, and this difference is larger when the nonwords used as foils are pronounceable than when they are not. How could the same stimuli produce two different drift rates? Ratcliff et al. hypothesized that the different dimensions of information that can be used to perform a LDT – such as semantic information, phonological information, orthographic information, or other kinds of lexical information – can be integrated into the drift rate when they contribute to the discriminability between words and nonwords. For example, in the experiments with unpronounceable random letter strings as nonwords, the difference in drift rates between words and nonwords was larger than when the nonwords were pronounceable pseudowords because the targets and the foils were different along a greater number of dimensions. Although Ratcliff et al. (2004a) did not commit to what these dimensions are or the computations involved in the transformation of this information into a drift rate, they labeled them 'lexical strength' and 'orthographic wordlikeness' (see Stone & Van Orden, 1993, for a similar formulation).

Another notable diffusion model account in the LDT relates to the effects of aging. It is well known that there is a slowdown due to aging in many tasks; the LDT is not an exception. Ratcliff et al. (2004b) used the diffusion model to account for aging effects in the LDT; the mean RT differences between old and young participants ranged from 156 ms (for high-frequency words in the context of random letter string foils) to 303 ms (for very low-frequency words in the context of pseudoword foils). Accuracy, on the other hand, showed an advantage for older participants (e.g., older participants' accuracy for very low frequency words was 0.91, while young participants' was only 0.81). To account for this pattern of results, they found that drift rates for the older and young subjects were about the same, but that the nondecision component (parameter T_{er}) was 80–100 ms longer for the older subjects than for the young subjects. They also found that the older subjects used larger decision thresholds (parameter a), which produced the higher accuracy for that group.

Not only can the diffusion model account for group differences, but it can also account for procedural differences. Gomez, Ratcliff, and Perea (2007) extended the model to account for differences in the go/no-go and the two-alternative forced choice task (the standard LDT). They concluded that even if the go/no-go task has only one explicit response ('go' alternative), the other response ('no-go' alternative) is associated with an implicit boundary. In addition, the go/no-go task tends to bias the process slightly towards the explicit response: the starting point is closer to the 'go' decision threshold than to the implicit 'no-go' boundary.

The empirical validation of the diffusion model parameters has occurred, most significantly, in perceptual tasks (e.g., Ratcliff & Rouder, 1998; Voss et al., 2004; Wagenmakers, 2009). There is, however, an important empirical validation study by Wagenmakers et al. (2008). The parameters of the diffusion model naturally map experimental manipulations like speed instructions ('Try to respond fast') and accuracy instructions ('Try to respond accurately'). In speed instructions, the decision boundaries should be closer to the starting point than in accuracy instructions. Similarly, when one category of items is presented more often than the other (e.g., words presented more frequently than nonwords), the starting point should be closer to the decision boundary for the more probable response. Given this mapping between the parameters of the model and the experimental manipulations, the model makes strong empirical predictions which Wagenmakers et al. (2008) validated.

With speed instructions (compared to accuracy instructions), error rates should increase and RTs decrease; error RTs should decrease relative to correct RTs; and the RT distributions' right-skewness should be less pronounced. All of these effects were found in the data. When the proportions of words vs nonwords are manipulated, the more probable stimuli should produce better accuracy and shorter RTs; errors for the more probable stimuli should be slower than correct responses (and vice versa for the less probable stimuli); and the RT distributions for the more probable stimuli should have less spread, and a shift to the left relative to the responses to the less probable stimuli. These effects were indeed found in the data, hence validating the model. The diffusion model accounted for all of the effects in the Wagenmakers et al. (2008) article allowing only two parameters to vary between the conditions of interest: boundary separation a and starting point z.

After considering the findings of these experiments, it is clear that the diffusion model has set a high bar. The strength of the diffusion model is that it can account for an impressive amount of detail in the data that goes way beyond mean RTs and accuracy. Although these details have not traditionally been reported or considered as benchmark phenomena in LDT research, they can provide more stringent tests for models. Ratcliff et al. (2004b) explicitly outlined a series of six benchmarks for models of the LDT. The work by Gomez et al. (2007) and Wagenmakers et al. (2008) adds another three benchmarks:

1. For words, accuracy increased and RT decreased (for both correct and error responses) as word frequency increased, and this was true whether the nonwords were random letter strings or pseudowords. The differences between the high- and low-frequency conditions were larger when the nonwords were pseudowords.
2. For words, RTs were shorter and accuracy was higher when the nonwords were random letter strings than when they were pseudowords.
3. For nonwords, correct responses had about the same RTs as correct responses for the slowest words. Responses were faster for random letter strings than for pseudowords, and accuracy was a little higher.
4. Most of the differences in RTs that occurred with increased word frequency were due to decreased skew of the RT distribution.
5. However, when the nonwords were pseudowords, there was a moderately large effect of frequency on the leading edge of the RT distribution. The leading edge for high-frequency words was shorter by 40 ms than the leading edges of the RT distributions for lower frequency words and nonwords.

When the nonwords were random letter strings, the differences were considerably smaller, about 13 or 14 ms, but still significant.

6. With random letter strings, error RTs were shorter than correct RTs. Error RTs were also shorter than correct RTs with pseudowords but only for fast participants.

7. In go/no-go LDT, accuracy for the explicit response will be higher than for the stimuli type associated with the 'go' response.

8. In speed instructions (compared to accuracy instructions), error rate should increase and RTs decrease; error RTs should decrease relative to correct RTs; and the RT distributions' right-skew should be less pronounced.

9. When the proportions of words vs nonwords are manipulated, the more probable stimuli should produce better accuracy and shorter RTs; errors for the more probable stimuli should be slower than correct responses (and vice versa for the less probable stimuli), and the RT distributions for the more probable stimuli should have less spread and a shift to the left relative to the responses to the less probable stimuli.

Limitations of the diffusion model

Although the diffusion model certainly raised the bar in terms of the level of precision in the quantitative fits, the model is not a model of lexical access or visual word recognition. Instead, it is a model of the decision stage of the LDT. As mentioned in the neural network section of this chapter, it has been suggested that some of the distributed neural networks could feed activation into the drift rate in the diffusion model. A full implementation of this idea is not available at this time. However, some recent efforts by Joordens, Piercey, and Azarbehi (2009) are noteworthy; they model word recognition with a Hopfield network similar to Masson's (1995). After the lexicon is learned test inputs can be presented. For each test stimulus, a harmony measurement (cf. Smolensky, 1986) is calculated at each cycle. Harmony grows as a function of time differently for words than for nonwords, and hence a referent curve can be determined. In a LDT trial, the harmony for the test string can be compared cycle by cycle to the referent curve; nonwords will tend to have lower harmony than the referent, and words will tend to have higher harmony. These differences could be the source of the noisy accumulation of evidence hypothesized by the diffusion model.

Norris (2009) has presented a critique to the diffusion model approach. I will discuss Norris's model in more detail in the next section, but for now I will mention one of his most important criticisms. The diffusion model implementation as described above assumes that the encoding time is the same for all categories of stimuli. That encoding time, arguably includes the time taken for lexical processes. Norris (2009) pointed out that assuming that all stimuli takes about the same time to be encoded seems implausible. Although I agree with Norris' main point, the effects of word frequency on encoding time are probably much smaller than the word frequency effects in the mean RT in the LDT (see also Donkin, Heathcote, Brown, & Andrews, 2009).

Bayesian approaches

Bayesian models of the LDT provide an implementation of the lexical aspect of the LDT, and share the sequential accumulation of evidence process with the diffusion model. Wagenmakers et al. (2004) and Norris (2006, 2009) are good examples of this approach.

REM-LD

Wagenmakers, Steyvers, Raaijmakers, Shiffrin, van Rijn, and Zeelenberg (2004) extended the Retrieving Effectively from Memory model (REM; Shiffrin & Styvers, 1997, 1998) to the lexical decision task (REM-LD). In the REM model, the memory for each word is represented as a vector of features. Some of the features in the vector encode content or item-information like lexical and ortho-graphic information, while other features represent the contextual information in which the item was experienced. This encoding is prone to errors, and it is assumed that each presentation of a known stimulus results in the addition and/or the updating the memory vector.

In the LDT, according to Wagenmakers et al., the contextual features are not as relevant as the content features. When an item is presented in a LDT trial, the number of features from the stimulus that are available to the matching process increases as a function of time. The stimulus features are matched to the features from each of the vectors in the memory representation (we can think of it as the lexicon), and the outcome of the noisy comparison process is a number of matches and mismatches. So, for each trace in memory (traces *1* to *j*), a likelihood ratio (λ_j) is obtained. λ_j is equal to the probability of observing the obtained number of matches given that the trace is the *same* as the probe, divided by the probability of observing the obtained number of matches given that the trace is *not the same* as the probe. The average of these likelihood ratios $\left(\frac{1}{n} \sum_{j=0}^{n} \lambda_j \right)$ is the posterior odds ratio φ, which is then transformed into the probability of respond-ing 'word' by a simple transformation $\varphi/(\varphi + 1)$.

The mechanism to generate nonword responses has been a point of contention among the different LDT models. In the MROM and DRC models, there is a temporal deadline, but this deadline mechanism is hard to reconcile with some of the data from Wagenmakers et al. (2008). The diffusion model assumes that there is a negative drift rate for nonwords, but some have questioned the meaning of a negative drift rate. Models like the REM-LD provide with a possible interpreta-tion of negative evidence generated by nonwords. In REM-LD, nonwords are not represented in memory, and hence negative evidence (evidence for nonwords) is obtained when the average likelihood of a probe being the same as any of the entries in memory is low.

An important limitation of the REM-LD model is that it has not been applied to the standard LDT procedure in which participants respond when they are ready to do so. Instead, the model was applied to data from signal-to-response experiments.

Wagenmakers et al. (2008) point out that the assumptions of the REM-LD model can easily be integrated with the sequential probability ratio test (SPRT) procedure (Wald, 1947; Laming, 1968). SPRT is a response execution rule in which at each point in time the probability ratio is $\dfrac{P_t(WORD \mid data)}{P_t(NOND \mid data)}$. If at time t this ratio exceeds one of the two preset bounds (lower bound for nonwords and upper bound for words) the corresponding response is executed with decision time t. Given that the SPRT is mathematically equivalent to a random walk model, it is very likely that some of the desirable properties of the diffusion model account of the LDT can be shared with an extension of the REM-LD, with the advantage that the REM-LD has a stronger commitment to the lexical processes involved in the LDT. To date, however, neither the SPRT nor a diffusion/random walk mechanism has been implemented in REM-LD, so the potential success/failure of this approach remains to be seen.

The Bayesian Reader model

Perhaps the most comprehensive model of the LDT is the Bayesian Reader (Norris & Kinoshita, in press; Norris, 2006, 2009). The ambitious scope of the Bayesian Reader (BR) includes accounts of the representation of the lexicon (Norris, 2006), the decision mechanism for the LDT (Norris, 2009), priming (Norris & Kinoshita, 2008) and the encoding of letter position (Norris, Kinoshita, & van Casteren, 2010). I will focus on the model of the LDT included in the Norris (2009) article.

The BR shares some of the mathematical properties of the diffusion model and the REM-LD. In these three models, optimal decisions are made based on accumulation of noisy evidence. The BR implements the SPRT, which is the (unimplemented) decision mechanism proposed by the REM-LD and, as mentioned before, is mathematically equivalent to a random walk (and hence the diffusion model). In spite of these similarities, the theoretical implications of the BR model are different than the diffusion model's. While the diffusion model proposes that different dimensions (e.g., lexical, orthographical, etc.) of information are integrated into a single drift rate, the Bayesian Reader makes optimal decisions based on multidimensional input.

Another major difference between the diffusion model and the BR is that while the diffusion model assumes that the encoding time (included in the T_{er} parameter) is the same for all stimuli and is independent of drift rate, the BR claims that there is no need for a distinction between encoding and decision processes. To some degree, the BR rose to the challenge set by the DM, to 'produce a lexical model that can account for their data' (Norris, 2009, p. 209).

Norris is critical of the DM's assumption of the drift rate being the outcome of a single source because when the input consists of letter strings there is no single perceptual dimension along which words and nonwords can be partitioned.

In the BR model, the stimulus is represented in a multi-dimensional perceptual space. Each word is represented by a concatenation of vectors; each of these vectors (with *size* = 26) represents a letter and concatenates *(size* = 26 × N) to represent a string of letters of length N that is the input to the model. Gaussian noise is added to the input vector in successive input samples, producing differences between the sample from the stimulus and the internal representation of the word. The number of samples necessary to identify a word depends on the size of the Gaussian noise.

The model performs lexical decision by calculating a multi-hypothesis sequential probability ratio test; it calculates the odds that a stimulus is a word vs a nonword (similarly to the REM-LD), and the size and direction of the step in the random walk is based on this ratio.

Like in the REM-LD, there is no explicit representation of nonwords. Norris has proposed two methods to estimate the nonword likelihood. In the first one (Norris, 2006), the model calculates the likelihood that the input is generated by a letter string that is at least one-letter different from a word. In the second one (Norris, 2009), the nonword likelihood is what is left over after summing the probability of the strings that form words: Nonword likelihood $= 1 - \sum_{j=1}^{m} P(LS_j)$, where LS_j is the product of the probabilities of the sequence of letters in the *j*th word in the lexicon.

So, unlike the DM in which the drift rate comes from a single source (like 'wordlikeness'), in the BR model the drift rate comes from as many sources as there are words in the lexicon. The DM takes a different approach: there is a separate drift rate for each condition in each experiment, which are the free parameters in the DM fits, while in the BR those drift rates emerge from the lexical process component of the model.

It must be noted, however, that some of the details of the Ratcliff et al. (2004b) data are not adequately fitted by the BR model. For example, in the current implementation of the BR error RTs tend to be shorter than correct RTs. In addition, the shift in the RT distribution for Experiment 1 seems to be underestimated by the BR (see Table 1 in Norris, 2009). Both of these effects are accounted for by the diffusion model thanks to its variability parameters. So, given that all other aspects of the DM and the BR models are equivalent, it would be reasonable to expect that refinements in the BR could produce more accurate fits.

Models of functional forms

Although the view of linear progress in science has been rightfully discredited, progress in our understanding of phenomena often emerges from finding functional forms that describe the relationship between two or more variables. The classic example from astronomy is Kepler's identification of functional forms that describe the orbits of planets. He could not have made such discovery without the precise observations by Tycho Brahe, and in turn, Newton could not have developed his laws of motion without Kepler. As Rouder, Speckman, Sun, Morey, and Iverson (2009) indicate, Kepler's formulations along with other identifications of functional forms (e.g., Weber–Fechner law) describe invariances (e.g., planets have elliptical orbits regardless of their size or orbital radius). Rouder et al. make a compelling case for invariances being of critical importance in the advancement of theory in cognitive psychology.

There have been recent efforts to find the functional form of the relationship between variables such as word frequency and performance in the lexical decision task. Although the search for functional forms per se does not need to commitment to the processes underlying the LDT, finding such functional forms might provide us with a firmer foundation to develop general theories of visual word recognition, and/or the mental lexicon.

There are different ways to explore this issue. In the last few years, there have been some influential articles which have dealt with LDT performance as a function of factors such as word frequency and contextual diversity (see Balota et al., this volume, Chapter 5). I will mention three such articles because they exemplify three different ways to relate to the types of model that have been the focus of this chapter.

In the first example of the relationship between LDT models and functional form, Murray and Forster (2004) champion a serial search model according to which the word access time should be linearly related to the frequency rank of a word, and not the frequency itself. Hence, the time increment in the access time should increase by the same amount when moving from one item to the next regardless of their actual word frequencies of the words. In this case, the model has the very desirable and commendable property of making an explicit prediction about functional forms. Although Murray and Forster (2004, 2008) argue that the fits of their model are more than adequate, this model was challenged recently by Adelman and Brown (2008). The work by Adelman and Brown represents a different approach to the search for functional forms.

Adelman and Brown (2008) tried to fit the relationship RT in a LDT as a function of two variables: word frequency and contextual diversity, under various transformations, including a rank transformation that depends on other properties of the corpus. They describe a bootstrapping method of testing models across different corpora, and derived the contending functional forms from current models of lexical decision. They found that the variability in the LDT data cannot be fully accounted by the rank word frequency hypothesis; according to their analysis, 'contextual diversity; (CD) is an important factor in LDT performance (Adelman, Brown, & Quesada, 2006). Although a serial search mechanism would be consistent with the *rank* contextual diversity, the rank-CD cannot account for the totality of the variability due to CD. Although there is an active debate on the interpretation of their findings (e.g., Murray & Forster, 2008; Norris, 2009), they provide with a valuable and rigorous tool to assess the form of the relationship between LDT performance and relevant factors.

The third approach worth mentioning is exemplified by Rouder, Tuerlinckx, Speckman, Lu, and Gomez (2008). Unlike Adelman and Brown (2008), and Murray and Forster (2008), Rouder et al.'s method does not have a strong foundation on lexical processing models. Instead, its efforts focus on dealing with three properties of RTs which in the authors' judgement need to be accounted for in order to adequately regress RT onto covariates such as word frequency:

1. There is significant individual variability that might distort the data when it is aggregated across participants.
2. The variance of the RT distribution is highly correlated with the mean RT in almost all two-choice tasks, which violates the assumption of equal variances, and in turn, biases the fits of possible functional form.
3. RTs do not have minima of zero, which is overlooked by log transformations which are frequently used in hierarchical models that regress on RT.

To deal with these three properties Rouder et al. provide a hierarchical regression model for regressing a Weibull parametrization (with parameters location, rate and shape) of RT distributions in a LDT. In their model, each participant has its own Weibull parameters, and the rate parameter is also indexed by item. Their regression model indicated that the RT decreases as a power function of word frequency due to the frequency effects on the rate of the Weibull distribution. There are two major limitations of this work; the first one is that only frequency (and not contextual diversity, for example) was considered. The second limitation is that Rouder's finding (the scale of the RT distribution decreasing 11% for every doubling of word frequency) does not have a clear theoretical interpretation. However, it is another valuable tool in the search for the relationship between LDT performance and word frequency.

Conclusion

Although the LDT has been one of the most widely used and analyzed tasks in psychology, there is an active and renewed interest in modeling the task itself and its relationship to factors such as word frequency, contextual diversity. In the last 10 years, the level of sophistication of the models and the methods is an excellent case study on current directions in mathematical modeling within cognitive science/psychology. Recent developments that have shaped the current landscape include the ambitious agenda set by the MROM and DRC models, the diffusion model raising the bar with the level of detail and accuracy of its account of LDT data, the emergence of Bayesian models that integrate an account of both lexical processes and decisional mechanism, and refinements in the methods used to regress LDT date on relevant factors.

---

*   The lexical decision task has been one of the most widely used the laboratory task in word recognition research. This has motivated researchers to try to understand the task itself.
*   Researchers have been trying to deconvolve the effects of the lexical processes from the effects related to performing the task itself.

> • History reflects the difference in modeling philosophies within the field of cognitive science, as well as the difference in focus of a diverse group of researchers. Within this diversity of approaches, current models can account for the data at an increasingly high level of detail.

References

Adelman, J. S. & Brown, G. D. A. (2008). Modeling lexical decision: The form of frequency and diversity effects. *Psychological Review, 115*, 214–229.

Adelman, J. S., Brown, G. D. A., & Quesada, J. F. (2006). Contextual diversity, not word frequency, determines word-naming and lexical decision times. *Psychological Science, 17*, 814–823.

Balota, D. A. & Chumbley, J. I. (1984). Are lexical decisions a good measure of lexical access? The role of word frequency in the neglected decision stage. *Journal of Experimental Psychology: Human Perception and Performance, 10*, 340–357.

Balota, D. A. & Chumbley, J. I. (1990). Where are the effects of frequency in visual word recognition tasks? Right where we said they were! Comment on Monsell, Doyle, & Haggard (1989). *Journal of Experimental Psychology: General, 119*, 231–237.

Besner, D., Twilley, L., McCann, R. S., & Seergobin, K. (1990). On the association between connectionism and data: Are a few words necessary? *Psychological Review, 97*, 432–446.

Busemeyer, R. & Diederich, A. (2010). *Cognitive modeling.* New York: Sage.

Carreiras, M., Perea, M., & Grainger, J. (1997). Effects of the orthographic neighborhood in visual word recognition: Cross-task comparisons. *Journal of Experimental Psychology: Learning, Memory, & Cognition, 23*, 857–871.

De Moor, W., Verguts, T., & Brysbaert, M. (2005). Testing the multiple in the multiple read-out model of visual word recognition. *Journal of Experimental Psychology: Learning, Memory, & Cognition, 31*, 1502–1508.

Dijkstra, X., Grainger, J., & van Heuven, W. (1999). Recognition of cognates and inter-lingual homographs: The neglected role of phonology. *Journal of Memory and Language, 41*, 496–518.

Donkin, C., Heathcote, A., Brown, S., & Andrews, S. (2009) Non-Decision Time Effects in the Lexical Decision Task. In N. A. Taatgen & H. van Rijn (eds), *Proceedings of the 31st Annual Conference of the Cognitive Science Society.* Austin, TX: Cognitive Science Society.

Forster, K. I. (1976). Repetition and frequency attenuation in lexical access. *Journal of Experimental Psychology: Learning, Memory, & Cognition, 10*, 680–698.

Gomez, R., Ratcliff, R., & Perea, M. (2007). Diffusion model of the go/no-go task. *Journal of Experimental Psychology: General, 136*, 389–413.

Gordon, B. (1983). Lexical access and lexical decision: Mechanisms of frequency sensitivity. *Journal of Verbal Learning & Verbal Behavior, 22*, 24–44.

Grainger, J. & Jacobs, A. M. (1994). A dual read-out model of word context effects in letter perception: Further investigations of the word superiority effect. *Journal of Experimental Psychology: Human Perception and Performance, 20*, 1158–1176.

Grainger, J. & Jacobs, A. M. (1996). Orthographic processing in visual word recognition: A multiple read-out model. *Psychological Review, 103*, 518–565.

Grainger, J., Dufau, S., & Ziegler, J. C. (2009). A new model of lexical decision: MROM+. In *50th Annual Meeting of the Psychonomic Society*, November 2009. Boston, MA.

Hunt, E. (2004). *The mathematics of behavior*. Cambridge, UK: Cambridge University Press.

Jacobs, A. M. & Grainger, J. (1992). Testing a semistochastic variant of the interactive activation model in different word recognition experiments. *Journal of Experimental Psychology: Human Perception and Performance, 18*, 1174–1188.

Jacobs, A. & Grainger, J. (1994). Models of visual word recognition: Sampling the state of the art. *Human Perception and Perfromance, 20*, 1311–1334.

Jacobs, A., Rey, A., Ziegler, J., & Grainger, J. (1998). MROM-P: An interactive activation, multiple readout model of orthographic and phonological processes in visual word recognition. In J. Grainger & A. Jacobs (Eds), *Localist connectionist approaches to human cognition* (pp. 147–188). Mahwah, NJ: Lawrence Erlbaum.

Joordens, S., Piercey, C. D., & Azarbehi, R. (2009). Modeling performance at the trial level within a diffusion framework: A simple yet powerful method for increasing efficiency via error detection and correction. *Canadian Journal of experimental Psychology/ Revue Canadienne de Psychologie Experimentale, 63*, 81–93.

Laming, D. R. J. (1968). *Information theory of choice-reaction times*. London: Academic Press.

Link, S. W. (1975). The relative judgment theory of two choice response time. *Journal of Mathematical Psychology, 12*, 114–135.

Link, S. W. & Heath, R. A. (1975). A sequential theory of psychological discrimination. *Psychometrika, 40*, 77–105.

Luck, S. (2005). *An introduction to the event-related potential technique (cognitive neuroscience)*. Cambridge, MA: The MIT Press.

McClelland, J. L. & Rumelhart, D. E. (1981). An interactive activation model of context effects in letter perception: I. An account of basic findings. *Psychological Review, 88*, 375–407.

Masson, M. E. J. (1995). A distributed memory model of semantic priming. *Journal of Experimental Psychology: Learning, Memory, and Cognition, 21*, 3–23.

Massaro, D. W. & Cowan, N. (1993). Information processing models: Microscopes of the mind. *Annual Review of Psychology, 44*, 383–425.

Meyer, D. E. & Schvaneveldt, R. W. (1971). Facilitation in recognizing pairs of words: Evidence of a dependence between retrieval operations. *Journal of Experimental Psychology, 90*, 227–234.

Morton, J. (1969). The interaction of information in word recognition. *Psychological Review, 76*, 165–178.

Morton, J. (1979). Facilitation in word recognition: Experiments causing change in the logogen model. In P. A. Kolers, M. E. Wrolstad, & H. Bouma (Eds), *Processing visible language* 1 (pp. 259–268). New York: Plenum.

Murray, W. & Forster, K. I. (2004). Serial mechanisms in lexical access: The rank hypothesis. *Psychological Review, 111*, 721–756.

Murray, W. S. & Forster, K. I. (2008). The rank hypothesis and lexical decision: A reply to Adelman and Brown (2008). *Psychological Review, 115*, 240–252.

Norris, D. (2006). The Bayesian reader: Explaining word recognition as an optimal bayesian decision process. *Psychological Review, 113*, 327–357.

Norris, D. (2009). Putting it all together: A unified account of word recognition and reaction-time distributions. *Psychological Review, 116*, 207–219.

Norris, D. & Kinoshita, S. (2008). Perception as evidence accumulation and bayesian inference: insights from masked priming. *Journal of Experimental Psychology: General, 137*, 434–455.

Norris, D. & Kinoshita, S. (in press). Reading through a noisy channel: Why there's nothing special about the perception of orthography. *Psychological Review*.

Norris, D., Kinoshita, S., & van Casteren, M. (2010). A stimulus sampling theory of letter identity and order. *Journal of Memory and Language, 62*, 254–271.

Paap, K. & Johansen, L. (1994). The case of the vanishing frequency effect: A retest of the verification model. *Journal of Experimental Psychology: Human Perception and Performance, 20*, 1129–1157.

Paap, K., Newsome, S. L., McDonald, J. E., & Schvaneveldt, R. W. (1982). An activation-verification model for letter and word recognition. *Psychological Review, 89*, 573–594.

Paap, K. R., McDonald, J. E., Schvaneveldt, R. W., & Noel, R. W. (1987). Frequency and pronounceability in visually presented naming and lexical decision tasks. In M. Coltheart (Ed.), *Attention and performance XII*. Hillsdale, NJ: Laurence Erlbaum Associates.

Perea, M., Carreiras, M., & Grainger, J. (2004). Blocking by word frequency and neighborhood density in visual word recognition: a task-specific response criteria account. *Memory and Cognition, 32*, 1090–1102.

Perea, M., Gomez, P., & Fraga, I. (2010). Masked nonword repetition effects in yes/no and go/no-go lexical decision: A test of the evidence accumulation and deadline accounts. *Psychonomic Bulletin & Review, 17*(3), 369–374.

Plaut, D. C. (1997). Structure and function in the lexical system: Insights from distributed models of word reading and lexical decision. *Language and Cognitive Processes, 12*, 765–805.

Plaut, D. C. & Booth, J. (2000). Individual and developmental differences in semantic priming: Empirical and computational support for a single-mechanism account of lexical processing. *Psychological Review, 107*, 786–823.

Ratcliff, R. (1978). A theory of memory retrieval. *Psychological Review, 85*, 59–108.

Ratcliff, R. (1981). A theory of order relations in perceptual matching. *Psychological Review, 88*, 552–572.

Ratcliff, R. & McKoon, G. (1997). A counter model for implicit priming in perceptual word identification. *Psychological Review, 104*, 319–343.

Ratcliff, R. & Rouder, J. N. (1998). Modeling response times for decisions between two choices. *Psychological Science, 9*, 347–356.

Ratcliff, R. & Rouder, J. N. (2000). A diffusion model analysis of letter masking. *Journal of Experimental Psychology: Human Perception and Performance, 26*, 127–140.

Ratcliff, R., Gomez, R., & McKoon, G. M. (2004a). A diffusion model account of the lexical decision task. *Psychological Review, 111*, 159–182.

Ratcliff, R., Thapar, A., Gomez, R., & McKoon, G. (2004b). A diffusion model analysis of the effects of aging in the lexical-decision task. *Psychology and Aging, 19*, 278–289.

Rouder, J. N., Tuerlinckx, R., Speckman, P., Lu, J., & Gomez, P. (2008). A hierarchical approach for fitting curves to response time measurements. *Psychonomic Bulletin and Review, 15*, 1201–1208.

Rouder, J. N., Speckman, P. L., Sun, D., Morey, R. D., & Iverson, G. (2009). Bayesian t-tests for accepting and rejecting the null hypothesis. *Psychonomic Bulletin & Review, 16*, 225–237.

Rubenstein, H., Lewis, S. S., & Rubenstein, M. A. (1971). Homographic entries in the internal lexicon: Effects of systematically and relative frequency of meanings. *Journal of Verbal Learning & Behavior, 10*, 57–62.

Rumelhart, D. E. & McClelland, J. L. (1982). An interactive activation model of context effects in letter perception: II. The contextual enhancement effect and some tests and extensions of the model. *Psychological Review, 89*, 60–94.

Seidenberg, M. S. & McClelland, J. M. (1989). A distributed, developmental model of word recognition and naming. *Psychological Review, 96*, 523–568.

Seidenberg, M. S. & McClelland, J. L. (1990). More words but still no lexicon: Reply to Besner et al. (1990). *Psychological Review, 97*, 447–452.

Shiffrin, R. M. & Steyvers, M. (1997). A model for recognition memory: REM: Retrieving Effectively from Memory. *Psychonomic Bulletin & Review, 4*, 145–166.

Shiffrin, R. M. & Steyvers, M. (1998). The effectiveness of retrieval from memory. In M. Oaksford & N. Chater (Eds). *Rational models of cognition* (pp. 73–95). Oxford, England: Oxford University Press.

Smolensky, R. (1986). Information processing in dynamical systems: Foundations of harmony theory. In D. E. Rumelhart & J. L. McClelland (Eds), *Parallel distributed processing. Explorations in the microstructure of cognition. Vol. 1: Foundations* (pp. 194–281). Cambridge, MA: MIT Press.

Stone, M. (1960). Models for choice-reaction time. *Psychometrika, 25*, 251–260.

Stone, G. & Van Orden, G. C. (1993). Strategic control of processing in word recognition. *Journal of Experimental Psychology: Human Perception and Performance, 19*, 744–774.

Stone, G. & Van Orden, G. C. (1994). Building a resonance framework for word recognition using design and system principles. *Journal of Experimental Psychology: Human Perception and Performance, 20*, 1248–1268.

Townsend, J. T. (1972). Some results concerning the identifiability of parallel and serial processes. *British Journal of Mathematical and Statistical Psychology, 25*, 168–199.

Voss, A., Rothermund, K., & Voss, J. (2004). Interpreting the parameters of the diffusion model: An empirical validation. *Memory & Cognition, 32*, 206–220.

Wagenmakers, E. J. (2009). Methodological and empirical developments for the Ratcliff diffusion model of response times and accuracy. *European Journal of Cognitive Psychology, 21*, 641–671.

Wagenmakers, E.-J., Steyvers, M., Raaijmakers, J. G. W., Shiffrin, R. M., van Rijn, H., & Zeelenberg, R. (2004). A model for evidence accumulation in the lexical decision task. *Cognitive Psychology, 48*, 332–367.

Wagenmakers, E. J., Ratcliff, R., Gomez, R., & McKoon, G. (2008). A diffusion model account of criterion shifts in the lexical decision task. *Journal of Memory and Language, 58*, 140–159.

Wald, A. (1947). *Sequential analysis*. New York: Wiley.

5 Megastudies

What do millions (or so) of trials tell us about lexical processing?

David A. Balota, Melvin J. Yap,
Keith A. Hutchison, and Michael J. Cortese

Many disciplines have an agreed-upon knowledge base for study. For cellular neuroscientists, it is the neuron, for geneticists, it is the genome, for some areas of chemistry, molecular interactions are the primary target. The success in these fields is in part due to the accumulation of a well-established set of principles. For example, in each of these domains there is a target knowledge base (i.e., the genome, the periodic table, etc.), which then allows researchers to investigate changes across different contexts and how the system interacts with other systems.

Within cognitive science, one might argue that words are a fundamental building block in psychology. Words have been central to developments in computational modeling (McClelland & Rumelhart, 1981), cognitive neuroscience (e.g., Petersen, Fox, Posner, Mintun, & Raichle, 1988, 1989), memory (Craik & Lockhart, 1972), psycholinguistics (Pinker, 1999), among many other areas. Words are wonderful stimuli because they have a relatively limited set of constituents (e.g., letters/phonemes) that can be productively rearranged to capture virtually all the meaning that humans convey to each other. In this light, one might argue that words, like cells for biologists, are a major building block of cognitive science.

If words are so fundamental to our discipline, then surely we must have accumulated an enormous wealth of information about how humans process words. Indeed, this is largely true. For example, psychologists and psycholinguists have identified many variables that appear to influence speeded lexical processing, including word frequency, familiarity, age of acquisition, imageability, number of meanings, letter length, phoneme length, syllable length, number of morphemes, syntactic class, orthographic neighborhood, phonological neighborhood, frequency of orthographic and phonological neighborhoods, spelling-to-sound consistency, among many others. Given the enormous effort that has been devoted to studying words, one would naturally assume that there is a well-specified set of constraints that one could use to accurately predict processing performance for any set of words. Specifically, there ought to be a standard set of assumptions about lexical processing that researchers have agreed upon.

In this chapter, we review a relatively recent approach to studying lexical processing, which involves developing large databases that are made available for researchers to study across three distinct domains; isolated visual word recognition, semantic priming, and recognition memory. One of the goals of this research endeavor is to help define the common set of principles that researchers can rely upon in better understanding how lexical processing influences critical aspects of cognition. This megastudy approach contrasts with the more traditional approach of factorial experiments targeting specific variables within small-scale studies. We will ultimately argue that progress in this field is going to depend on a judicious combination of targeted factorial studies and large scale databases.

Factorial studies of lexical processing

The vast majority of studies of words have involved standard factorial studies in which investigators cross-targeted variables. For example, one might be interested in the interaction between word frequency and length (i.e., number of letters). Hence, the researcher will select a set of items (typically 10–20) that fit the four (or more) cells of the experimental design by crossing word frequency and length.

As noted, the standard factorial approach has yielded a wealth of knowledge. However, there are also some limitations. First, a critical assumption of this approach is that one can equate stimuli on all other relevant variables to fit the critical cells within such designs. Given the plethora of variables available, this is clearly a daunting task (see Cutler, 1981, for a discussion of this point). Second, one needs to worry about list context effects. Specifically, it is possible that by loading up on a given variable, one may actually be modulating the effect of this variable. For example, if one is interested in spelling-to-sound regularity effects, it is possible that other similarly spelled words could influence the obtained effects (consider a list which contains both HINT and PINT; see Seidenberg, Waters, Sanders, & Langer, 1984). Indeed, there is clear evidence of overall list context effects across a number of variables in the literature (see Lupker, Brown, & Colombo, 1997; Monsell, Patterson, Graham, Hughes, & Milroy, 1992; Zevin & Balota, 2000). Third, most variables are not categorical, but are continuous in nature. Moreover, it is unlikely that variables are linearly related to the behavior of interest. By arbitrarily setting a categorical boundary for a variable that is nonlinearly scaled (e.g., word frequency), one may either magnify or diminish the influence of the variable. Along these same lines, one loses statistical power by turning a continuous variable into a categorical variable (see Cohen, 1983; Humphreys, 1978; Maxwell & Delaney, 1993). Finally, one needs to worry about experimenter biases in selection of items. Forster (2000) has demonstrated that experimenters have implicit knowledge about how lexical variables drive performance in a given task. Hence, it is possible that such knowledge may inadvertently influence item selection.

The megastudy approach

A complementary approach to factorial designs is to let the language define the stimuli, as opposed to selecting stimuli based on a limited set of criteria. This indeed is the megastudy approach reviewed here. If there is an agreed-upon useful database, then researchers may use this dataset to explore the influence and interrelationships amongst targeted variables and also test contemporary theoretical models in a more continuous manner instead of the categorical manner which has dominated model development.

Of course, there are also potential limitations to the megastudy approach. One concern is that researchers may exploit the dataset. For example, one could resample multiple times from the large dataset and capitalize on chance to find 'significant' effects of theoretical interest. We believe that the normal peer-review process is sufficiently sensitive to such sampling possibilities, and have not seen megastudy databases misused in this manner. A more important problem is that the large databases may not be stable enough to detect more subtle effects. That is, there may be sufficient error variance in the databases to decrease sensitivity to variables that appear to be well-established in the factorial literature. Interestingly, this possibility has been raised recently by Sibley, Kello, and Seidenberg (2009). Because of the potential importance of this concern, we will briefly address this issue.

Sibley et al. (2009) argued that one should be cautious in relying on megastudy databases because these databases may not be sensitive to more subtle manipulations in the literature that have important theoretical implications. To pursue this issue, they tested the adequacy of megastudies for finding an important interaction between spelling-to-sound consistency/regularity and word frequency. Specifically, high-frequency words are typically influenced less by spelling-to-sound consistency/regularity than are low-frequency words. They correctly argued that these variables have been critical in the development of models of word naming. Therefore, Sibley et al. selected the items from published studies investigating these variables, and attempted to determine if the same pattern would be observed when the item means were obtained from the megastudies. Sibley et al. examined the stability of consistency effects across four different datasets, and indeed there was variability across the datasets with respect to producing the pattern. Here, we simply investigate the stability of the effects using the English Lexicon Project (ELP), because this has been the most well explored database to date and includes a wide range of both monosyllabic and multisyllabic words. At its completion, the ELP was by far the largest megastudy (approximately 20 times larger than other English datasets), although as described below, there are recent databases approaching its size. Finally, this dataset is readily available for researchers to access via the website (http://elexicon.wustl.edu), along with a search engine that affords access to a rich set of lexical characteristics.

In their paper, Sibley et al. (2009) focused on mean *raw* item naming response time (RT) data. However, in the ELP, different participants contribute to the mean RT of any item, and it is therefore more appropriate to look at z-scored RTs instead of raw RTs, as suggested by Balota, Yap, Cortese, Hutchison, Kessler, Loftus, Neely, et al. (2007). In this way, no subject disproportionately influences the item means. Of course, it is also useful to look at the accuracy data. To explore this, we recently used the ELP to conduct analyses similar to Sibley et al.'s, and the collective results are remarkably consistent with published studies. For example, Seidenberg (1985) observed an interaction between spelling-to-sound consistency and word frequency. In our analysis of the Seidenberg items taken from the ELP dataset, the mean z-scores clearly were indeed in the same direction, albeit non-significant, while the accuracy data was significant and clearly replicated the Seidenberg (1985) pattern. Turning to Seidenberg et al. (1984), the ELP dataset again produced the same reliable interaction in all three dependent measures (i.e., raw RTs, z-scored RTs, accuracy). Turning to Papp and Noel (1991), who did not report the results from statistical tests, the ELP produced an interaction in the same direction for z-scores ($p = .07$), and the interaction was again reliable in accuracy in the predicted direction. Jared (2002) observed main effects of consistency and word frequency with her stimuli, with no interaction. This pattern was reliably replicated in the accuracy data of the ELP dataset with her items, and also in the pattern of mean z-scores and raw RTs. Finally, Taraban and McClelland (1987: 613) did *not* report a reliable frequency by regularity interaction for their stimuli, but in separate tests did report a reliable effect of regularity for low-frequency words, but not for high-frequency words. Indeed, in the ELP, there is a regularity effect for Taraban and McClelland low-frequency words in both accuracy and z-scores, but not for high-frequency words. In sum, we view the data from the ELP as being remarkably consistent with the critical studies that have manipulated both spelling-to-sound regularity and word frequency. Instead of only questioning the ELP database, it would be useful for the field to test the reliability of standard effects in the lexical processing literature across different institutions for a baseline. In fact, given the likelihood of idiosyncratic effects of list context and voice-key measurement issues, we were surprised (and pleased) by the level of stability. Clearly, based on the above analyses, it appears that the ELP does quite well in producing the standard effects regarding spelling-to-sound regularity/consistency and word frequency.

One might also ask if other standard interactions are observed in the ELP database. As indicated in Balota et al., (2004) and Yap and Balota (2009), many standard interactions reported in the literature (i.e., length by frequency, orthographic N by frequency, orthographic N by length) are well-replicated in the ELP. Most importantly, if the ELP had an extraordinary amount of error variance, one might expect little variance in the total dataset to be accounted for by standard lexical variables. However, this is clearly not a problem in the ELP. For example, Balota et al. accounted for 49% and 42% of the variance in speeded pronunciation and lexical decision latencies respectively for monosyllabic words. Moreover, Yap and Balota (2009) accounted for over 60% of the variance for all monomorphemic multisyllabic words with standard predictors. Because it is likely that there are still unknown variables and possible better ways of conceptualizing current variables (i.e., nonlinear functions), the current estimates may underestimate the amount of variance accounted for (see Rey, Courrieu, Schmidt-Weigand, & Jacobs, 2009, for further discussion).

Of course, the stability of these datasets is an important issue for testing current computational models. If indeed the datasets are not stable/reliable, then the utility of these datasets would be minimized. Indeed, Spieler and Balota (1997) were initially surprised by the relatively small amount of variance captured by standard computational models. For example, for the monosyllabic dataset, 10.1% was captured by the Seidenberg and McClelland model, and 3.3% was captured by the Plaut, McClelland, Seidenberg, and Patterson (1996) model. In contrast, word frequency, orthographic neighborhood size and length accounted for 21.7% of the variance. Hence, it is not the case that one can simply dismiss the poor fits due to error-prone datasets.

Thus, in developing models of word recognition, researchers have become more interested in using accounted for variance as one useful (but not only) metric of evaluating model performance. In addition, Perry, Zorzi, and Ziegler (2010) have labeled an additional metric called the Yap and Balota criteria, which basically involves the *specific* proportion of variance in model performance accounted for by different variables (also see Sibley and Kello, this volume, Chapter 2). Of course, there are multiple ways of evaluating model adequacy. The point we are emphasizing here is simply that a possible lack of stability of the megastudy datasets is not a reason to dismiss this useful constraint on model development (see Adelman, Marquis, & Sabatos-DeVito, 2011, for further discussion of explained and unexplained variance in word recognition performance).

We shall now turn to a selective review of what we have learned from the megastudy approach at a more empirical level. We will first discuss studies of isolated word recognition, which are by far the most well investigated. We will then turn to more recent developments in the domains of semantic priming and episodic recognition memory performance.

Isolated word recognition performance

In addition to providing a testbed for evaluating computational models of visual word recognition, there are three additional contributions from megastudies to better understand lexical processing. First, these datasets allow researchers to rigorously evaluate the strength of relatively novel variables that theoretically should modulate word recognition. Second, the databases allow for one to compare the relative predictive power of competing metrics. Third, the datasets allow for a finer-grained assessment of the functional relationships (e.g., linear vs nonlinear) between lexical variables and word recognition performance.

Evaluating the influence of novel variables

Megastudies are very useful for benchmarking new variables by evaluating whether they account for additional variance above and beyond traditional variables. In an early example of such work, Treiman, Mullennix, Bijeljac-Babic, and Richmond-Welty, (1995) explored readers' sensitivity to the consistency of spelling-sound mappings at different grain sizes (Ziegler & Goswami, 2005). A word is considered consistent if its pronunciation matches that of most similarly spelled words. For example, PINT is inconsistent because the pronunciation of its rime (vowel and following consonants, i.e., -INT) conflicts with that of similarly spelled words (e.g., HINT, MINT, TINT). At the time the Treiman et al. paper was published, the dominant view was that spelling–sound relations were most appropriately described at the level of graphemes and phonemes, and Treiman et al. were interested in whether consistency defined for higher-order units (e.g., rimes) was also able to predict speeded pronunciation performance. On the basis of regression analyses of two independent megastudies (consisting of 1327 and 1153 words respectively), they demonstrated that the consistency of higher-order rime units indeed reliably accounted for pronunciation variance, after the consistency of individual graphemes and other variables were controlled for. To strengthen the general conclusions from the megastudies, Treiman et al. also conducted additional factorial studies where rime consistency was manipulated. Importantly, the results from these studies converged nicely with the findings from the megastudies, suggesting that large-scale and factorial studies provided complementary perspectives on phenomena of interest.

The Treiman et al. (1995) study focused on monosyllabic consonant-vowel-consonant (CVC) words. Chateau and Jared (2003) carried out a megastudy (including 1000 words) where they compared the consistency of various orthographic segments in six-letter disyllabic words. Specifically, they obtained measures of spelling-sound consistency for simple (i.e., C_1, V_1, C_2) and higher-order (i.e., C_1V_1, V_1C_2) orthographic segments in the first and second syllables. In addition, they computed consistency for the BOB (body-of-the-BOSS; Taft, 1992) which includes the first vowel and as many following consonants to form a legal word ending (e.g., the BOB for VERTEX is ERT). They found that the consistency of the BOB and the second-syllable vowel predicted pronunciation performance, confirming that readers were sensitive to the consistency of multiple grain sizes when pronouncing words aloud.

Other theoretically motivated variables whose validity have been evaluated using megastudy data include imageability (Cortese & Fugett, 2004), age of acquisition (Cortese & Khanna, 2008), semantic richness (Yap, Tan, Pexman, & Hargreaves, 2011a), a new measure of orthographic similarity called Levenshtein Orthographic Distance (Yarkoni, Balota, & Yap, 2008), a new measure of phonological similarity called the Levenshtein Phonological Distance measure (see http://elexicon.wustl.edu), contextual diversity (i.e., the number of contexts a word appears in; Adelman, Brown, & Quesada, 2006), phonographic neighborhood size (i.e., the number of neighbors that are both orthographic and phonological; Adelman & Brown, 2007), and Sensory Experience Rating (Juhasz, Yap, Dicke, Taylor, & Gullick, 2011), a new variable motivated by the grounded cognition framework which indexes the degree to which a word evokes sensory/perceptual experiences. The general strategy is to assess the extent to which a novel predictor accounts for unique variance in megastudies, after other correlated variables have been controlled for. While a full description of these studies is outside the scope of this chapter, the studies listed above have shed light on the role of semantic variables on word recognition (Cortese & Fugett, 2004; Cortese & Khanna, 2008; Juhasz, Yap, Dicke, Taylor, and Gullick, 2011; Yap et al., 2011a), the influence of a new orthographic distinctiveness metric that can be used for long words and outperforms the traditional measure of orthographic neighborhood size (Yarkoni et al., 2008), and the superiority of contextual diversity (Adelman et al., 2006) and phonographic neighborhood size (Adelman & Brown, 2007) over raw word frequency and orthographic neighborhood size respectively. Finally, it is noteworthy that the megastudy approach has also been used to provide evidence *against* the reliability of a new variable (see Kang, Yap, Tse, & Kurby, 2011, for an example).

Comparing competing metrics

Megastudies are also ideal for adjudicating between competing measures of the same construct. For example, word frequency is one of the most studied variables in cognitive science. Although many frequency counts are available, most researchers unfortunately continue to rely on the Kučera and Francis (1967; KF67) norms, which are dated and based on a relatively small corpus of written texts. Brysbaert and New (2009), using lexical decision data from recently published large-scale data, compared a number of frequency counts, including KF67, HAL (Hyperspace Analog to Language; Burgess & Livesay, 1998), CELEX (Center for Lexical Information; Baayen, Piepenbrock, & van Rijn, 1993), TASA (Touchstone Applied Science Associates; Zeno, Ivens, Millard, & Duvvuri, 1995), and BNC (British National Corpus; Leech, Rayson, & Wilson, 2001). KF67, CELEX, TASA, and BNC are based on written texts, while HAL is based on internet newsgroup postings. The proportion of variance each frequency measure accounted for in lexical decision performance from the ELP was used as a criterion of its quality. These were all evaluated against an intriguing new frequency measure (SUBTL) based on a 50-million word corpus comprising film and television subtitles. A subtitle-based corpus possesses the advantages of being more reflective of day-to-day spontaneous language exposure and is also relatively easy to accumulate. Indeed, the analyses conclusively demonstrated that KF67 frequency was clearly the worst measure (replicating studies by Balota, Cortese, Sergent-Marshall, Spieler, & Yap, 2004; Zevin & Seidenberg, 2004), whereas subtitle-based frequency accounted for more variance than the other leading frequency measures. Interestingly, Yap, Balota, Brysbaert, and Shaoul (2011a) have also shown that a measure of rank frequency (simply the rank order of word frequency values instead of their actual frequency, see Forster, this volume, Chapter 3) predicts very similar amounts of variance. In the examples in this section, word frequency was the construct of interest but in principle, a similar strategy can be used to compare different instantiations of other constructs. Indeed, this is precisely what Yarkoni et al. (2008) reported in their comparison of the new Levenshtein Distance measure and the standard orthographic N measure (see Davis, this volume, Chapter 9, for a discussion of orthographic neighborhood structure).

Exploring functional relationships amongst variables in word recognition

Large-scale data have been used productively to explore the functional relationships between lexical variables and word recognition performance. For example, word recognition researchers have tended to focus on linear relationships between variables and response times, but it is clear that non-linear contributions also need to be taken into account (see Baayen, Feldman, & Schreuder, 2006).

Consider the relationship between word length in letters and response times. It is commonly assumed that the relationship between length and word recognition performance (as reflected by tasks such as lexical decision, speeded pronunciation, perceptual identification, and eye tracking) is linear, and that word recognition latencies increase monotonically as a function of length. However, this view is complicated by inconsistent results across tasks and studies. Specifically, some studies find inhibitory effects (length and response times positively correlated), others find facilitatory effects (negative correlation), while yet others yield null effects (see New, Ferrand, Pallier, & Brysbaert, 2006, for a review). New et al. explored this inconsistency by conducting regression analyses on a dataset of lexical decision latencies for over 33,000 words (ranging from 3 to 13 letters) from the English Lexicon Project (Balota et al., 2007). They observed an intriguing U-shaped relationship between length and lexical decision latencies, whereby length was facilitatory for 3–5-letter words, null for 5–8-letter words, and inhibitory for 8–13-letter words. Hence, to the extent that different investigators are using stimuli of different lengths, this U-shaped relationship provides a partial explanation for the varied results across different experiments. More recently, Yarkoni et al. (2008) have suggested that this nonlinear function may be accommodated by differences in the orthographic neighborhood characteristics as reflected by the novel Levenstein Distance metric, discussed in the previous section.

The functional form of the relationship between word frequency and word recognition latencies has also been receiving considerable attention in the literature (see Forster, this volume, Chapter 3). Traditionally, researchers have assumed that a linear relationship exists between the logarithm of frequency and recognition times. However, recent models have begun to make explicit predictions about the form of the frequency effect (see Adelman & Brown, 2008, for a review). For example, Norris' (2006) Bayesian Reader model predicts a logarithmic relationship between word frequency and lexical decision latencies; this model conceptualizes readers as optimal Bayesian decision-makers who use Bayesian inference to combine perceptual information with knowledge of prior probability during word recognition. In contrast, Murray and Forster's (2004) serial search model of lexical access predicts that RTs will be 'directly related to the rank position of a word in a frequency-ordered list, not to its actual frequency or to any transform of it' (p. 723). Finally, instance-based models, which are predicated on the assumption that each encounter with a word leaves a memory trace (e.g., Goldinger, 1998; Logan, 1988), predict that frequency and latencies are represented as a power function. Using large-scale datasets, Adelman and Brown (2008) evaluated the rank frequency function against other functional forms (e.g., logarithmic and power functions) and concluded that the empirical data appeared to be most consistent with some versions of the instance-based models (but see Murray & Forster, 2008). Clearly, without these large-scale data-bases one would not be able to test the functional form of this theoretically important relationship.

Identifying the unique predictive power of targeted variables

The ultimate goal of factorial studies is to afford a better understanding of the influence of theoretically motivated variables. This goal has been somewhat elusive, for the various reasons discussed in the Introduction. As noted, it is difficult to control for the many variables that have been shown to influence word recognition (Cutler, 1981), since many of these variables are correlated. Megastudies minimize these problems by having the language, rather than the experimenter, select the stimulus set, and using regression analyses to control for correlated variables.

The studies by Treiman et al. (1995) and Chateau and Jared (2003) described earlier exploit this approach for exploring spelling-to-sound consistency, but Balota et al. (2004) were the first to explore the effects of a comprehensive array of variables on word recognition. Specifically, they examined the unique predictive power of surface variables (phonological features in the onsets), lexical variables (e.g., measures of consistency, frequency, familiarity, neighborhood size, and length), and semantic variables (e.g., imageability and semantic connectivity) on word recognition performance for virtually all monomorphemic monosyllabic words. They also compared lexical decision to pronunciation data to study task-dependent effects, and young adult to older adult performance to study the effects of aging. Space limits preclude a full description of the study, but Balota et al. were able to demonstrate that the influence of many variables were modulated by the nature of the task, hence shedding light on a number of empirical controversies. For example, surface variables, length, neighborhood size, and consistency accounted for more variance in pronunciation, compared to lexical decision, because of the pronunciation task's emphasis on generating phonology. In contrast, word frequency and semantics better predicted lexical decision, because of lexical decision's reliance on familiarity-based information for discriminating between familiar words and unfamiliar nonwords (e.g., Balota & Chumbley, 1984). There was also an interesting age-related dissociation where older adults were more influenced by objective frequency while younger adults were more influenced by subjective frequency (i.e., subjective ratings of a word's frequency; Balota, Pilotti, & Cortese, 2001), suggesting that standard frequency estimates based on written texts may be better tuned to the older adult lexicon.

To a large extent, the visual word-recognition literature has been overwhelmingly dominated by the study of monosyllabic words, because these are relatively simple stimuli to work with. However, monosyllabic words only constitute a small minority of a person's lexicon, and it is unclear if behavioral effects reported for monosyllabic words generalize to longer multisyllabic words. The Chateau and Jared (2003) study discussed earlier is noteworthy for being the first large-scale exploration of multisyllabic words. However, they were predominantly interested in how consistency influences the pronunciation of six-letter disyllabic words.

Using data from the ELP, Yap and Balota (2009) extended the work by Balota et al. (2004) and Chateau and Jared (2003) by using hierarchical regression analyses to identify the effects of surface, lexical, and semantic variables for 6115 monomorphemic multisyllabic words. In addition to considering the role of traditional variables (e.g., frequency, length, orthographic neighborhood size), they also explored variables specific to multisyllabic words (e.g., stress pattern, number of syllables). Importantly, processing of multisyllabic words does not appear to radically differ from the processing of monosyllabic words. However, there were also a number of surprising differences. First, onset characteristics, which account for considerable variance in monosyllabic pronunciation, are far less influential in multisyllabic pronunciation. This may suggest differences in the emphasis on onsets during production in the monosyllabic words compared to the more complex multisyllabic words. Second, number of syllables was positively correlated with both lexical decision and pronunciation latencies, even after controlling for a host of variables. This suggests that multiple codes mediate lexical access and output processes, and the syllable is one of those codes. Third, the analyses included novel measures of orthographic and phonological distinctiveness (Levenshtein measures; Yarkoni et al., 2008) to complement traditional measures (e.g., orthographic neighborhood size) that are not optimized for long words. The interesting finding here is that words which have relatively close visually and phonologically confusable neighbors produced faster response latencies in both naming and lexical decision performance, which is inconsistent with a simple competitive lexical identification process.

Stable individual differences revealed in the ELP

Interestingly, there has been relatively little work in the visual word recognition literature on the reliability of measures of lexical processing within individuals (see Andrews, Volume 2, Chapter 3). This issue is important for a number of reasons. First, if one is ultimately interested in extending visual word recognition models based on lexical processing studies to individuals who have breakdowns in reading performance, e.g., individuals with developmental dyslexia, then one needs to be concerned about the stability of the lexical processing tasks within individuals. Second, in evaluating the adequacy of computational models, it is possible that the mean performance across individuals at the item level should not simply be fit to one static model, because a single model will miss the important diversity across individuals. Third, there may indeed be important tradeoffs in the effects of variables (such as spelling-to-sound correspondence vs lexical-semantic processing), which provide important information on how mechanisms associated with specific variables may tradeoff across individuals.

Of course, in order to investigate the stability of lexical processing one needs to have sufficient number of observations of a large number of participants to obtain stable estimates at different points in time. The ELP affords an excellent database to examine stability since it contains naming or lexical decision perform-ance for a large number of participants responding to a large set of different words (and nonwords in LDT) across two sessions, separated by a 24-hour to a 1-week interval. Yap, Balota, Sibley, and Ratcliff (2012) recently undertook this endeavor, and found that the participants in the ELP database provided consider-able consistency in performance across these sessions in mean performance, reaction time distributional parameters (such as estimates from the ex-Gaussian function, see Balota & Yap, 2011), and even estimates from the diffusion model (see Ratcliff, Gomez, & McKoon, 2004), and sensitivity to individual lexical variables such as word frequency. Moreover, this database indicated that subjects who had higher vocabulary in general produced faster response latencies, more accurate word recognition performance, and *attenuated* sensitivity to lexical vari-ables. Finally, there was no evidence of tradeoffs in lexical and non-lexical processing across individuals. Clearly, megastudies such as the ELP provide useful information regarding basic aspects of individual differences in lexical processing and are only just beginning to be explored.

To summarize, the work described in this section has provided interesting new constraints on current models and future theory development. While megastudies clearly cannot (and indeed should not) replace well-designed factorial studies for establishing what the benchmark effects should be, they provide a powerful complementary, convergent approach for investigating visual word recognition.

Extending the megastudy approach beyond English

The megastudy approach to isolated word recognition has recently been deve-loping to understand lexical processing in other languages. To our knowledge, there are now two published recent megastudies in non-English languages (note that Keuleers, Lacey, Rastle, & Brysbaert, 2012, have a paper on the British lexicon): The French Lexicon Project (FLP; Ferrand, New, Brysbaert, Keuleers, Bonin, Méot, et al., 2010) and a study of 14,000 Dutch mono- and disyllabic words and nonwords (Keuleers, Diependaele, & Brysbaert, 2010). As an adjunct to the English Lexicon Project, these databases offer a number of benefits. For example, consider the FLP. In addition to stimulating psycholinguistic research in French, researchers can also develop a better understanding of the similarities and differences between English and French, which might yield insights into research aimed at teasing apart language-specific from language-general proc-esses. For example, although English and French are both alphabetic languages,

French is far more morphologically productive, has more transparent mappings from spelling to sound, and has unambiguous syllable boundaries (Ferrand et al., 2010). In the FLP, lexical decision latencies for 38,840 French words and nonwords were collected; due to financial and logistical constraints, speeded pronunciation data have not yet been collected. Although the FLP has only been recently completed, it has already yielded a number of noteworthy findings. Similar to English, a frequency measure based on subtitles predicted lexical decision variance better than book-based frequency estimates. Interestingly, the intriguing quadratic length effect seen in the ELP data (see earlier discussion; New et al., 2006) was also replicated in the FLP, indicating that the non-linear effects of length generalize across languages and are also not specific to the methodological idiosyncrasies of the ELP.

Yap, Balota, Brysbaert, and Shaoul (2010b) have also recently developed a megastudy for Malay. Malay, a language spoken by about 250 million people in Indonesia, Malaysia, Brunei and Singapore, contrasts well with English, due to its very shallow alphabetic orthography (i.e., spelling–sound mappings are predictable and transparent), simple syllabic structures, and transparent affixation. Speeded pronunciation and lexical decision latencies were collected for 9592 Malay words, and regression analyses revealed some interesting processing differences between Malay, a shallow orthography, and English, a deeper orthography. For example, word *length* predicted Malay word recognition performance far better than word frequency. In contrast, frequency is the best predictor in English word recognition. This is consistent with the idea that transparent orthographies heavily implicate a frequency-insensitive sublexical mechanism that assembles pronunciations using a limited set of spelling-sound rules (see Frost, Katz, & Bentin, 1987). Although frequency effects were greatly attenuated in Malay, they were nonetheless reliable, demonstrating that lexical processing plays a role even in very shallow orthographies.

Megastudies have also been used to make other types of cross-linguistic comparisons. Using a progressive demasking task, Lemhöfer, Dijkstra, Schriefers, Baayen, Grainger, and Zwitserlood (2008) compared the word recognition performance of French, German, and Dutch bilinguals for the same set of 1025 monosyllabic English words. English was the second language for these bilinguals. Regression analyses were used to examine the data, and a large number of within-language (e.g., length, word frequency, morphological characteristics, semantic characteristics) and between-language (e.g., cognate status, number of orthographic neighbors in the *first* language) variables were included as predictors. Lemhöfer et al. noted that there was substantial overlap in response time distributions between the three bilingual groups, suggesting that word recognition performance in English generalizes to different bilingual groups with distinct mother tongues. More interestingly, word recognition performance of all three groups was primarily driven by within-language characteristics, i.e., the characteristics of the target language, English. The characteristics of the first language played a relatively limited role in influencing English word recognition. Finally, comparisons of the bilingual groups against a control native English-speaking group yielded subtle but interesting differences. For example, both written and spoken frequency independently influenced word recognition performance in nonnative speakers, while only spoken frequency had an effect for native speakers. Effects of word frequency were also stronger for nonnative, compared to native, speakers.

In sum, the development of megastudies across different languages already has shed some interesting observations on language-specific vs language-general principles. Although the first steps have already been initiated (indeed there are interesting ongoing megastudies of other languages such as Slovenia; Repovs, personal communication), a future goal of this work would be to establish links across languages in these large databases to provide insights into the mapping of orthography onto meaning, and eventually the mapping of phonology onto meaning, in speech perception. Such a cross-language repository of lexical processing would greatly facilitate our understanding of fundamental characteristics of language. At one level, it would be useful to have an international consortium established to test individuals on identical experimental platforms to insure comparability across the languages, and participants. On the other hand, it would also be useful to have more participants from a wide variety of backgrounds. Indeed, a promising study by Dufau, Dunabeitia, Moret-Tatay, McGonigal, Peeters, Alaorio, et al. (2011) has recently initiated a large international lexical decision study that relies on a common smart-phone platform that participants all over the world can access freely. Data collection has been remarkably fast using this approach, accumulating as many observations in months that the ELP took years to accomplish. Possibly, this approach will lay the foundation of a multilingual psycholinguistic resource, containing performance and lexical characteristics for multiple languages.

Megastudies of semantic priming

Although much has been gleaned about the processes underlying isolated word recognition from both factorial and megastudy approaches, words are typically not recognized in isolation, and there is an extensive literature concerning the influence of semantic/associative context on word recognition (see McNamara, 2005; Jones & Estes, accompanying volume). In the semantic priming paradigm, participants are presented with a target word (e.g., TABLE) for a speeded response (typically pronunciation or lexical decision) that was immediately preceded by either a related (e.g., CHAIR) or an unrelated (e.g., WATCH) prime word. The semantic priming effect refers to the consistent finding that people respond faster to target words preceded by related, relative to unrelated, primes. If one merely wished to demonstrate the existence of semantic priming, then the factorial limitations described earlier would not impede progress because semantic priming researchers typically counterbalance primes and targets across subjects by repairing the same prime-target pairs to create unrelated pairs. Thus, any facilitation in responding to targets could not be due to item selection differences between related and unrelated conditions.

Simple demonstrations of priming, however, are no longer the primary issue of interest. Today, researchers use the semantic priming paradigm as a tool to better understand the organization and retrieval of semantic knowledge. In doing so, researchers select sets of items that differ on a dimension deemed relevant for semantic priming. For example, researchers may test how priming differs as a function of target characteristics such as word frequency (Becker, 1979), regularity (Cortese, Simpson, & Woolsey, 1997), or imageability (Cortese et al., 1997). Alternatively, researchers may examine priming as a function of prime-target relatedness using measures such as forward associative strength (FAS), backward association strength (BAS; Hutchison, 2002; Shelton & Martin, 1992; Thomson-Schill, Kurtz, & Gabrieli, 1998), semantic feature overlap (McRae & Boisvert, 1998; Moss, Ostrin, Tyler, & Marslen-Wilson, 1995), type of semantic relation (Hodgson, 1991), global co-occurrence (Jones, Kintsch, & Mewhort, 2006; Lund, Burgess, & Atchley, 1995), or relational similarity (Estes & Jones, 2006).

Such factorial designs, while important, can distort the relative importance of the variable of interest in accounting for semantic priming. Primes and targets from different item sets often are not matched on potentially important variables. For instance, studies examining priming for categorically related (e.g., HORSE–DONKEY) vs associatively related (e.g., THIRSTY–WATER) pairs often confound type of relation with target frequency such that associatively related targets are often higher in frequency (Bueno & Frenk-Mastre, 2008; Ferrand & New, 2003; Williams, 1996). Since low-frequency words typically show larger priming effects (Becker, 1979), this can artificially inflate the importance of categorical, relative to associative, relations (see Hutchison, 2003).

In addition to matching problems, list context effects also plague factorial semantic priming studies. McKoon and Ratcliff (1995) showed that priming of a particular type of semantic relation (e.g., synonyms or antonyms) is modulated by the proportion of similar types of relations within a list, even when the overall proportion of related items in the list (i.e., the relatedness proportion) is held constant (also see Becker, 1980). Therefore, including many such items within a list likely inflates priming for that particular type of relation (e.g., category members, script-relations, antonyms, etc.). Supporting this argument, Hutchison (2003) observed that priming from perceptually-similar items (e.g., COIN–PIZZA) only occurs when such items constitute a majority of the list. In addition to relation types, the salience of specific item characteristics (e.g., word frequency, regularity, imageability, etc.) is also increased when participants are presented with extreme values on variables in factorial studies.

Finally, as noted earlier, the methodological problems inherent in categorizing continuous variables also apply to semantic priming. Selecting items high or low on a particular dimension can reduce the power to detect true relationships between variables and can even produce spurious effects that do not truly exist when the entire sample is considered (Cohen, Cohen, West, & Aiken, 2003). Most importantly, the use of extreme scores fails to capture the importance of the variable across its full range. If a variable is really an important factor in priming, it should capture the magnitude of priming, not just its presence or absence (McRae, De Sa, & Seidenberg, 1997).

In addition to comparing priming effects across different types of relations and items, researchers have also compared priming effects across different groups of participants including young vs older adults (Balota & Duchek, 1988; Laver & Burke, 1993), and those high vs low perceptual ability (Plaut & Booth, 2000), reading ability (Betjemann & Keenan, 2008), vocabulary (Devitto & Burgess, 2004; Yap & Balota, 2009) and working memory capacity (Hutchison, 2007; Kiefer et al., 2007).[1] As with items, subjects from different populations likely differ in many ways other than the variable of interest and it is impossible to match on everything. One particularly critical difference is often baseline RT. If RTs are not first standardized within participants, priming effects from the slower group will be artificially inflated, often creating a significant group × priming interaction (Faust, Balota, Spieler, & Ferraro, 1999). This methodological flaw can then leave theorists attempting to explain such hyper-priming among their clinical population. In addition, selecting extreme groups on a dimension (e.g., high vs low reading ability) can over- or underestimate the importance of that dimension in priming among the general population.

Hutchison, Balota, Cortese, and Watson (2008)

In an early attempt to highlight, and partially circumvent, such item selection problems, Hutchison et al. (2008) examined priming for 300 strong forward associate pairs (e.g., CAT–DOG) among 108 younger and 95 older adults. Priming effects were measured across both lexical decision and pronunciation tasks using both short (200 ms) and long (1200 ms) stimulus onset asynchrony (SOA) conditions. Because the items were initially selected based upon FAS, this variable was somewhat restricted in range (99% between 0.50 and 0.94). However, there was considerable variability in the other prime-target relation variables examined (global co-occurrence, backward associative strength) and in both prime and target lexical characteristics (frequency, length, orthographic neighborhood). In addition to these variables, baseline RTs for target words were obtained through the use of a neutral prime condition (i.e., the prime BLANK) and RTs for the prime words that were available from the ELP website (another example of the use of such megastudy databases).

Reaction times were first standardized across participants to control for individual differences in baseline RT and variability. Then z-scores for items (averaged across the z-scores calculated within each participant) were obtained in related and unrelated conditions. Multiple regression analyses were then used to predict standardized priming for each item based upon characteristics of the primes and targets (length, log printed word frequency, orthographic neighborhood, baseline RT) as well as the prime-target relatedness variables FAS, BAS, and Latent Semantic Analysis (LSA; Landauer & Dumais, 1997). Across tasks, priming effects were well predicted by the prime characteristics, target characteristics, and prime-target relatedness measures.

There were a number of findings relevant to the present discussion. First, collapsing across tasks, priming at the 200-ms SOA was greater following related primes that were short, high in frequency, and had few orthographic neighbors. Thus, under such time constraints, priming likely depends upon one's ability to quickly identify the prime word. Second, priming effects were greater for targets that had long baseline RTs, especially within the LDT. These two findings are problematic for any previous or future priming study that uses different prime and/or target words across item sets. In some cases, both primes and targets differ across item sets (e.g., categorical vs associatively related items) whereas in other cases a researcher will contrast priming for the same target (e.g., ANGER) preceded by one of two different related primes (e.g., a synonym RAGE vs an antonym HAPPY). In either case, differential priming effects may be determined entirely by the lexical characteristics of the different items themselves, rather than to any type of prime-target relation per se.

In addition, when collapsed across SOA, FAS predicted RT and error priming in both tasks whereas BAS predicted priming only in the LDT. This pattern is consistent with Neely's (1991) three-process model of semantic priming in which a backwards semantic-matching mechanism contributes to priming in the LDT, but not in pronunciation. This model appropriately predicts that backward relations (from the target to the prime) should increase priming for LDT only.

Finally, LSA similarity did not predict priming in any of the four task × SOA conditions. This finding is problematic for global co-occurrence as a major factor in producing semantic priming. Even though LSA was able to predict that priming would occur in this study (i.e., related items had higher LSA values than unrelated items), it could not predict differences in the degree of semantic priming among related items. In summary, this preliminary regression study of semantic priming has important methodological and theoretical implications for the study of semantic priming and semantic memory.

The Semantic Priming Project (SPP)

The SPP (Hutchison, Balota, Cortese, Neely, Niemeyer, & Bengson, 2011) is an attempt to greatly extend the methodology of Hutchison et al. (2008) to a broader range of items and subjects. Like its predecessor, the ELP, the SPP is a National Science Foundation funded collaborative effort among four universities (Montana State University; University of Albany, SUNY; University of Nebraska, Omaha; and Washington University in St Louis) to investigate a wide range of both item and individual differences in semantic priming. The resulting database (see http://spp.montana.edu) will hopefully aid researchers throughout the world to advance theories and computational models of the processes that allow humans to use context during word recognition.

SPP priming task

A total of 768 native-English-speaking healthy young adults with normal or corrected-to-normal vision were recruited for the semantic priming task: 256 in speeded pronunciation and 512 in lexical decision. Each participant responded to

1661 target words preceded by either a related or unrelated prime. Related pairs were selected from the Nelson, McEvoy, and Schreiber (2004) association norms with the constraint that no item occurred more than twice in the study (once as a prime and once as a target, presented on different days). For each target, a first associate prime (for which the target is the first associate given) and a randomly selected other associate prime (i.e., the target is not the first associate given) were chosen. Unrelated trials were created by randomly re-pairing items within the first and other sets of related pairs. Experimental trials were separated into two sessions with two blocks of trials within each session (a 200-ms SOA block and a 1200-ms SOA block, counterbalanced).

SPP item measures

For item-specific characteristics, the SPP includes the measures (length, frequency, orthographic neighborhood, ELP RT and error rate) used by Hutchison et al. (2008). In addition to these measures, the SPP includes measures of concreteness, imageability, bigram frequency, phonological onset, part-of-speech, and polysemy. For prime-target relational characteristics, the SPP will also include associative measures such as FAS, BAS, associative rank order, semantic measures such semantic feature overlap, connectivity, and type of semantic relation (e.g., synonym, antonym, category coordinate, etc.), and global co-occurence measures such as BEAGLE (Jones et al., 2006) and HAL (Burgess, 1998). The inclusion of such a broad range of variables across the large sample of items in the priming task should greatly increase our understanding of the extent to which item characteristics and types of relatedness contribute to semantic priming.

SPP individual difference measures

As was done for the ELP, we have obtained information about each participant's gender, age, education level, ethnic background, knowledge of non-English languages (e.g., fluency in a second or third language), amount of reading per week on a seven-point scale, circadian rhythm, and self-rated health information. In addition to these measures, the SPP includes measures of reading comprehension, vocabulary, and attentional control (operation span task, Stroop task, and antisaccade task, taken from Hutchison, 2007). As noted previously, performance on each of these measures has been linked to semantic priming performance for various items or under various conditions.

Targeted audience for the website

We anticipate that this database will be an invaluable tool for researchers developing theories of semantic priming and models of semantic memory. Of primary importance is identifying variables crucial for predicting priming across the database. For instance, is semantic priming more accurately predicted by primary word association, number of overlapping features, or similarity in global co-occurrence? The answer to this question is central to understanding the basic structure of semantic memory. Overall predictability can be tested as well as possible interactions between predictor variables. For instance, perhaps normative association strength (or associative rank order) will produce larger influences on priming when feature overlap and/or global co-occurrence is low, or vice-versa. Perhaps these effects are further modulated by SOA, attentional control, vocabulary, or some combination of these.

This project should also serve as a tool for researchers interested in generating hypotheses for future factorial experiments of semantic priming and actually conducting virtual experiments by accessing the database. In addition, researchers from other areas (e.g., memory, perception, neuroimaging, neuropsychology) will be able to use this database to select items that produce large, medium, or small priming effects and are equated along a number of relevant dimensions. Finally, researchers interested in examining populations such as children, aphasics, schizophrenics, Alzheimer's patients, or healthy older adults could use patterns of priming in this database as a control to test predicted deviations for their population under certain conditions or with certain types of stimuli.

A megastudy of recognition memory

The megastudy approach is obviously not limited to investigations of psycholinguistic variables in lexical decision and pronunciation performance. This approach can be extended across many domains of cognition. For example, item characteristics (e.g., word frequency, concreteness/imageability, orthographic neighborhood size, spelling-to-sound regularity) have also been examined in factorial studies of recognition memory. However, item analyses have been surprisingly rare in the memory literature. Therefore, it is difficult to know if an effect is consistent across items and generalizes to the population of items (Clark, 1973, see special issue of *Journal of Memory and Language* Volume 59, Issue 4, 2008 for detailed discussion of these issues). This is problematic because models of recognition memory do indeed make predictions about particular classes of items, and clearly could be tested at the item level.

Cortese, Khanna, and Hacker (2010) have recently reported the first megastudy of episodic word recognition.[2] The Cortese et al. study provides recognition memory estimates (e.g., hits, false alarms, etc.) for 3000 monosyllabic words. This set of words was selected because estimates for key predictor variables such as imageability and age of acquisition (AoA) were readily available for the majority of these words. In two studies, participants completed 30 study and test lists consisting of 50 and 100 monosyllabic words, respectively, across two 2-hour sessions. The main difference between studies was that in Study 1, participants determined the study duration for each word whereas in Study 2, each word was presented for 2000 ms during study. Across participants, each word was responded to as an old or new item about equally often. The dependent measures were hit rate, false alarm rate, hit minus false alarm rate, d', and C (Snodgrass & Corwin, 1988). Each of these dependent variables was initially analyzed via multiple regression in which eight predictor variables (see below) were entered simultaneously. Of the 3000 words used in the studies, there were 2578 for which predictor variable values were available. The results across the two studies were very similar (supporting the stability of the data) so the data reported here have been collapsed across studies.

The results of the Cortese et al. (2010) study are useful for the following reasons: First, these data can be used to assess theories of recognition memory. For example, most theories (e.g., Glanzer, Adams, Iverson, & Kim, 1993) predict that items which produce a high hit rate should also produce a low false alarm rate and vice versa (i.e., the mirror effect which yields a negative correlation between hits and false alarms across items). In addition, item noise models (e.g., McClelland & Chappell, 1998) predict that memory will be hampered for items that are similar to many other items. Hypothetically, this similarity could occur at any level (e.g., orthography, phonology, semantics). For highly similar items, there will be more feature matches between the test items and memory representations, increasing the false alarm rates for these items. In addition, one might also hypothesize that individual features will be weakly stored in highly similar words, and this would produce a lower hit rate as well. We can test these possibilities by investigating the influence of orthographic and phonological measures as reflected by the recently developed Levenshtein distance metrics. Semantic similarity may be captured by Age of Acquisition effects. Finally, by regressing the dependent recognition memory measures onto a set of targeted predictor variables, one has the advantage of capturing unique variance of each of the predictor variables, with other variables controlled. Previous research has identified a number of item characteristics that influence recognition memory, but the *relative* influence of each factor remains largely unknown.

The results from this study yielded a number of intriguing observations. Across items, the mean hit rate was 0.72 (SD = 0.10) and the mean false alarm rate was 0.20 (SD = 0.09). The set of predictor variables accounted for 45.9% of the variance in hit rates, 14.9% of the variance in false alarm rates, and 29.2% of the variance in hits minus false alarms. Interestingly, contrary to the prediction that item hit rates should be negatively related to their false alarm rates, hit rates were positively correlated with false alarm rates ($r = 0.145$, $p < .0001$). Hence, when one looks at the item level, as opposed to the factor level, there is not much support for the mirror effect. This is particularly compelling because the same items served as old and new items on the recognition test, and so any idiosyncratic item information that drives hits should also increase false alarms.

The results also indicated that traditional measures of recognition memory including hits minus false alarms and d' were positively correlated with imageability, AoA, and negatively related with word frequency, phonological and orthographic similarity, and word length. Interestingly, imageability and length were the two strongest predictors. Consistent with item noise models, item similarity effects were observed for both phonological density and orthographic density measures. These findings suggest that items sharing similarities with many other items are less distinct (i.e., associated with more noise) and more difficult to recognize. In addition, there were effects of age of acquisition that may tap into semantic similarity. It is again important to note that the effects of AoA were above and beyond the correlated influence of the related variables.

In sum, the results from the mega recognition memory study have yielded a number of intriguing findings that further our understanding of episodic recognition. Based on these results, it appears that the mirror effect in episodic recognition does not naturally extend to the item level. Moreover, there is some support for item noise models suggesting that there are strong similarity effects along orthographic, phonological, and semantic measures. Finally, imageability and word length provide unique predictive power in recognition performance above and beyond correlated variables of word frequency and familiarity. Clearly the megastudy approach to episodic recognition nicely exemplifies the utility of this approach to models of episodic recognition.

Conclusions

The present chapter reviews evidence of the utility of the megastudy approach in providing further leverage in understanding cognitive performance across a number of distinct domains. As we have emphasized throughout this chapter, we are not suggesting that this is the only way to study such domains, but believe that it is indeed important to use converging evidence across both factorial and megastudy approaches. Hopefully, the megastudies will nurture the development of cumulative datasets that serve to lay the foundation of accepted findings and principles that appear to be common place in other scientific disciplines.

- Megastudies of visual word recognition involve the collection behavioral responses across a large set of participants and items. Such databases provide a complementary, converging approach to the standard factorial studies that dominate the literature.
- Recently, there has been a concern raised that data from megastudies may not be sensitive enough to pick up some subtle effects in the word recognition literature. We directly addressed this issue and showed that the concern is not substantiated in the largest megastudy database available, the English Lexicon Project.
- The megastudy literature was reviewed to demonstrate the utility of this approach in a) the evaluation of extent computational models, b) the development of new models (e.g., models of multisyllabic word processing), c) the evaluation of hitherto unexplored variables (e.g., Levenstein Distance measures), d) comparing the predictive power of multiple measures of the same variable (e.g., the functional form of various word frequency norms), e) comparing the predictive power of different measures (e.g., word frequency vs letter length), f) measuring individual differences in sensitivity to lexical properties.

- Although the megastudy approach was originally developed in the visual word recognition domain in English, this approach has now been extended to other languages (e.g., Dutch, French, German, and Malay), and to other behavioral domains such as Semantic Priming and Episodic Word Recognition. These newer studies were also reviewed.

Acknowledgments

We thank James Adelman and two anonymous reviewers for their comments on this chapter. This work was supported by NSF BCS 0001801 and NSF BCS 0517942.

Notes

1 Both Hutchison (2007) and Kiefer et al. (2005) actually included subjects within the full range of working memory capacity in their studies for their correlational analyses, but included the extreme-groups analyses mainly for illustrative purposes.
2 It should be noted however, that in an analyses of items drawn from 13 experiments, Rubin and Friendly (1986), conducted regression analyses to predict free recall performance for 925 nouns. They found that imageability, emotionality, and the likelihood of being generated as an associate via free association (i.e., availability) were the best predictors of free recall.

References

Adelman, J. S. & Brown, G. D. A. (2007). Phonographic neighbors, not orthographic neighbors, determine word naming latencies. *Psychonomic Bulletin & Review, 14*, 455–459.

Adelman, J. S. & Brown, G. D. A. (2008). Modeling lexical decision: The form of frequency and diversity effects. *Psychological Review, 115*, 214–227.

Adelman, J. S., Brown, G. D. A., & Quesada, J. F. (2006). Contextual diversity, not word frequency, determines word naming and lexical decision times. *Psychological Science, 17*, 814–823.

Adelman, J. S., Marquis, S. J., Sabatos-DeVito, M. G., & Estes, Z. (2012). *The unexplained nature of reading*. Manuscript submitted for publication.

Baayen, R. H., Piepenbrock, R., & van Rijn, H. (1993). *The CELEX lexical database*. Philadelphia, PA: Linguistic Data Consortium, University of Pennsylvania.

Baayen, R. H., Feldman, L. B., & Schreuder, R. (2006). Morphological influences on the recognition of monosyllabic monomorphemic words. *Journal of Memory & Language, 55*, 290–313.

Balota, D. A. & Chumbley, J. I. (1985). The locus of word-frequency effects in the pronunciation task: Lexical access and/or production? *Journal of Memory & Language, 24*, 89–106.

Balota, D. A. & Duchek, J. M. (1988). Age-related differences in lexical access, spreading activation, and simple pronunciation. *Psychology & Aging, 3*, 84–93.

Balota, D. A. & Yap, M. J. (2011). Moving beyond the mean in studies of mental chronometry: The power of response time distributional analyses. *Current Directions in Psychological Science, 20*, 160–166.

Balota, D. A., Pilotti, M., & Cortese, M. J. (2001). Subjective frequency estimates for 2,938 monosyllabic words. *Memory & Cognition, 29*, 639–647.

Balota, D. A., Cortese, M. J., Sergent-Marshall, S. D., Spieler, D. H., & Yap, M. J. (2004). Visual word recognition of single-syllable words. *Journal of Experimental Psychology: General, 133*, 283–316.

Balota, D. A., Yap, M. J., Cortese, M. J., Hutchison, K.A., Kessler, B., Loftus, B., Neely, J. H., Nelson, D. L., Simpson, G. B., & Treiman, R. (2007). The English lexicon project: A user's guide. *Behavior Research Methods, 39*, 445–459.

Becker, C. A. (1979). Semantic context and word frequency effects in visual word recognition. *Journal of Experimental Psychology: Human Perception & Performance, 5*, 252–259.

Becker, C. A. (1980). Semantic context effects in visual word recognition: An analysis of semantic strategies. *Memory & Cognition, 8*, 493–512.

Betjemann, R. S. & Keenan, J. M. (2008). Phonological and semantic priming in children with reading disability. *Child Development, 79*, 1086–1102.

Brysbaert, M. & New, B. (2009). Moving beyond Kučera and Francis: A critical evaluation of current word frequency norms and the introduction of a new and improved word frequency measure for American English. *Behavior Research Methods, 41*, 977–990.

Bueno, S. & Frenk-Mastre, C. (2008). The activation of semantic memory: Effects of prime exposure, prime-target relationship, and task demands. *Memory & Cognition, 36*, 882–898.

Burgess, C. (1998). From simple associations to the building blocks of language: Modeling meaning in memory with the HAL model. *Behavior Research Methods: Instruments & Computers, 30*, 188–198.

Burgess, C. & Livesay, K. (1998). The effect of corpus size in predicting RT in a basic word recognition task: Moving on from Kucera and Francis. *Behavior Research Methods, Instruments, & Computers, 30*, 272–277.

Chateau, D. & Jared, D. (2003). Spelling-sound consistency effects in disyllabic word naming. *Journal of Memory & Language, 48*, 255–280.

Clark, H. (1973). The language-as-fixed-effect fallacy: A critique of language statistics in psychological research. *Journal of Verbal Learning & Verbal Behavior, 12*, 335–339.

Cohen, J. (1983). The cost of dichotomization. *Applied Psychological Measurement, 7*, 249–53.

Cohen, J., Cohen, P., West, S. G., & Aiken, L. S. (2003). *Applied multiple regression/ correlation analysis for the behavioral sciences.* (3rd Ed.). Mahwah, NJ: Lawrence Erlbaum Associates.

Cortese, M. J. & Fugett, A. (2004). Imageability ratings for 3,000 monosyllabic words. *Behavior Research Methods, Instruments & Computers, 36*, 384–387.

Cortese, M. J. & Khanna, M. M. (2008). Age of acquisition ratings for 3000 monosyllabic words. *Behavior Research Methods, 40*, 791–794.

Cortese, M. J., Simpson, G. B., & Woolsey, S. (1997). Effects of association and imageability on phonological mapping. *Psychonomic Bulletin & Review, 4*, 226–231.

Cortese, M. J., Khanna, M. M., & Hacker, S. (2010) Recognition memory for 2,578 monosyllabic words. *Memory, 18*, 595–609.

Craik, F. I. M. & Lockhart, R. S. (1972). Levels of processing: A framework for memory research. *Journal of Verbal Learning & Verbal Behavior, 11*, 671–684.

Cutler, A. (1981). Making up materials is a confounded nuisance: or Will we be able to run any psycholinguistic experiments at all in 1990? *Cognition, 10*, 65–70.

Dufau, S., Dunabeitia, J. A., Moret-Tatay, C., McGonigal, A., Peeters, D., Alaorio, F., Balota, D. A., Brysbaert, M., Carreiras, M., Ferrand, L., Ktoir, M., Perea, M., Rastle, K., Sasburg, O., Yap, M. J., Ziegler, J. C., & Grainger, J. (2011). Smart phone, smart science: How the use of Smartphones can revolutionize research in cognitive science. *PLoS ONE* 6(9): e24974.

Devitto, Z. & Burgess, C. (2004). Theoretical and methodological implications of language experience and vocabulary skill: Priming of strongly and weakly associated words. *Brain and Cognition*, *55*, 295–99.

Faust, M. E., Balota, D. A., Spieler, D. H., & Ferraro, F. R. (1999). Individual differences in information-processing rate and amount: Implications for group differences in response latency. *Psychological Bulletin*, *125*, 777–99.

Ferrand, L. & New, B. (2003). Semantic and associative priming in the mental lexicon. In P. Bonin (Ed.), *Mental lexicon: Some words to talk about words* (pp. 25–43). Hauppage, NY: Nova Science Publishers.

Ferrand, L., New, B., Brysbaert, M., Keuleers, E., Bonin, P., Méot, A., Augustinova, M., & Pallier, C. (2010). The French Lexicon Project: Lexical decision data for 38,840 French words and 38,840 pseudowords. *Behavior Research Methods*, *42*, 488–496.

Forster, K. I. (2000). The potential for experimenter bias effects in word recognition experiments. *Memory & Cognition*, *28*, 1109–1115.

Frost, R., Katz, L., & Bentin, S. (1987). Strategies for visual word recognition and orthographical depth: A multilingual comparison. *Strategies*, *13*, 104–115.

Glanzer, M., Adams, J. K., Iverson, G. J., & Kim, K. (1993). The regularities of recognition memory. *Psychological Review*, *100*, 546–567.

Goldinger, S. D. (1998). Echoes of echoes? An episodic theory of lexical access. *Psychological Review*, *105*, 251–259.

Humphreys, L. G. (1978). Research on individual differences requires correlational analysis, not ANOVA. *Intelligence*, *2*, 1–5.

Hutchison, K. A. (2002). The effect of asymmetrical association on positive and negative semantic priming. *Memory & Cognition*, *30*, 1263–1276.

Hutchison, K. A. (2003). Is semantic priming due to association strength or featural overlap? A *micro*-analytic review. *Psychonomic Bulletin & Review*, *10*, 785–813.

Hutchison, K. A. (2007). Attentional control and the relatedness proportion effect in semantic priming. *Journal of Experimental Psychology: Learning, Memory, & Cognition*, *33*, 645–662.

Hutchison, K. A., Balota, D. A., Cortese, M., & Watson, J. M. (2008). Predicting semantic priming at the item-level. *Quarterly Journal of Experimental Psychology*, *61*, 1036–1036.

Hutchison, K. A., Balota, D. A., Cortese, M. J., Neely, J. H., Niemeyer, D. P., & Bengson, J. J. (2011). The Semantic Priming Project: A web database of descriptive and behavioral measures for 1,661 nonwords and 1,661 English words presented in related and unrelated contexts. http://spp.montana.edu, Montana State University.

Hodgson, J. M. (1991). Informational constraints on pre-lexical priming. *Language and Cognitive Processes*, *6*, 169–205.

Jared, D. (2002). Spelling-sound consistency and regularity effects in word naming. *Journal of Memory & Language*, *46*, 723–750.

Jones, M. N., Kintsch, W., & Mewhort, D. J. K. (2006). High-dimensional semanticspace accounts of priming. *Journal of Memory & Language*, *55*, 534–552.

Juhasz, B. J., Yap, M. J., Dicke, J., Taylor, S. C., & Gullick, M. M. (2011). Tangible words are recognized faster: The grounding of meaning in sensory and perceptual systems. *The Quarterly Journal of Experimental Psychology*, *64*, 1683–91.

Kang, S. H. K., Yap, M. J., Tse, C-S., & Kurby, C. A. (2011). Semantic size does not matter: 'Bigger' words are not recognised faster. *The Quarterly Journal of Experimental Psychology*, *64*, 1041–1047.

Kučera, H. & Francis, W. (1967). *Computational analysis of present-day American English*. Providence, RI: Brown University Press.

Keuleers, E., Diependaele, K., & Brysbaert, M. (2010). Practice effects in large-scale visual word recognition studies. A lexical decision study on 14000 Dutch mono- and disyllabic words and nonwords. *Frontiers in Language Sciences, Psychology, 1*, 174.

Keuleers, E., Lacey, P., Rastle, K., & Brysbaert, M. (2012). The Britsh lexicon project: Lexical decision data for 28,730 monosyllabic and disyllabic English words. *Behavior Research Methods, 44*, 287–304.

Landauer, T. K. & Dumais, S. T. (1997). A solution to Plato's problem: The latent semantic analysis theory of acquisition, induction, and representation of knowledge. *Psychological Review, 104*, 211–240.

Laver, G. D. & Burke, D. M. (1993). Why do semantic priming effects increase in old age? A meta-analysis. *Psychology and Aging, 8*, 34–43.

Leech, G., Rayson, P., & Wilson, A. (2001). *Word frequencies in written and spoken English: Based on the British National Corpus*. London: Longman.

Lemhöefer, K., Dijkstra, A., Schriefers, H., Baayen, R. H., Grainger, J., & Zwitserlood, P. (2008). Native language influences on word recognition in a second language: A megastudy. *Journal of Experimental Psychology: Learning, Memory, & Cognition, 34*, 12–31.

Logan, G. D. (1988). Toward an instance theory of automatization. *Psychological Review, 95*, 492–527.

Lund, K., Burgess, C., & Atchley, R. A. (1995). Semantic and associative priming in high-dimensional semantic space. In J. D. Moore & J. F. Lehman (Ed.), *Proceedings of the 17th annual meeting of the Cognitive Science Society*, (pp. 660–665). Pittsburgh, PA: Lawrence Erlbaum Associates.

Lupker, S. J., Brown, P., & Colombo, L. (1997). Strategic control in a naming task: Changing routes or changing deadlines? *Journal of Experimental Psychology: Learning, Memory, & Cognition, 23*, 570–590.

McClelland, J. L. & Rumelhart, D. E. (1981). An interactive activation model of context effects in letter perception: Part 1. An account of basic findings. *Psychological Review, 88*, 375–407.

McClelland, J. L. & Chappell, M. (1998). Familiarity breeds differentiation: A subjective-likelihood approach to the effects of experience in recognition memory. *Psychological Review, 105*, 724–760.

McKoon, G. & Ratcliff, R. (1995). Conceptual combinations and relational contexts in free association and in priming in lexical decision and naming. *Psychonomic Bulletin & Review, 2*, 527–533.

McNamara, T. P. (2005). *Semantic Priming: Perspectives from memory and word recognition*. New York, NY: Psychology Press.

McRae, K. & Boisvert, S. (1998). Automatic semantic similarity priming. *Journal of Experimental Psychology: Learning, Memory, & Cognition, 24*, 558–572.

McRae, K., De Sa, V. R., & Seidenberg, M. S. (1997). On the nature and scope of featural representations of word meaning. *Journal of Experimental Psychology: General, 126*, 99–130.

Maxwell, S. E. & Delaney, H. D. (1993). Bivariate median splits and spurious statistical significance. *Psychological Bulletin, 113*, 181–190.

Monsell, S., Patterson, K., Graham, A., Hughes, C. H., & Milroy, R. (1992). Lexical and sublexical translations of spelling to sound: Strategic anticipation of lexical status. *Journal of Experimental Psychology: Learning, Memory, & Cognition, 18*, 452–467.

Moss, H. E., Ostrin, R. K., Tyler, L. K., & Marslen-Wilson, W. D. (1995). Accessing different types of lexical semantic information: Evidence from priming. *Journal of Experimental Psychology: Learning, Memory, & Cognition, 21*, 863–883.

Murray, W. S. & Forster, K. I. (2004). Serial mechanisms in lexical access: The rank hypothesis. *Psychological Review, 111*, 721–756.

Murray, W. S. & Forster, K. I. (2008). The rank hypothesis and lexical decision: A reply to Adelman and Brown (2008). *Psychological Review, 115*, 240–251.

Neely, J. H. (1991). Semantic priming effects in visual word recognition: A selective review of current findings and theories. In Besner, D. & Humphreys, G. W. (Eds) *Basic processes in reading: Visual word recognition.* (pp. 264–336). Hillsdale, NJ, USA: Lawrence Erlbaum Associates, Inc.

Nelson, D. L., McEvoy, C. L., & Schreiber, T. (2004). The University of South Florida word association, rhyme and word fragment norms. *Behavior Research Methods, Instruments, & Computers, 36*, 402–407.

New, B., Ferrand, L., Pallier, C., & Brysbaert, M. (2006). Re-examining word length effects in visual word recognition: New evidence from the English Lexicon Project. *Psychonomic Bulletin & Review, 13*, 45–52.

Norris, D. (2006). The Bayesian reader: Explaining word recognition as an optimal Bayesian decision process. *Psychological Review, 113*, 327–357.

Paap, K. R. & Noel, R. W. (1991). Dual route models of print to sound: Still a good horse race. *Psychological Research, 53*, 13–24.

Perry, C., Ziegler, J. C., & Zorzi, M. (2010). Beyond single syllables: Large-scale modeling of reading aloud with the Connectionist Dual Process (CDP++) model. *Cognitive Psychology, 61*, 106–151.

Petersen, S. E., Fox, P. T., Posner, M. I., Mintun, M., & Raichle, M. E. (1988). Positron emission tomographic studies of the cortical anatomy of single-word processing. *Nature, 331*, 585–589.

Petersen, S. E., Fox, P. T., Posner, M. I., Mintun, M., & Raichle, M. E. (1989). Positron emission tomographic studies of the processing of single words. *Journal of Cognitive Neuroscience, 1*, 153–170.

Pinker, S. (1999). *Words and rules: The ingredients of language.* New York: HarperCollins.

Plaut, D. C. & Booth, J. R. (2000). Individual and developmental differences in semantic priming: Empirical and computational support for a single-mechanism account of lexical processing. *Psychological Review, 107*, 786–823.

Plaut, D. C., McClelland, J. L., Seidenberg, M. S., & Patterson, K. (1996). Understanding normal and impaired word reading: Computational principles in quasi-regular domains. *Psychological Review, 103*, 56–115.

Ratcliff, R., Gomez, P., & McKoon, G. (2004). A diffusion model account of the lexical decision task. *Psychological Review, 111*, 159–182.

Rey, A., Courrieu, P., Schmidt-Weigand, F., & Jacobs, A. M. (2009). Item performance in visual word recognition. *Psychonomic Bulletin & Review, 16*, 600–608.

Rubin, D. C. & Friendly, M. (1986). Predicting which words get recalled: Measures of free recall, availability, goodness, emotionality, and pronunciability for 925 nouns. *Memory & Cognition, 14*, 79–94.

Seidenberg, M. S. (1985). The time course of phonological code activation in two writing systems. *Cognition, 19*, 1–30.

Seidenberg, M. S., Waters, G. S., Sanders, M., & Langer, P. (1984). Pre and post-lexical loci of contextual effects on word recognition. *Memory & Cognition, 12*, 315–328.

Shelton, J. R. & Martin, R. C. (1992). How semantic is automatic semantic priming? *Journal of Experimental Psychology: Learning, Memory, & Cognition, 18*, 1191–1210.

Sibley, D. E., Kello, C. T., & Seidenberg, M. S. (2009). *Error, error everywhere: A look at megastudies of word reading.* Proceedings of the Annual Meeting of the Cognitive Science Society. Amsterdam, The Netherlands.

Snodgrass, J. G. & Corwin, J. (1988). Pragmatics of measuring recognition memory. Applications to dementia and amnesia. *Journal of Experimental Psychology: General, 117*, 34–50.

Spieler, D. H. & Balota, D. A. (1997). Bringing computational models of word naming down to the item level. *Psychological Science, 8*, 411–416.

Taft, M. (1992). The body of the BOSS: Subsyllabic units in the lexical processing of polysyllabic words. *Journal of Experimental Psychology: Human Perception & Performance, 18*, 1004–1014.

Taraban, R. & McClelland, J. L. (1987). Conspiracy effects in word pronunciation. *Journal of Memory & Language, 26*, 608–631.

Thompson-Schill, S. L., Kurtz, K. J., & Gabrieli, J. D. E. (1998). Effects of semantic and associative relatedness on automatic priming. *Journal of Memory and Language, 38*, 440–458.

Treiman, R., Mullennix, J., Bijeljac-Babic, R., & Richmond-Welty, E. D. (1995). The special role of rimes in the description, use, and acquisition of English orthography. *Journal of Experimental Psychology: General, 124*, 107–136.

Williams, J. N. (1996). Is automatic priming semantic? *European Journal of Cognitive Psychology, 22*, 139–151.

Yap, M. J. & Balota, D. A. (2009). Visual word recognition of multisyllabic words. *Journal of Memory & Language, 60*, 502–529.

Yap, M. J., Balota, D. A., Brysbaert, M., & Shaoul, C. (2010a). *Are three frequency measures better than one? Creating a composite measure of word frequency.* Unpublished manuscript.

Yap, M. J., Rickard Liow, S. J., Jalil, S. B., & Faizal, S. S. B. (2010b). The Malay lexicon project: A database of lexical statistics for 9,592 words. *Behavior Research Methods, 42*, 992–1003.

Yap, M. J., Tan, S. E., Pexman, P. M., & Hargreaves, I. S. (2011). Is more always better? Effects of semantic richness on lexical decision, speeded pronunciation, and semantic classification. *Psychonomic Bulletin & Review, 18*, 742–750.

Yap, M. J., Tse, C-S., & Balota, D. A. (2009). Individual differences in the joint effects of semantic priming and word frequency revealed by RT distributional analyses: The role of lexical integrity. *Journal of Memory and Language, 61*, 303–325.

Yap, M. J., Balota, D. A., Sibley, D. E., & Ratcliff, R. (2012). Individual differences in visual word recognition: Insights from the English Lexicon Project. *Journal of Experimental Psychology: Human Perception and Performance, 38*, 53–79.

Yarkoni, T., Balota, D. A., & Yap, M. J. (2008). Beyond Coltheart's N: A new measure of orthographic similarity. *Psychonomic Bulletin & Review, 15*, 971–979.

Zeno, S. M., Ivens, S. H., Millard, R. T., & Duvvuri, R. (1995). *The educator's word frequency guide.* Brewster, NY: Touchstone Applied Science.

Zevin, J. D. & Balota, D. A. (2000). Priming and attentional control of lexical and sublexical pathways during naming. *Journal of Experimental Psychology: Learning, Memory, & Cognition, 26*, 121–135.

Zevin, J. D. & Seidenberg, M. S. (2004). Age-of-acquisition effects in reading aloud: Tests of cumulative frequency and frequency trajectory. *Memory & Cognition, 32*, 31–38.

Ziegler, J. & Goswami, U. (2005). Reading acquisition, developmental dyslexia, and skilled reading across languages: A psycholinguistic grain size theory. *Psychological Bulletin, 131*, 3–29.

6 Methodological issues with words

James S. Adelman

Studies in visual word recognition (and other areas of psycholinguistics) very frequently rely on comparing words (or other items) of different types on response time (RT), accuracy or some other measure, and such studies have been conducted since at least as early as the time of Cattell (1886). Studies of this type are conducted to discover the properties of the underlying visual word recognition system of the participants. For instance, if one is interested in the hypothesis that there is a stage or component of the system that processes each letter one by one (Coltheart, Rastle, Perry, Langdon, & Ziegler, 2001; Whitney, 2001, propose such a component, though I oversimplify the consequences), the number of letters – that is, the length of the word – involved should affect the time taken to read a word. It is therefore of interest whether longer words – such as YEARN, PERCH, PROSE or FLECK – take more time to read than do shorter words – such as CAN, HAT, LOT or MAN – as predicted. But it should be clear that the comparison proposed by my examples is unfair: my short words are fairly common, and my long words are somewhat rarer. If the longer words did turn out to take more time to read, it would be unclear whether this was because of their length, the amount of experience participants had with them, or some other factor. To demonstrate the effect, we require that *all other things being equal* long words take more time to read than short words. This chapter is about the problem of these other things – nuisance lexical factors – in three parts concerning: (i) the lexical factors we know about that might be nuisances but we may control; (ii) the statistical basis for protecting against spurious results that derive from not only idiosyncrasies of participants, but also yet-to-be-discovered lexical factors; and (iii) some pitfalls that are to be avoided when selecting stimuli and analysing such studies.

Controlling words

The first problem with these other relevant properties of words is that there are so many of them. As long as 30 years ago, researchers were expressing despair as to the possibility of selecting words that were matched on every possible variable (Cutler, 1981). The extent of the problem might be appreciated by examining a list of variables that one might consider controlling, due to their known effect on visual word recognition, though it is unlikely that one would in fact control for all of these, and it is unlikely that this list is complete. This list is followed by some indications of where one might source the relevant information.

Some variables to control

Word frequency

This is among the earliest studied variables in visual word recognition (Cattell, 1886), and among the most studied in cognitive psychology. Frequency is sometimes measured in occurrences or parts per million (opm), or otherwise in raw count, the number of times the word occurred in the sample of language (corpus) from which the estimate is taken. A frequent word is read more quickly and accurately than its rare counterpart. This effect shows diminishing returns: the RT difference between a 1 opm word and a 10 opm word is more than that between all opm word and a 20 opm word. In the low-to-mid frequency range, a ratio rule applies: the difference between a 1 opm word and a 10 opm word is about the same as that between a 10 opm word and a 100 opm word. To adjust this property, a logarithmic (log.) transformation is often applied. If we take the common (base 10) logarithm (written $\log_{10}$) of the values in my preceding statement it reads: the difference between a $0 \log_{10}$ opm word and a $1 \log_{10}$ opm word is about the same as that between a $1 \log_{10}$ opm word and a $2 \log_{10}$ opm word. This makes comparing the log. values (or the average of the log. frequencies in each condition) more sensible than doing so on opm or raw values. However, the frequency effect is barely apparent in the higher frequency range, above a few hundred opm (e.g., Gordon & Caramazza, 1985). As a result, the log. transformation alone is becoming rarer in regression analyses, and replaced by more complex polynomials or splines.

Contextual diversity

When assembling a frequency count, several documents are examined for the number of times a word occurs. Contextual diversity (or context frequency or context variability) is the number of documents in which the word occurs, indicating the variety of contexts or situations in which the word has been experienced – TORNADO and OUTLOOK are similar in frequency, but OUTLOOK occurs in far more contexts. We (Adelman, Brown, & Quesada, 2006) have claimed that this variable accounts for the existence of word frequency effects; words occurring in more contexts take less time to read (and are also usually more frequent).

Orthographic neighbourhood size

Orthographic neighbours are words that may be formed from one another by replacing one letter with another in its place (e.g., DOVE and COVE are orthographic neighbours). The neighbourhood size of a word is the number of neighbours it has (Coltheart's *N*; Coltheart, Davelaar, Jonasson, & Besner, 1977).

Under most situations, higher *N* words are facilitated in RT and accuracy, but this may not hold when competition between words is emphasised, such as identification with degraded (brief/dim/noise-splattered) stimuli (see Andrews, 1997; Mathey, 2001, for reviews).

Phonological neighbourhood size

Visual word recognition researchers usually define phonological neighbours analogously to orthographic neighbours, but with phonemes in place of letters[1] (e.g., HEART is a phonological neighbour of CART). Phonological *N* is also claimed to be facilitatory (Yates, 2005).

Phonographic neighbourhood size

Phonographic neighbours are words that are both orthographic and phonological neighbours, and phonographic *N* is the count of these (Peereman and Content, 1997). Figure 6.1 illustrates the relationships. Of the orthographic neighbours, only those that are phonographic neighbours are facilitatory in reading aloud (Adelman & Brown, 2007). Whilst there is some evidence that phonological neighbours may only be facilitatory when they are phonographic neighbours (Adelman & Brown, 2008), this is probably due to the absence of feedback consistency (see below) in the regressions (cf. the experiments of Mulatti, Reynolds, & Besner, 2006, who controlled this variable).

Levenshtein-distance based neighbourhood measures

Another alternative neighbourhood measure has been suggested by Yarkoni, Balota, and Yap (2008). This generalises the idea of neighbourliness into the idea of distance – the number of changes (replacements, deletions or insertions) that are needed to get from one word from the other. The average distance of the nearest 20 words is used, known as OLD20 when applied to orthography and PLD20 when applied to phonology.

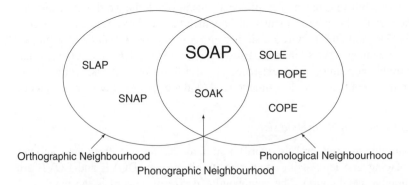

Figure 6.1 Neighbourhoods of SOAP.

Spelling–sound regularity and position of irregularity

Some models of visual word recognition (notably the dual-route cascaded model: Coltheart, Curtis, Atkins, & Haller, 1993, 2001; Coltheart, this volume, Chapter 1) posit a set of spelling–sound rules that are applied to generate a plausible pronunciation of a letter string. Words that follow these rules are known as regular words, and those that do not are known as exception words. Exception words are read slower than regular words, and this effect is more pronounced for low frequency words (Seidenberg, Waters, Barnes, & Tanenhaus, 1984). Moreover, this effect is more pronounced for those words whose irregularity affects early phonemes (Rastle & Coltheart, 1999) – the delay in a word like ONCE compared to control is greater than that in MONK. Due to the complexities of matching exception words, they are rarely included in studies that are not intended to examine the regularity effect.

Spelling–sound (feedforward) consistency

Other models of visual word recognition (notably Plaut, McClelland, Seidenberg, & Patterson, 1996) use procedures that construct pronunciations in a graded fashion, and are said to be sensitive to consistency, the extent to which other words agree with its match of spelling to sound. Most commonly, this is operationalised in terms of rime friends and enemies, the rime being the part of a syllable from the vowel onwards (e.g., -INT is the rime of TINT and -AIR is the rime of STAIR). Words whose ending makes them look as though they should rhyme, and in fact do, are friends of one another, whilst those that do not rhyme despite having the same ending are enemies of one another (e.g., MINT and TINT are friends, but PINT is an enemy of both). Words with many friends and few or no enemies are said to be consistent. If this needs to be quantified as a single number, the consistency ratio is taken to be the ratio $\frac{friends}{friends + enemies}$ where *friends* and *enemies* are taken as one of (i) the number of different words in each category, a type ratio; (ii) the sum of the frequencies of the words in each category, a token ratio; or (iii) the sum of the log. of the frequencies of the words in each category, a log. tokens ratio. Similar ratios are sometimes calculated for the onset of the word (i.e., the part of the word before the vowel), or other ways of splitting the word.

Feedback (sound–spelling) consistency

In addition, feedback consistency is measured analogously to the usual (feedforward) spelling–sound consistency but with the roles of spelling and sound reversed (e.g., PAIR and STAIR are friends, but BEAR is their feedback enemy). It is known as feedback consistency because it presumably reflects an influence of the (incomplete) response on the stimulus, rather than from the stimulus to the response (which is the forwards direction).

First phoneme or onset

When the RT is given by the start of speech (i.e., in reading aloud) it becomes important to control for non-psychological effects to do with the measurement of RT, which might be associated with the articulatory-motor aspects of speech and the process of detecting the start of speech (particularly when this is done mechanically with a voice key; see, e.g., Rastle & Davis, 2002). When items are picked for such experiments, items are therefore paired off so that each group of items has the same selection of onsets. In regressions, it is more common to concentrate on the initial phoneme, with some researchers choosing to code its acoustic features (e.g., Balota, Cortese, Sergent-Marshall, Spieler, & Yap, 2004).

Length

It is common to control length in letters, in phonemes, and in syllables.

Bigram frequency

Although the effect on word recognition is not clear, it is still fairly common to control the frequency with which adjacent letter pairs are used; for instance NT is common, but UA is rare. The count is usually based on word types (not their frequency) and may take into account the position of the bigram within the word.

Morphological properties

A word's morphological structure – its construction from components (morphemes) that have meaning (e.g., WALK = WALK + ED or HEADBOARD = HEAD + BOARD) – and its morphological family – those words sharing the same base-word (e.g., WALK, WALKS, WALKED, WALKING, WALKER) – may also be important. Whilst a common attempt to circumvent this is to use single-morpheme words, this does not appear to be sufficient, as there may be effects of morphological family size, frequency of the entire morphological family etc. for these words (Baayen, Feldman, & Schreuder, 2006).

Rating-based measures

A variety of meaning- or experience-based ratings have been shown to affect visual word recognition, which are sometimes controlled, particularly if a new meaning-based measure is being tested. Such measures include concreteness, imageability, valence and familiarity. Due to the difficulty of obtaining sufficient data to measure age of acquisition, participant estimates of the age at which words are learnt are commonly used in their place.

Some sources of words and variables for English

Elexicon

The Elexicon project web site (http://elexicon.wustl.edu/; Balota, Yap, Cortese, Hutchison, Kessler, Loftis, et al., 2007) contains many of the variables that are relevant to control for many words, as well as data from word naming and lexical decision. The variables include frequency counts from USENET (Burgess & Livesay, 1998) and word frequency and contextual diversity from a subtitle corpus (Brysbaert & New, 2009); all the neighbourhood variables (phonographic N is labelled OG_N); phonological information that includes a whole transcription, number of phonemes and of syllables; morphological transcriptions and number of morphemes; and bigram frequency information.

CELEX

CELEX (Baayen, Piepenbrock, & Gulikers, 1995) contains commonly used phonological transcriptions, frequencies, part of speech information, and morphological transcriptions. The transcriptions can be processed to produce a variety of derived statistics. Some care is required with the morphological information, as derivational informational about lemmas (basewords) is contained separately from the inflectional informational about individual words, and with the frequency information, which is present for the surface form of words as well as each possible meaning of a word (and due to rounding the values of the latter do not always add up to the former).

Lexicall

Lexicall (currently at http://lexicall.widged.com/) provides access or links to a variety of databases, which include the Gilhooly and Logie (1980) norms for age of acquisition, imagery, concreteness, familiarity, and ambiguity measures, the Clark and Paivio (2004) norms for imageability and familiarity, and the Cortese and Fugett (2004) imageability norms, among others.

MRC Psycholinguistic Database

Among the databases in the Lexicall list is the MRC database (Wilson, 1988). This database has been widely used, because it brought together several contemporary sources in one place. However, many of those sources have been extended or superseded.

Testing words

In most of psychology (and hence much of psychologists' statistical training), statistical tests are conducted with the participant as the unit of observation.

One observes the mean effect over participants, and estimates the stability of the estimate of the effect on the basis of the variability and number of participants. If the stability is such that it is unlikely that the observed effect would have occurred were the true effect (averaged over participants) zero, then one declares the result significant. There are two reasons to look at stability in this way: in order to ignore inexplicable *noise*, and in order to examine the population average whilst ignoring individual participant idiosyncrasies. The distinction between these two sources of instability is often ignored, because they are conflated in simple designs, but becomes critical when there are other sources of instability in the data.

In word recognition experiments, there is such a further source of instability: individual word idiosyncrasies; even when extensive attempts have been made to control the stimuli, there will inevitably be uncontrolled variables that affect the RTs observed in the experiment. After all, if one knew *all* the factors affecting visual word recognition, there would be no need to conduct the experiment.[2]

In the following, I describe how these sources of variability are combined into a single model to produce relevant statistical tests, building up from simpler designs and models. These analyses are split into four pairs of cases: (i) the participants-only between-subjects cases, which set the background, and illustrate a commonly misunderstood point about averaging: in appropriate designs, it is a technique to reduce computation without discarding information; (ii) the participants-only within-subjects cases, which illustrate the importance of differences in subjects' susceptibility to the effect of interest; (iii) items-only cases, which illustrate the difference in analysis between listwise and itemwise matching (yoking); and (iv) cases including both subject and item variability. That is, the simpler analyses illustrate the key points that are needed to understand the last-named pair of cases.

For the interested reader, the model specifications are accompanied by R (R Development Core Team, 2010) code to fit the models and produce the significance tests; these assume the dataset is loaded correctly into dataset and that condition, subject, item, and yoke (matching group) are factors, with Y being the dependent variable.

The participants-only between-subjects cases

Case 1: One-factor between-subjects designs, assuming subjects do not differ

I start with some simple cases to introduce the notation. The first design involves two groups of n trials from q different conditions $C1$, $C2$, etc. These trials are taken to be the same, except for the manipulation, and idiosyncratic noise for the trial; subject differences are ignored (perhaps because there is only one subject and it isn't really a between-subjects design). For some trial number m, which is in condition Ci, the observation $y_{(i)m}$ as being the sum of μ_i, the mean for conditions Ci and a *random* noise component $\varepsilon_{(i)m}$ (The i is in parentheses because the value of m tells you the value of i.) That is,

$$y_{(i)m} = \mu_i + \varepsilon_{(i)m},$$

> i : conditions
> m : trials

```
summary(aov(Y ~ condition, dataset))
or summary (lm (Y ~ condition, dataset))
```

and under the null hypotheses, all the μ are equal. Each ε is treated as independently normally distributed with variance σ^2 and mean zero.

It is, however, more convenient for our purposes to phrase everything relative to the overall mean (or intercept) μ, and treat condition effects as differences (κ_i) from the overall mean. That is, once μ is set to be the mean, all the κ must add up to zero. For instance, in the two group case, if the $C1$ group are 10 ms above the mean, the $C2$ group must be 10 ms below the mean. If the null hypothesis is true, the means are equal, and therefore the κ are all zero. That is:

$$y_{(i)m} = \mu_i + \kappa_i + \varepsilon_{(i)m},$$

> i : conditions
> m : trials

```
summary (aov (Y ~ condition, dataset))
or summary (lm (Y ~ condition, dataset))
```

Table 6.1 shows how a particular data set can come about when the null hypothesis is true. Table 6.2 shows how that same data set can come about when the alternative hypothesis is true. Table 6.3 shows how that same data set has to be interpreted under the null hypothesis, whilst Table 6.4 shows the interpretation under the alternative hypothesis. Note that that Tables 6.3 and 6.4 do not perfectly match either manner in which the data could have been generated. From this point, the standard F-test for this situation can be justified in several ways, of which two are important for our purposes: the argument from mean squares which is the traditional way based on estimates of variance – the analysis of

Table 6.1 A set of data that might occur under the null hypothesis for Case 1

Observation (m)	Condition (i)	Mean (μ)	Effect of C (κᵢ)	Residual (ε₍ᵢ₎ₘ)	y₍ᵢ₎ₘ
1	1	500	0	−15	485
2	1	500	0	−5	495
3	1	500	0	5	505
4	2	500	0	−10	490
5	2	500	0	20	520
6	2	500	0	20	520
Sum of squares:			0	$SSE = 1175$	

Table 6.2 A set of data that might occur under the alternative hypothesis for Case 1; in fact the same data as Table 6.1

Observation (m)	Condition (i)	Mean (μ)	Effect of C (κ_i)	Residual ($\varepsilon_{(i)m}$)	$y_{(i)m}$
1	1	500	−10	−5	485
2	1	500	−10	5	495
3	1	500	−10	15	505
4	2	500	10	−20	490
5	2	500	10	10	520
6	2	500	10	10	520
Sum of squares:			$SSC = 600$	$SSE = 575$	

Table 6.3 Fit to the data from Tables 6.1 and 6.2 for the null hypothesis for Case 1

Observation (m)	Condition (i)	Mean ($\hat{\mu}$)	Effect of C ($\hat{\kappa}_i$)	Residual ($\hat{\varepsilon}_{(i)m}$)	$y_{(i)m}$
1	1	502.5	0	−17.5	485
2	1	502.5	0	−7.5	495
3	1	502.5	0	2.5	505
4	2	502.5	0	−12.5	490
5	2	502.5	0	17.5	520
6	2	502.5	0	17.5	520
Sum of squares:			0	$SSE = 1137.5$	

Table 6.4 Fit to the data from Tables 6.1 and 6.2 for the alternative hypothesis for Case 1

Observation (m)	Condition (i)	Mean ($\hat{\mu}$)	Effect of C ($\hat{\kappa}_i$)	Residual ($\hat{\varepsilon}_{(i)m}$)	$y_{(i)m}$
1	1	502.5	−7.5	−10	485
2	1	502.5	−7.5	0	495
3	1	502.5	−7.5	10	505
4	2	502.5	7.5	−20	490
5	2	502.5	7.5	10	520
6	2	502.5	7.5	10	520
Sum of squares:			$SSC = 337.5$	$SSE = 800$	

variance (ANOVA) – and the argument from log-likelihood (fit), which is a more general model fitting and testing principle. For the simpler cases here these suggest the same tests, because the log-likelihood for relevant models with normal distributions is closely linked to the unexplained variance. For more complex cases, however, the approaches will diverge.

ARGUMENT FROM EXPECTED MEAN SQUARES

One indicator of how strong the variability due to the difference between conditions is the variability in the estimated κ values – that is, $\hat{k}$ values – under the alternative hypothesis. This is quantified as the sum of squares due to C, $SSC = \sum_j \tilde{\kappa}_i^2$. However, some of the variability in the κ_i comes about due to the noise (i.e., chance), and the expected (average over replications) value of SSC can be found to be $E(SSC) = (q-1)\sigma^2 + \sum_j k_i^2$. To determine if there is an effect, we need to judge if SSC is made up of only noise, or a real effect plus some noise. To do this, we need to know how big the noise is, and therefore we note that the expected value of the sum-squared error under the alternative is $E(SSE) = (N-q-2)\sigma^2$. The mean squares are then constructed as $MSC = SSC/(q-1)$, and $MSE = SSE/(N-q-2)$. The test statistic (F-value) is MSC/MSE. If the null hypothesis is true, then we expect MSC and MSE to both be around σ^2 (because $\sum_j k_i^2 = 0$), and to follow the relevant F distribution. If the alternative is true, then we expect MSC to be bigger than MSE (because $\sum_j k_i^2 > 0$) and F to be noticeably greater than 1.

ARGUMENT FROM LIKELIHOOD (FIT)

A quantitative estimate of the quality of fit of a model is the SSE, which under appropriate conditions is proportional to the (maximum profile) log-likelihood – that is, the most generous estimate of the probability that the data might occur under the model in question. It should be clear that smaller SSE corresponds to a better fit, and that this value depends on the random component of the model, the ε. The question is whether the extra parameter (mean) in the more complicated model is worth it: The alternative hypothesis needs m means, where the null hypothesis makes do with just 1. The improvement per parameters is clearly $\frac{SSE(null) - SSE(alt)}{q-1}$ – that is, the change in fit divided by the number of parameters needed to make the change[3]. Unfortunately, this value depends on σ^2, which we again estimate with the MSE from the alternative. Dividing one by the other leads to the same F as before.

Whilst the mean-squares argument relies on the specifics of the design, the likelihood argument can be generalised more readily to take into account missing data, covariates and dependencies in the data. Among the extensions that have been made on this basis is mixed-effects modelling (e.g., Laird & Ware, 1982). Versions of this approach allow the inclusion of non-nested (crossed) sources of variability. Whilst the technique better estimates variances in designs without replicates, Baayen, Davidson, and Bates (2008) found that in the complete unyoked design considered below (they did not examine the yoked one), the significance test for the effect of interest was superior for the mean-squares approach.

Case 2: One-factor between-subjects designs, assuming subjects do differ

We could in principle add a term to the equation to allow for differences between subjects, so on the mth observation from subject j:

$$y_{(i)m} = \mu + \kappa_i + \pi_{(i)j} + \varepsilon_{(i)jm},$$

i : conditions

j : participants

m : trials

```
summary(aov (Y ~ condition + Error (subject), dataset))
or lmer(Y ~ condition + (1|subject), dataset)
```

with both the π – reflecting a modification to the observation idiosyncratic to the subject – and ε – reflecting the trial-to-trial noise – values being random. Note that with only one condition observed per subject, we cannot distinguish whether π reflects a difference in intercept, slope, or both. First considering the case where there is only one value per subject (in my example, a total of six trials coming from a total of six participants), Table 6.5 shows the resulting estimated values under the alternative hypothesis; it is clear that the ε values do no work, and all the calculation could occur with π values in their place, leading to the same analysis; we say that $\pi_{(i)j}$ and the corresponding $\varepsilon_{(i)j(m)}$ are aliased.

It is only slightly harder to see that something similar is true when each subject contributes more than one observation. Examine the estimated values for the alternative and null hypothesis for a new data set in Tables 6.6 and 6.7 respectively. It should be apparent that the individual data points can change in a way that does not affect the participant means, so that the $\hat{\varepsilon}$ values will change, but neither the $\hat{\pi}$ nor the $\hat{\alpha}$ will, in either model. As a consequence, the variability in the ε only has its influence on the α through its influence on the π, not directly. It follows that the test should be based on the $\hat{\pi}$ sum-of-squares (i.e., use *MSC/ MSP*). Although I do not discuss the details, this heuristic argument can be made more thorough on the basis of calculating the expected mean squares, or by decomposing the likelihood into terms based on the nested levels of the data set.

Table 6.5 Fit to the data for the alternative hypothesis for Case 2

Participants (j)	Condition (i)	Mean ($\hat{\mu}$)	Effect of C ($\hat{\kappa}_i$)	Participants effect ($\hat{\pi}_{(i)j}$)	Residual ($\hat{\varepsilon}_{(i)j}$)	$y_{(i)j}$
1	1	502.5	−7.5	−10	0	485
2	1	502.5	−7.5	0	0	495
3	1	502.5	−7.5	10	0	505
4	2	502.5	7.5	−20	0	490
5	2	502.5	7.5	10	0	520
6	2	502.5	7.5	10	0	520
Sum of squares:			SSC = 337.5	SSP = 800	0	

Table 6.6 Fit to further data for the alternative hypothesis for Case 2

Participants (j)	Condition (i)	Mean ($\hat{\mu}$)	Effect of C ($\hat{\kappa}_i$)	Participants effect ($\hat{\pi}_{(i)j}$)	Residual ($\hat{\varepsilon}_{(i)m}$)	$y_{(i)j}$
1	1	495	15	−10	5	505
1	1	495	15	−10	−5	495
2	1	495	15	0	10	520
2	1	495	15	0	−10	500
3	1	495	15	10	20	540
3	1	495	15	10	−20	500
4	2	495	−15	−10	10	480
4	2	495	−15	−10	−10	460
5	2	495	−15	10	3	493
5	2	495	−15	10	−3	487
6	2	495	−15	0	11	491
6	2	495	−15	0	−11	469
Sum of squares:			MSC = 2700	MSP = 800	MSE = 1510	

Table 6.7 Fit to further data for the null hypothesis for Case 2

Participants (j)	Condition (i)	Mean ($\hat{\mu}$)	Effect of C ($\hat{\kappa}_i$)	Participants effect ($\hat{\pi}_{(i)j}$)	Residual ($\hat{\varepsilon}_{(i)m}$)	$y_{(i)j}$
1	1	495	0	5	5	505
1	1	495	0	5	−5	495
2	1	495	0	15	10	520
2	1	495	0	15	−10	500
3	1	495	0	25	20	540
3	1	495	0	25	−20	500
4	2	495	0	−25	10	480
4	2	495	0	−25	−10	460
5	2	495	0	−5	3	493
5	2	495	0	−5	−3	487
6	2	495	0	−15	11	491
6	2	495	0	−15	−11	469
Sum of squares:			0	MSP = 3500	MSE = 1510	

As a consequence, we can ignore the individual trials, and take the average for each subject, replacing the model with

$$\bar{y}_{(if)} = \mu + \kappa_i + \pi_{(i)j} + \bar{\varepsilon}_{(i)j},$$
$$= \mu + \kappa_i + \pi_{(i)j}.$$

i : condition

j : participant

```
datasetr <-aggregate(dataset, list(subject = dataset$subject,
    condition = dataset$condition), mean);
summary(aov (Y ~ condition, datasetr))
```

Participants-only within-subjects cases

*Case 3: One-factor within-subjects designs, assuming
subjects differ in intercept*

Of course, a more realistic design for the psycho linguistic case has the same
subjects in each condition. We might consider a model that is basically the same
as before, with subject adjustments to intercept, but now the condition is not
determined by the subject, it is determined by the trial (the word on that trial):

$$y_{(i)m} = \mu + \kappa_i + \pi_j + \varepsilon_{(i)jm}.$$

i : condition
j : participant
m : trial

```
summary(aov(Y ~ subject+condition, dataset))
or summary(lm(Y ~ subject+condition, dataset))
or lmer(Y ~ condition+(1|subject), dataset))
```

This is not usually the recommended solution, however, because it assumes
that all participants have the same underlying size of effect: Variability in the
effects shown across participants is only due to trial-to-trial variation, not to any
difference between the participants themselves. This does not correspond to
the traditional idea of subjects being randomly sampled: if subjects are
randomly sampled, not only is there a random (intercept) effect of subject, every
interaction involving subjects should be considered random, *including the
subject-by-condition interaction* because the size of the condition effect can be
seen as dependent on the (random) subject; that is, the condition effect is a property
of the subjects.[4]

*Case 4: One-factor within-subject designs, assuming subjects differ in intercept
and effect size*

Of course, one can extend the model to correct for this by including variability
between participants in the observed effect:

$$y_{i(j)m} = \mu + \kappa_i + \pi_j + \gamma_{ij} + \varepsilon_{i(j)m},$$

i : subjects
j : conditions
m : trials

```
summary(aov(Y ~ condition+Error(subject)), dataset)
or lmer(Y ~ condition+(condition|subject), dataset)
```

γ_{ij} being the divergence from the mean effect π_j in condition j for participant i. As previously (because items are not considered), trials within participants within conditions have no explanatory role. The sum-of-squares for κ can be tested against the sum-of-squares for γ. Indeed, the model can be reduced thus:

$$\bar{y}_{(ij)} = \mu + \kappa_i + \pi_j + \gamma_{ij} + \bar{\varepsilon}_{(i)j},$$
$$= \mu + \kappa_i + \pi_j + \gamma_{ij}.$$

i : conditions

j : participants

```
datasetr < -aggregate(dataset, list(subject = dataset$subject,
  condition = dataset$condition), mean);
summary(aov (Y ~ condition + Error(subject), datasetr))
```

Tests of this form are the usual by-subjects F_1 (or t_1) test. Again, this averaging is a useful computational convenience that arises from the fact that all the information needed for inference is contained in the average.

The items-only cases

So far none of these models have incorporated the properties of the items other than the one of interest, the problem with which my discussion began. On the one hand, there is the vast array of known variables that we can attempt to control. Indeed, we must attempt to control these if we are not to be subject to criticism for the properties of ouractual items. If our selection procedure tends to select items that differ on an irrelevant variable, our comparison will not achieve its goal. At the very least, then, the conditions must not differ significantly on any of these known variables; that is, the list in each condition must match each other list on each variable (known as listwise matching).

Even once this is done, one may still have the misfortune (or perhaps fortune, if one likes publishing results regardless of their truth value) to have selected items that differ in some unknown (or merely unexamined) variable that is not the factor of interest. Presumably such unknown factors exist, because if we knew all factors, we would have no cause to look for a new one in our study; indeed, for a commonly used selection of monosyllabic words, Adelman, Marquis and Sabatos-DeVito (2012), estimate that of the non-noise variance in word naming response times due to properties of words other than the first phoneme, only around a third is due to properties of that are currently known to affect response times (though a larger estimate would be obtained with a broader selection of words; for instance, Yap & Balota, 2009, obtained a lower bound that was higher than this without correcting for noise variance).

Case 5: Unyoked items

Including some such unknown variability, we can use the following model for the RT for trial m with the item k, which is in condition i:

$$y_{(i)km} = \mu + \kappa_i + \lambda_{(i)k} + \varepsilon_{(i)km},$$

i : condition
k : word
m : trials

```
summary(aov(Y ~ condition + Error(item), dataset)
or datasetr < -aggregate(dataset,list(item = dataset$item,
   condition = dataset$condition), mean);
summary(aov(Y ~ condition + Error(item)), datasetr))
or lmer(Y ~ condition + (1|item),dataset)
```

this being a between-items analogy to the between-participants case, where the λ represent the difference of the items from the mean of their condition, assumed to be due to unknown variance. There is therefore the option of reducing the overall computation required by first calculating the mean per item for the significance test – rather than using the complete model – as the $\hat\varepsilon$ carry no relevant information; the sum-of-squares of the κ is tested against that of the λ. This gives the by-items or F_2 (or t_2) test.

Case 6: Yoked items

However, the variability among the items (λ) in that model with such a design comes from both the known, controlled, factors and the unknown factors. However, we would wish it to only reflect the unknown factors, because we have constructed the items so that the known factors do not produce a difference between the conditions. One option, not discussed in detail here, is to include the controlled factors as covariates.[5] The other is to perform the matching at the level of the individual items, so that an item in one condition is 'yoked' to an item in each of the other conditions.[6] This suggests the following model:

$$Y_{(i)kl(m)} = \mu + \alpha_i + \upsilon_i + \lambda_{(i)k(l)} + \varepsilon_{(i)kl(m)},$$

i : condition
k : word
l : yoking group
m : trial

```
summary(aov(Y ~ condition + Error(yoke + item), dataset))
or datasetr < -aggregate(dataset, list(item = dataset$item,
   condition = dataset$condition), yoke = dataset$yoke), mean);
summary(aov(Y ~ condition + Error(item)), datasetr))
or lmer(Y ~ condition + (condition|yoke), dataset)
```

where *l* is the yoking group. In the context of this pairwise matching, the λ still capture variability among like-condition items due to unknown factors, but they only capture variability due to known factors to the extent that matching has failed. In most cases, the reduction in this variance more than compensates the reduction in degrees of freedom, resulting in increased power. Again, averaging the items reduces the computation required to obtain the F_2 (or paired t_2) test.

Including both subject and item variability

If we are concerned about the influence of *both* the participant idiosyncrasies in susceptibility to the effect of interest *and* the uncontrollable item idiosyncrasies not due to the effect of interest, we require a test that protects against both. This would need to be based on a model that incorporates both:

$$Y_{i(j)k} = \mu + \kappa_i + \pi_j + \gamma_{ij} + \lambda_{(i)k} + \eta_{(i)jk},$$

	i : condition
	j : participant
	k : word

```
summary(aov(Y ~ condition*subject*item))
    and then calculated F' by hand
or lmer(Y ~ condition+(condition|subject)+(1|item))
```

in the unyoked case for participant *j*'s response time to item *k*, which is in condition *i*, assuming each participants does not repeat an item so that η includes both the noise (that was previously called ε) and any idiosyncratic participant-item interaction; and

$$Y_{i(j)k(l)} = \mu + \kappa_i + \pi_j + \gamma_{ij} + \upsilon_l + \nu_{jl} + \lambda_{(i)k(l)} + \eta_{(i)jk(l)},$$

	i : conditions
	j : participant
	k : word
	l : yoking group

```
summary(aov(Y ~ condition*subject*yoke))
    and then calculated F' by hand
or lmer(Y ~ condition+(condition|subject)+(condition|yoke))
```

in the yoked case, the ν representing idiosyncratic participant response to the matching variables.

H. H. Clark (1973) considered how to test the effect κ in this model. Neither F_1 nor F_2 is appropriate if one examines the expected sums-of-squares. Moreover, the model cannot be simplified in a way that estimates the excess variability in the κ in a single variance. Clark described an appropriate approximate F-statistic, known as F', that can be formed from manipulation of the sums of squares ($F' = (MSC + MS[C \times P \times I])/(MS[C \times P] + MSI)$). Though the complete decomposition of the sums of squares is simple with modern-day computing power, at the time, it was necessary to approximate this still further with *minF'*, which can be calculated from the easily computed F_1 and F_2 statistics. Reporting F_1 and F_2 and their associated *p*-values has become common, although these *p*-values cannot produce a solution to Clark's problem.

An alternative approach, discussed in the context of linear mixed-effect models, is to use the residual maximum-likelihood estimates. This allows principled estimation of the standard errors of the $\hat{\kappa}$, though the resulting statistic again only approximates a standard distribution, so that numerical evaluation is recommended (Baayen et al., 2008). It is worth emphasising that to be a solution to Clark's (1973) problem, with conditions formed by items and a within-subjects design, subject differences in effect size must be included in the model; that is, lmer (Y ~ condition + (1 | subject) + (1 | item)) will not solve the problem because (like Case 3 above) it omits subject differences in effects.

Mistakes in controlling and testing words

The goals of matching stimuli and including item variability in statistical analyses are similar – namely, to avoid being misled by nuisance variables – but the problems from and potential solutions to known and unknown nuisance variables are distinct. We can, unsurprisingly, do more to counteract the effects of the known nuisance variables than the unknown. To minimise spurious results and maximise genuine results, we must do the best we can in both cases: we should neither treat known nuisances as though they were unknown, nor treat unknown nuisances as though they were absent.

A particular concern arises from the *systematic* relationships between lexical variables. Such systematic relationships are common, and may arise because of pressures of language evolution; for instance, it is useful to allow commonly used words to become shorter to improve the efficiency of communication (if it is not at too great an expense in terms of other concerns). Indeed, longer words are on average less frequent than shorter words.

It can be seen that this may lead to misleading results. Imagine a world in which the cognitive mechanisms of reading are not sensitive to the length, but they are sensitive to frequency, such that frequent words are read quicker. A typical long word is less frequent than a typical short word, therefore a typical long word will be read slower than a typical short word, even without causal cognitive effect (even if there is a causal chain of some sort, because, e.g., over the life of a language, frequent words are more likely to become abbreviated). Uninformative comparison sets like the example at the start of this chapter – in which length and frequency are confounded – are not merely an outlying possibility that might arise to bad luck, they are typical. For this reason, simple *random selection* is of no use.

Making the conditions appear equivalent – not significantly different on some test – on nuisance variables may be achieved by several means, but some of them only achieve the appearance of equivalence, rather than actual equivalence.

One of these is *selection by deletion*, that is, taking a poorly matched list and removing the extreme items that contribute most to the discrepancy until the lists appear matched. But a non-significant result does not reliably indicate lack of a difference in the average outcome of the procedure, let alone in the specific outcome on any occasion – which will usually be just-not-significant in the expected direction. Indeed, the relevance of the significance test is unclear: for any given experiment, the properties of its set of test items is of interest – as this will determine the confounding of the experiment – not that of the average set of test items produced by the selection procedure.

Moreover, deletion runs into the general risks of *selecting too few items*. First, quite large differences in the nuisance variables can lead to non-significant results with few items; this can lead to heavily confounded experiments. Second, if one takes into account by-item variability, having few items is detrimental to the power of the experiment.

Using other, subjective, criteria for deletion can also run into difficulties; one may end up deleting slow items from the condition one wishes to be fast, and fast items from the condition one wishes to be slow in a spurious manner. This experimenter bias is sometimes known as *Forster fibbing*, after Forster (2000) demonstrated that researchers would certainly be able to do this using explicit knowledge available in their estimates of which of pairs of matched words would be given faster lexical decisions. Even if the distortion is not made deliberately, such judgements may influence choices of words if the procedure is not automated.

More generally, *listwise matching* exhibits problems of power, when there is only matching on average, rather than all items being similar, because of the within-condition variability. This can be ameliorated somewhat with a mixed strategy of control on average, plus covariate adjustment (i.e., ANCOVA), though this tends to resemble a regression approach common with mega-studies anyway (see Balota et al., this volume, Chapter 5).

Nevertheless, this approach implies the assumption that there are no interactions among the controlled nuisance variables, and this could be rather troublesome (unless such interactions are also covaried). For instance, recall the frequency by regularity interaction (Seidenberg et al., 1984): Whilst rare exception words are read more slowly (say, 500 ms) than common exception words (say, 465 ms), the frequency effect is smaller for regular words, though rare regular words (say, 475 ms) are still read more slowly than rare exception words (say, 460 ms). Therefore, as illustrated in Table 6.8, it is possible to match frequency and regularity across two conditions, but still expect a difference due to the interaction. Therefore, if the interactions are not also controlled (as would be achieved by pairwise matching), spurious results can occur.

Conclusion

Comparisons between lists of words differing on a critical property continue to be a major feature of visual word recognition research, despite the difficulties

Table 6.8 Words differing in some property C, and listwise matched on frequency and regularity (but not the interaction). Even if C has no effect, the expected RTs [$E(RT)$] differ on average. Regularity is dummy-coded (0 = exception; 1 = regular)

Condition C=1				*Condition C=2*			
Word	log. frequency	Regularity	$E(RT)$	Word	log. frequency	Regularity	$E(RT)$
rouse	1	0	500	reap	1	1	475
wield	1	0	500	wag	1	1	475
hole	3	1	460	heard	3	0	465
wet	3	1	460	watch	3	0	465
Mean	2	0.5	480		2	0.5	470

described above, and the availability of the complementary mega-study approach (see Balota et al., this volume, Chapter 5). Words have properties other than the critical one, and the design and analyses of studies need to take into account properties known to affect visual word recognition and – to the extent that it is possible – unknown properties, by appropriate matching of stimuli and statistical testing.

- A key problem when trying to identify the effect of characteristics (e.g., length, frequency, neighbourhood size) of words on behaviour is that when identifying relevant words, other characteristics may differ. Moreover, many lexical characteristics are confounded in the language at large (e.g., frequent words tend to be shorter).
- A great number of possible confounding characteristics are known to affect behavior, and this chapter listed some sources for these variables. These can be used to match items, or to perform regressions or ANCOVAs involving these predictors.
- Nevertheless, still other yet-to-be-identified characteristics probably have an effect. Even if they are not confounded in the language, chance confounding can occur with the selection of items – just as it can with the selection of people.
- This chapter introduces the basis of statistical techniques that are available to take into account differences that are systematically linked to people or items, as well as other 'noise' sources of variability. Particular care is needed to ensure that the fact that an *effect* (or its size) – not just the average RT (or intercept) – may depend on each particular *person* is accounted for in the analysis.
- Overall, considerable care is needed to ensure results from studies comparing words are not questionable.

Notes

1 In spoken word recognition research, deletion/insertion of a phoneme is usually also permitted.
2 And there is no way to tell if one knows all-but-one or all-but-two or all-but-x of the factors.
3 Of course, *SSE* (*null*) is often called the total sum of squares, and *SSE* (*alt*) = *SSE* (*null*)– *SSC* is the usual simplifying formula for *SSE*.
4 Nor does the Case 3 model correspond to treating subjects or the subject-by-condition interaction as a traditional fixed effect.
5 This may seem strange to use in addition to controlling the mean, but even when controlled across conditions, a variable will produce within-condition variability.

6   The relationship ought to be transitive, so there are pairs if there are two conditions or sextuplets if there are six conditions.

References

Adelman, J. S. & Brown, G. D. A. (2007). Phonographic neighbors, not orthographic neighbors, determine word naming latencies. *Psychonomic Bulletin & Review, 14,* 455–459.

Adelman, J. S. & Brown, G. D. A. (2008). Methods of testing and diagnosing models: Single and dual route cascaded models of word naming. *Journal of Memory and Language, 59,* 524–544.

Adelman, J. S., Brown, G. D. A., & Quesada, J. F. (2006). Contextual diversity, not word frequency, determines word-naming and lexical decision times. *Psychological Science, 17,* 814–823.

Adelman, J. S., Marquis, S. J., Sabatos-DeVito, M. G., & Estes, Z. (2012). *The unexplained nature of reading aloud.* Manuscript submitted for publication.

Andrews, S. (1997). The effect of orthographic similarity on lexical retrieval: Resolving neighborhood conflicts. *Psychonomic Bulletin & Review, 4,* 439–461.

Baayen, R. H., Piepenbrock, R., & Gulikers, L. (1995). *The CELEX Lexical Database (Release 2)* [CD-ROM]. Philadelphia: Linguistic Data Consortium, University of Pennsylvania.

Baayen, R. H., Feldman, L. B., & Schreuder, R. (2006). Morphological influences on the recognition of monosyllabic monomorphemic words. *Journal of Memory and Language, 53,* 496–512.

Baayen, R. H., Davidson, D. J., & Bates, D. M. (2008). Mixed-effects modeling with crossed random effects for subjects and items. *Journal of Memory and Language, 59,* 390–412.

Balota, D. A., Cortese, M. J., Sergent-Marshall, S. D., Spieler, D. II., & Yap, M. J. (2004). Visual word recognition of single-syllable words. *Journal of Experimental Psychology: General, 133,* 283–316.

Balota, D. A., Yap, M. J., Cortese, M. J., Hutchison, K. I., Kessler, B., Loftis, B., Neely, J. H., Nelson, D. L., Simpson G. B., & Treiman, R. (2007). The English Lexicon Project. *Behavior Research Methods, 39,* 445–459.

Brysbaert, M. & New, B. (2009). Moving beyond Kucera and Francis: A critical evaluation of current word frequency norms and the introduction of a new and improved word frequency measure for American English. *Behavior Research Methods, 41,* 977–990.

Burgess, C. & Livesay, K. (1998). The effect of corpus size in predicting reaction time in a basic word recognition task: Moving on from Kucera and Francis. *Behavior Research Methods, Instruments and Computers, 30,* 211–257.

Cattell, J. M. (1886). The time taken up by cerebral operations. *Mind, 11,* 377–392. Retrieved from http://psychclassics.yorku.ca.

Clark, H. H. (1973). The language-as-fixed-effect fallacy: A critique of language statistics in psychological research. *Journal of Verbal Learning and Verbal Behavior, 12,* 335–359.

Clark, J. M. & Paivio, A. (2004). Extensions of the Paivio, Yuille, and Madigan (1968) norms. *Behavior Research Methods, Instruments and Computers, 36,* 371–383.

Coltheart, M., Davelaar, E., Jonasson, J. X., & Besner, D. (1977). Access to the internal lexicon. In S. Dornic (Ed.), *Attention and performance VI* (pp. 535–555). Hillsdale, NJ: Erlbaum.

Coltheart, M., Curtis, B., Atkins, P., & Haller, M. (1993). Models of reading aloud: Dual-route and parallel-distributed-processing approaches. *Psychological Review, 100,* 589–608.

Coltheart, M., Rastle, K., Perry, C., Langdon, R., & Ziegler, J. (2001). DRC: A dual route cascaded model of visual word recognition and reading aloud. *Psychological Review, 108,* 204–256.

Cortese, M. J. & Fugett, A. (2004). Imageability ratings for 3,000 monosyllabic words. *Behavior Research Methods, 36,* 384–387.

Cutler, A. (1981). Making up materials is a confounded nuisance, or: Will we be able to run any psycholinguistic experiments at all in 1990? *Cognition, 10,* 65–70.

Forster, K. I. (2000). The potential for experimenter bias effects in word recognition experiments. *Memory & Cognition, 28,* 1109–1115.

Gilhooly, K. & Logie, R. (1980). Age of acquisition, imagery, concreteness, familiarity, and ambiguity measures for 1,944 words. *Behavior Research Methods and Instrumentation, 12,* 395–427.

Gordon, B. & Caramazza, A. (1985). Lexical access and frequency sensitivity: Frequency saturation and open/closed class equivalence. *Cognition, 21,* 95–115.

Laird, N. M. & Ware, J. H. (1982). Random-effects models for longitudinal data. *Biometrics, 38,* 963–974.

Mathey, S. (2001). L'influence du voisinage orthographique lors de la reconnaisance des mots écrits [The influence of orthographic neighbourhood on visual word recognition]. *Revue Candienne de Psychologie Expérimentale/Canadian Journal of Experimental Psychology, 55,* 1–23.

Mulatti, C., Reynolds, M. G., & Besner, D. (2006). Neighborhood effects in reading aloud: New findings and new challenges for computational models. *Journal of Experimental Psychology: Human Perception and Performance, 32,* 799–810.

Peereman, R. & Content, A. (1997). Orthographic and phonological neighborhoods in naming: Not all neighbors are equally influential in orthographic space. *Journal of Memory and Language, 37,* 382–410.

Plaut, D. C., McClelland, J. L., Seidenberg, M. S., & Patterson, K. (1996). Understanding normal and impaired reading: Computational principles in quasi-regular domains. *Psychological Review, 103,* 56–115.

R Development Core Team. (2010). R: A language and environment for statistical computing [Computer software manual]. Vienna, Austria. Available from http://www.R-project.org.

Rastle, K. & Coltheart, M. (1999). Serial and strategic effects in reading aloud. *Journal of Experimental Psychology: Human Perception and Performance, 25,* 482–503.

Rastle, K. & Davis, M. H. (2002). On the complexities of measuring naming. *Journal of Experimental Psychology: Human Perception and Performance, 28,* 307–314.

Seidenberg, M. S., Waters, G. S., Barnes, M. A., & Tanenhaus, M. K. (1984). When does irregular spelling or pronunciation influence word recognition. *Journal of Verbal Learning and Verbal Behavior, 23,* 383–404.

Whitney, C. (2001). How the brain encodes the order of letters in a printed word: The SERIOL model and selective literature review. *Psychonomic Bulletin & Review, 8,* 221–243.

Wilson, M. D. (1988). The MRC Psycholinguistic Database: Machine Readable Dictionary, Version 2. *Behavior Research Methods, Instruments and Computers, 20,* 6–11.

Yap, M. J. & Balota, D. A. (2009). Visual word recognition of multisyllabic words. *Journal of Memory and Language, 60*, 502–529.

Yarkoni, T., Balota, D., & Yap, M. (2008). Moving beyond Coltheart's *N: A* new measure of orthographic similarity. *Psychonomic Bulletin & Review, 15*, 971–979.

Yates, M. (2005). Phonological neighbors speed visual word processing: Evidence from multiple tasks. *Journal of Experimental Psychology: Learning, Memory, and Cognition, 31*, 1385–1397.

7 Brain asymmetry and visual word recognition

Do we have a split fovea?

Marc Brysbaert, Qing Cai, and
Lise Van der Haegen

Most people have left hemisphere dominance for spoken word production

The brain is divided into two halves, but both hemispheres do not process information in exactly the same way. One of the first findings about the consequences of brain damage was that speech problems were more likely after injuries to the frontal part of the left brain half than after injuries to the right brain half. This finding was first established in the 19th century by the French scientists Marc Dax and Paul Broca and remains a basic tenet of neuropsychology. For instance, after a review of a group of patients with unilateral brain damage, Bryden, Hecaen, and De Agostini (1983) concluded that about half of the right-handed patients had speech problems after left-hemisphere lesions (36 out of 70) against only 10% after right-hemisphere lesions (five out of 60).

Recent studies have extended the clinical findings to the healthy population. For instance, Pujol, Deus, Losilla, and Capdevila (1999) used brain imaging (fMRI) to determine the relative activity of the frontal lobes in the left and the right cerebral hemispheres of 50 right handers and 50 left handers, who took part in a word-generation task. The participants were presented with a letter (e.g., F) and had to silently generate words starting with that letter. Pujol et al. used a laterality index defined as $100 * (L-R)/(L+R)$, L being the number of measurement units (voxels) active in the left hemisphere, and R being the number of voxels active in the right hemisphere. Figure 7.1 shows the results of the study, which are typical for all later studies examining brain dominance and can be summarised as follows: (i) the vast majority of participants show more activity in the left frontal cortex during word generation than in the right frontal cortex; (ii) the asymmetry is on average larger in right-handers than in left-handers; (iii) most participants show some activity in the right frontal cortex as well (i.e., the laterality index is not +100), and (iv) a small number of left-handers show a reversed dominance, with significantly more activity in the right hemisphere than in the left hemisphere. The percentages of people with reverse dominance usually quoted in the literature are 25% for left-handers and 5% for right-handers (Knecht, Drager, Deppe, Bobe, Lohmann, Floel, et al., 2000; Loring, Measor, Lee, Murro, Smith, Flanigin, et al., 1990). However, in our own work with university students we find that only about 10% of the left-handers are clearly

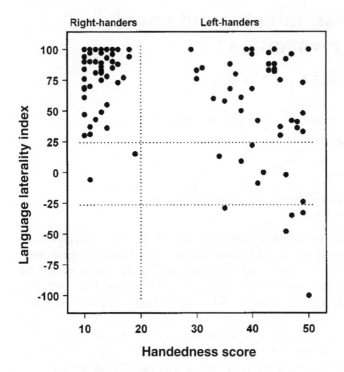

Figure 7.1 Correlation between handedness (measured from extreme right [score 10] to extreme left [score 50]) and activation laterality in the inferior frontal gyrus. The authors defined laterality scores larger than +25 as evidence for left hemisphere dominance, scores lower than −25 as evidence for right hemisphere dominance, and scores in-between as evidence for bilateral speech control. Source: Pujol et al., 1999.

right-dominant for spoken language generation, a figure that seems to agree with Pujol et al.'s data in Figure 7.1 (Van der Haegen, Cai, Seurinck, & Brysbaert, 2011).

Does speech dominance have implications for visual word recognition?

An important question is to what extent brain dominance for spoken language generation has implications for word reading. This need not be the case, as the former involves action control whereas the latter concerns visual perception. In addition, both activities depend on different parts of the brain. Visual word recognition predominantly makes use of the lower back part of the brain (i.e., the occipital and the temporal lobes) and not of the frontal lobes involved in speech production. So, there would be no anatomical contradiction between unilateral processing for spoken language production in the frontal lobes and bilateral processing for visual word recognition in the occipito-temporal part of the brain. As a matter of fact, some of the early evidence with split-brain patients suggested exactly this organisation.

Split-brain patients are patients who had their corpus callosum sectioned for the treatment of otherwise intractable epilepsy. This surgery disconnected the left and the right cerebral hemispheres and was used in those cases where an epileptic focus provoked uncontrolled activity in the opposite brain half. By disconnecting the two hemispheres, it was possible to reduce the seizures. Gazzaniga (1983) presented a review of the research with these patients, which seemed to suggest quite extensive spoken and written language understanding in the isolated right hemisphere, but no speech output. For instance, split-brain patients seemed to understand visual words flashed to the right hemisphere (assessed by asking them to identify the corresponding object with the left hand), but were not able to name the words. In the same review, however, Gazzaniga (1983) criticised the studies and came to the conclusion that the evidence for right hemisphere language comprehension was not very strong, because it could be due to experimental flaws in the early studies and it was limited to very few participants. For instance, he argued that only three of the 28 patients from the East Coast sample demonstrated evidence of right-hemisphere language. A different view was defended by Zaidel (1983), who took issue with Gazzaniga's conclusions and suggested that a better summary of the right hemisphere language capacities in split-brain patients was: 'no speech, good auditory language comprehension, and moderate reading'.

The question to what extent word reading is lateralised got a major impetus from modern neuroscience techniques. Two particularly interesting studies were published by Cohen and colleagues (Cohen, Dehaene, Naccache, Lehericy, Dehaene-Lambertz, Henaff, et al., 2000, Cohen, Lehericy, Chochon, Lemer, Rivaud, & Dehaene, 2002). In these studies, Cohen et al. showed that a region in the left occipito-temporal junction was crucially involved in visual word recognition (Figure 7.2). This region was active independent of the position of the word in the visual field and, in particular, whether or not the word was initially projected to the left hemisphere. Cohen et al. called this area the 'visual word form area' (VWFA) and claimed that information from written words had to pass through it to access the associated semantic and phonological memory representations.

Cai and colleagues (Cai, Lavidor, Brysbaert, Paulignan, & Nazir, 2008; Cai, Paulignan, Brysbaert, Ibarrola, & Nazir, 2010) investigated whether the left lateralisation of the visual word form area was caused by the laterality of the frontal language processing areas or could be explained by other factors favouring the left hemisphere, such as left hemisphere dominance for detailed form perception or the left–right reading direction of the language tested. Cai et al. (2008) determined the laterality of spoken word production for a group of French-speaking right- and left-handers with a paradigm similar to Pujol et al. (1999) and selected four left-handers with clear right hemisphere dominance. All four of these participants had the visual word form area in the right hemisphere, suggesting that interactions between the anterior and the posterior language areas are indeed

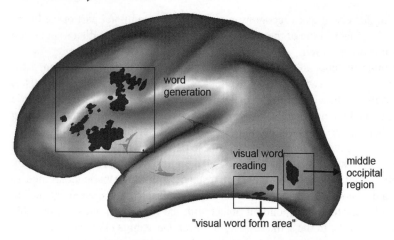

Figure 7.2 Figure of the left hemisphere showing the frontal areas active in word generation and the visual word form area, as postulated by Cohen and colleagues.
Posterior to the visual word form area is a part of the occipital cortex, the
middle occipital gyrus, that is also particularly active in written word recognition. It is left lateralised in typical healthy participants as well (Gold & Rastle,
2007), but was not correlated with the activity in the frontal language areas in
Cai et al. (2010).

responsible for the lateralisation of the visual word form area. A person with
speech control in one hemisphere is very likely to have the visual word form area
in the same hemisphere (see Cornelissen, Kringelbach, Ellis, Whitney, Holliday,
& Hansen, 2009, for evidence of rapid interactions between the occipito-temporal
cortex and the left inferior frontal gyrus in visual word recognition).

Cai et al. (2010) repeated the Cai et al. (2008) study with 11 participants who
were left-dominant for language generation and five participants who were right-
dominant (participants were again French-speaking). Ten of the 11 left-dominant
participants showed higher activation in the visual word form area of the left
hemisphere; and four out of five right-dominant participants showed higher activation in the right hemisphere, suggesting that the correlation between the asymmetry of the language generation areas and the word reading areas may not be
100%. Another published exception involved a German-speaking person with left
frontal dominance for speech production and right temporal dominance for
spoken word recognition (Jansen, Deppe, Schwindt, Mohammadi, Sehlmeyer, &
Knechts, 2006).

All in all, the evidence collected thus far indicates that the interactions between
the frontal and occipito-temporal brain areas are so important for language
processing that chances are very high that the visual word form area will be
lateralised to the same side as the language production areas. This is particularly
surprising for the right-dominant participants who read from left to right, because

for these participants most of the words are initially transmitted to the left hemisphere during reading, as we will see in the next section.

Brain asymmetry and parafoveal word recognition

The lateralisation of the visual word form area most likely has an impact on parafoveal word recognition. This is word recognition a few letter positions to the left or to the right of the fixation location (central vision is usually referred to as foveal vision). Indeed, the organisation of the visual system is such that stimuli in the left visual field (LVF) are initially sent to the right brain half, whereas stimuli in the right visual field (RVF) are sent to the left brain half. This is because the optic fibres from the nasal hemiretina (i.e., the side towards the nose) cross at the optic chiasm and project to the contralateral cerebral hemisphere (Figure 7.3). This organisation is interesting for survival, because it allows humans to notice more rapidly whether an important moving stimulus (food or predator) is situated to the left or to the right. As a result, it presumably got

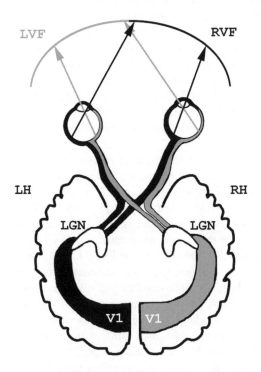

Figure 7.3 Organisation of the visual system. Because the optic fibres coming from the nasal halves of the retina cross to the other hemisphere, all stimuli presented to the left of the fixation location are initially sent to the right cerebral hemisphere and all stimuli presented to the right of the fixation location are initially sent to the left cerebral hemisphere. LGN = Lateral Geniculate Nucleus.

selected by evolutionary pressure. As we will see later, psychologists disagree about whether the separation between LVF (left visual field) and RVF (right visual field) is sharp (i.e., a split fovea) or whether there is a small overlap of LVF and RVF in the middle of the visual field (i.e., a bilaterally projecting fovea). LGN, ; LH/RH, left hemisphere/right hemisphere.

The fact that words are recognised better in RVF than LVF was first documented in the 1950s, although the effect initially was not attributed to cerebral dominance but to reading-related attentional processes. Mishkin and Forgays (1952) investigated the left–right differences for English and Yiddish words (the latter is a language read from right to left), and reported a RVF advantage for English words, but a tendency towards an LVF advantage for Yiddish words (a finding shortly afterwards reported by Orbach, 1952, as well). Heron (1957, Experiment 5) also observed a RVF advantage in English readers when strings of letters were presented either to the left or to the right of the fixation location, but a LVF advantage when the letter strings were presented simultaneously in RVF and LVF or straddled each other in central vision. Heron attributed these findings to reading-related attentional biases in English. In his view, English-reading participants have a tendency to start reading at the leftmost word of a line of text and to proceed from there to the end of the line. So, when two words are presented simultaneously in LVF and RVF, attention will first go to the word in LVF (the first word on the line) and then move to RVF. In contrast, when a word is presented either in LVF or in RVF, attention can immediately shift to the word that is presented and presumably this is easier from the fixation point to the word in RVF (in line with the normal left-to-right reading direction) than from the fixation point to the word in LVF (a movement which resembles the return-sweep needed to bring the eyes from the last word on one line of text to the first word of the next line).

Further research, however, established a genuine influence of brain dominance in the RVF advantage for words, even though other factors such as reading habits and the distribution of information within words play a role as well. The first important finding was that a significant RVF word advantage is observed for languages read from right to left, such as Hebrew and Arabic, when reaction times to the words are measured rather than recognition rates for very briefly presented stimuli (e.g., Faust, Kravetz, & Babkoff, 1993; Ibrahim & Eviatar, 2009; Lavidor, Ellis, & Pansky, 2002). Second, the RVF advantage has been found to be smaller for left-handers than for right-handers (e.g., Bryden, 1982, pp. 61–63), in line with the reduced left language dominance in this group. Finally, it was shown that people with right language production dominance, as measured with fMRI, have a LVF advantage for words rather than the typical RVF advantage (Hunter & Brysbaert, 2008; Van der Haegen et al., 2011).

Parafoveal word recognition plays a role in text reading, as can be concluded from studies in which the upcoming words are masked until the eyes land on them. Eye movements in reading are characterised by a sequence of fixations and short fast eye movements, called saccades (see the chapter by Schotter and Rayner in the accompanying volume, Chapter 4). Verbal information is extracted during the fixations and mainly consists of the word being fixated, but also of the word next to it and sometimes the second next word. Rayner, Well, Pollatsek, and Bertera (1982, Experiment 1) concluded this from an English reading study in which three viewing conditions were compared: (1) a condition in which none of the upcoming words next to the currently fixated word was visible; (2) a condition in which one word was visible in the right parafovea; and (3) a condition in which two parafoveal words were visible. Reading rate in the condition with no parafoveal preview was 212 words per minute; in the condition with one parafoveal word visible it was 309 words per minute; and in the condition with two parafoveal words visible it was 339 words per minute, close to the reading speed when the full text was visible all the time (348 words per minute). The finding that reading is more efficient when participants have information of the words next to the one they are currently fixating is called the parafoveal preview benefit effect (e.g., Rayner, 1998).

The fact that word information can be extracted more efficiently from RVF than LVF may be one of the factors that have contributed to the predominance of the left-to-right reading direction in the world (another factor that has been proposed is that it may be easier to write from left to right with the dominant right hand; e.g., Bradshaw & Nettleton, 1983). Given the direct access of RVF parafoveal vision to the dominant left hemisphere, it makes more sense to have the upcoming word(s) in this visual field than in LVF. The languages read from right to left (such as Arabic, Farsi, Hebrew) require more interhemispheric information transfer to process the upcoming words in parafoveal vision in the dominant hemisphere. Interestingly, these languages tend to have a more compact writing system (e.g., vowels are omitted), so that the average saccade length can be reduced (5.5 characters instead of 7–9 characters in languages read from left to right; Pollatsek, Bolozky, Well, & Rayner, 1981). More information close to the fixation position makes sense if extra information needs to be transferred between hemispheres, as callosal connections are better for central vision.

Brain asymmetry and foveal word recognition: the bilateral projection theory vs the split-fovea theory

A more contentious issue is whether brain asymmetry also has consequences for the processing of centrally fixated words. The general assumption, both among psycholinguistics and among laterality researchers, has been that laterality is not involved in this case, that the LVF and RVF overlap in central vision, and that foveally presented words are transmitted simultaneously to the left and the right cerebral hemisphere. Surprisingly, this conclusion is not based on a lot of empirical evidence. Three arguments are usually put forward (for more extensive discussions, see Brysbaert, 1994, 2004; Ellis & Brysbaert, 2010; Lavidor & Walsh, 2004).

The first argument is the existence of macular sparing in hemianopia. Hemianopia refers to the loss of vision in LVF or RVF after a one-sided stroke or brain injury. In the majority of patients (but not in all) there is some preserved vision in the centre of the visual field, which can be interpreted as evidence for a bilaterally projecting fovea. Unfortunately, a review of the literature does not provide a compelling case for this interpretation. Two problems are mentioned. The first is that macular sparing often is due to spared tissue in the affected hemisphere. Because central vision occupies a large part of the visual cortex, which in addition is less susceptible to strokes, central vision has the highest chances of surviving brain injury. This explains why macular sparing is so variable, going from nearly 0° to over 5° (e.g., McFadzean, Hadley, & Condon, 2002; Trauzettel-Klosinski & Reinhard, 1998). The second problem concerns the precision with which spared vision has been measured in the cases of limited macular sparing. Eye movements are rarely controlled properly and researchers do not take into account the fact that the light flashes they use are likely to be visible over a wider area than the directly stimulated part of the retina (due to the light scatter). When Reinhard and Trauzettel-Klosinski (2003) controlled for both variables in patients without spared tissue in the affected hemisphere, they were unable to find evidence for macular sparing within the limits of their technique (0.5° from the fixation location).

The second argument refers to five physiological studies published in the 1970s–1980s (Stone, Leicester, & Sherman, 1973; Bunt, Minckler, & Johanson, 1977; Bunt & Minckler, 1977; Leventhal, Ault, & Vitek, 1988; Fukuda, Sawai, Watanabe, Wakakuwa, & Morigiwa, 1989). In these studies, one optic tract of various species of monkeys was sectioned or stained and the authors examined which ganglion cells of the retinas projected to this tract. By comparing the retinas of the left and the right eyes they could measure the amount of overlap between the nasal and the temporal hemiretina. From these studies it was concluded that there is a naso-temporal overlap of some 1–3° wide. In particular Bunt and Minckler (1977, p. 1445) made the explicit claim that 'A 1°-wide strip centered on the vertical meridian has been found in which ipsilaterally and contralaterally projecting ganglion cells intermingle. This strip expands to a width of 3° at the fovea, …' The claim of 3° overlap in central vision has been strongly contested in the physiological and ophthalmological literatures because (1) the overlap of foveal vision in Bunt and Minckler's studies could not be measured directly but had to be inferred; and (2) because Bunt and Minckler's estimate does not agree with the conclusions drawn by the other researchers. As for the first problem, it is well known that the fovea does not contain ganglion cells. This part of the retina entirely consists of receptors (which is why visual acuity is so high in foveal vision). So, in all studies mentioned above the left and the right foveas did not contain any stained cells and the amount of overlap had to be inferred from stained ganglion cells around the fovea. From the observation of a limited number of stained ganglion cells in the 'wrong' hemiretina Bunt and Minckler drew the sweeping conclusion that the entire fovea was bilaterally presented. This is surprising, given that the other authors proposed much smaller estimates (of at most 1°) and noticed that the amount of overlap was smaller towards the fovea than further in the periphery (suggesting an even smaller overlap in the fovea itself). Wyatt (1978) further questioned Bunt and Minckler's estimate because the number of 'wrongly' stained ganglion cell was far too small to get projections from the entire fovea. Finally, Tootell, Switkes, Silverman, and Hamilton (1988) used a technique of neuronal staining in the visual primary cortex that did allow them to directly trace the naso-temporal overlap in foveal vision, and they concluded equally strongly (p. 1531) 'We find neither a duplication nor an overrepresentation of the vertical meridian.' Still, Bunt and Minckler's estimate of the foveal overlap is the one that made it into the psychological literature (Bourne, 2006; Jordan & Paterson, 2009; Lindell & Nicholls, 2003).

Finally, several researchers have pointed to null-effects as evidence for a bilaterally projecting fovea. For instance, Marzi, Mancini, Sperandio, and Savazzi (2009) asked participants to respond as fast as possible with their left or right hand to small light flashes presented in LVF or RVF. They reported that participants respond 6 ms faster when the stimulus and the responding hand were on the same side than when they were on opposite sides. However, this was only true when the stimuli were presented 6° from the fixation location, but not when they were presented 1° from the fixation location. From this finding, Marzi et al. concluded that (p. 3007) 'This pattern of results is consistent with a nasotemporal overlap at 1° and a complete lateralization at 6°. Both hemiretinae contribute to the overlap area which can be considered as responsible for foveal sparing in hemianopic patients.' Similarly, Jordan, Paterson, and Stachurski (2008) flashed words (such as SNOW) very briefly at various eccentricities and asked participants to choose which of two alternatives (SNOW–SHOW) had been presented. Jordan et al. reported a RVF advantage when the words were presented at an eccentricity of 2°, but not when they were presented at an eccentricity of less than 1°. They also interpreted this as evidence against the idea of a split fovea. As often happens in research, for each of these null effects there is a series of other studies reporting significant effects. So, Harvey (1978), Haun (1978), and Lines and Milner (1983) all reported significantly faster ipsilateral than contralateral responses for eccentricities well below 1° in the paradigm used by Marzi et al. (2009). Similarly, Fendrich and Gazzaniga (1989) and Hunter, Brysbaert, and Knecht (2007), among others, reported evidence incompatible with Jordan et al.'s (2008) conclusion. Some of this evidence will be summarised below (see also Ellis & Brysbaert, 2010, for a more detailed discussion).

The optimal viewing position in left- and right-dominant individuals

Brysbaert (1994) argued that the influence of brain asymmetry on foveal word recognition is easy to investigate. All one has to do is to compare a group of left-dominant participants with a group of right-dominant participants on the recognition of centrally presented short words. If there is a bilateral representation of the fovea, both groups should perform the same (as both hemispheres have immediate access to the information). In contrast, if the fovea is split, performance on foveally presented words should correlate with that of parafoveally presented words. More specifically, if participants show a RVF advantage for parafoveal word recognition, they should be faster at recognising words after fixation on the first letter (which makes the whole word fall in RVF) than after fixation on the last letter. Similarly, if they show a LVF advantage, they should be faster to recognise words after fixation on the last letter than after fixation on the first letter. Brysbaert (1994) presented some preliminary evidence in favour of the split fovea, but the research topic only really took off once it was possible to reliably assess cerebral dominance in healthy participants.

As indicated above, reliable and valid assessment of cerebral dominance for language production became available with the introduction of fMRI. Pujol et al. (1999), for instance, could have compared the performance of a group of five right-dominant left-handers to that of a control group on the basis of the data shown in Figure 7.1. Such a comparison was made by Hunter et al. (2007), who diagnosed a small group of left-handers with right speech dominance and a group of left-handers with left speech dominance. The authors made use of the Optimal Viewing Position (OVP) paradigm (Figure 7.4, left panel; see also Brysbaert and Nazir, 2005, for a review of the task). Participants were asked to fixate the centre of a computer screen (indicated by two fixation lines) and words were presented in such a way that the participants looked on the first, the second, the third, …, or the last letter of the stimulus word. They had to name the word as fast as possible.

The right panel of Figure 7.4 shows the speed with which the left- and right-dominant participants could name four-letter words as a function of the letter on which they fixated when the word appeared. As predicted by the split-fovea view, the left dominant participants were faster to name the word when it appeared in such a way that they were looking at the word beginning than when they were looking at the end. In contrast, the right dominant participants were faster to name the words when they fixated on the end than when they fixated on the beginning. The effect for right dominant participants was not completely the reverse of that of the left-dominant participants, in line with the finding that the asymmetry of the Optimal Viewing Position effect is not entirely due to cerebral dominance, but also influenced by the reading direction and the fact that word beginnings in general are more informative than word ends (Brysbaert & Nazir, 2005). Because the stimuli were slightly more than 1.5° wide, the different OVP-curves for right and left dominant participants allow us to firmly reject the possibility of a 3° foveal overlap, although they may not completely rule out the possibility of a smaller overlap (e.g., smaller than 1°).

Other evidence for a split fovea

Ellis, Lavidor, and colleagues have argued that the split fovea theory predicts more similarities between foveal and parafoveal word recognition. In principle, if the split fovea view is correct, every difference between RVF and LVF that has been documented should have its equivalent in foveal vision. For instance, it has been shown that word recognition suffers more from word length in LVF than in RVF. Lavidor, Ellis, Shillcock, and Bland (2001) examined whether the same was true for foveal vision, and indeed they observed that word recognition times

Fixation
position

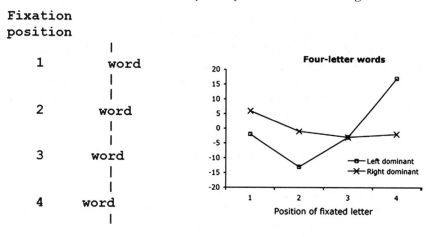

Figure 7.4 Left panel: Illustration of the Optimal Viewing Position paradigm with four-letter words. A trial starts with the appearance of two vertical lines slightly above and below the centre of the computer screen. Participants are asked to fixate between the two lines. After a brief interval a four-letter word is presented between the lines. Participants have to name the word as fast as possible. On different trials, the word is presented in such a way that participants look on the first, the second, the third, or the last letter. Right panel: Word naming times of four-letter words (relative to the group average) for left dominant and right-dominant participants as a function of the fixation position within the word. Participants with left speech dominance named foveally presented four-letter words faster when they were presented in such a way that the participants were fixating on the second letter, whereas participants with right speech dominance had an advantage for words presented in such a way that participants were fixating on the last letter. Notice that the effect is gradual, not only present for fixations on the extreme letter positions but also for fixations on the inner letters. Reproduced with permission from MIT Press from Hunter, Z. R., Brysbaert, M., and Knecht, S. (2007). Foveal word reading requires interhemispheric communication. *Journal of Cognitive Neuroscience, 19*, 1373–1387. © MIT Press.

depended strongly on the number of letters to the left of the fixation location but not on the number of letters to the right of the fixation location.

Ellis, Brooks, and Lavidor (2005) started from the finding that cAsE aLtErNa-TiOn has a more detrimental effect in RVF than in LVF and again showed that foveal word processing was affected by case alternation in exactly the same way. That is, the detrimental effect of case alternation was stronger for letters to the right of the fixation location than for letters to the left. Lavidor, Hayes, Shillock, and Ellis (2004) further showed that foveal word recognition speed depends on the number of words with a similar beginning but not on the number of words with a similar end, in line with the finding that a large number of orthographically similar words (so-called neighbours) speed up lexical decision more in LVF than in RVF.

Finally, Hsiao, Shillcock, and Lee (2007) measured the EEG-signals while Chinese-speaking participants silently named centrally presented Chinese two-character words. Hsiao found that the EEG-signal in the left hemisphere was more affected when the phonetic radical was the right character of the word than when it was the left character; the reverse was observed in the right hemisphere. Apparently, the phonological information disclosed by the phonetic radical was initially picked up by the contralateral hemisphere only.

When does interhemispheric integration take place? The early vs the late integration account

If one accepts that interhemispheric communication is needed for foveal word recognition, the logical next question is where in word processing the integration takes place. Two different views have been proposed.

The first view, called the early integration account, states that interhemispheric integration occurs before word processing proper starts. Word recognition does not begin until all letter information has arrived in the dominant hemisphere. An example of this approach is Whitney's (2001) SERIOL model of word recognition. In this model, words are processed serially from the first to the last letter. To make this possible, Whitney argued, it is necessary that the information from the word end (presented in RVF) is inhibited by the information from the word beginning (presented in LVF) until the latter information has arrived in the left hemisphere. Evidence for such an inhibition process was recently presented by Van der Haegen and Brysbaert (2011). They showed that the usual RVF advantage for word naming can be turned into a LVF advantage by presenting irrelevant letter information nearby in the opposite visual half field. Thus, a word presented to the right of fixation location is inhibited strongly by irrelevant letter information presented to the left, whereas irrelevant information presented to the right helps word recognition in LVF, at least when the two stimuli are in close proximity. This finding is similar to the one reported by Heron in 1957 (see above), but with a different interpretation (interhemispheric inhibition instead of reading-related attentional biases).

Shillcock, Ellison, and Monaghan (2000) proposed a late-integration theory. According to their computational model of word recognition, each hemisphere starts processing on the basis of the letters it received, and the two outputs are integrated at a later stage. As a result, word processing is different when a word is fixated on the first, the middle, or the last letter. When the word is fixated on the first letter, nearly all information falls in RVF and, hence, is projected to the left hemisphere, which takes care of the processing. In contrast, if the word is fixated on the last letter, nearly all information falls in LVF and is sent to the right hemisphere, which attempts to identify the word. Finally, in the case of central fixation, each hemisphere receives half of the information and starts to generate possible word candidates on the basis of the information it received and on the basis of an estimate of the total word length. According to Shillcock et al.'s (2000) model, the asymmetry of the OVP effect is not due to the extra time needed for interhemispheric transfer of information initially sent to the nondominant hemisphere but to differences in the efficiency of visual word recognition according to the amount of information received by each hemisphere and the effectiveness of the division of labour between both hemispheres.

To decide between both the early and the late integration account, Van der Haegen, Brysbaert, and Davis (2009) started from the finding that words are primed more when two of their letters are transposed than when the corresponding letters are replaced by different letters (Perea & Lupker, 2003, 2004). So, participants are faster to recognise the target word JUDGE when it is preceded by the prime JUGDE than when it is preceded by the prime JUNPE, arguably because letter positions are not encoded very strictly (Davis, this volume, Chapter 9). Van der Haegen et al. (2009) reasoned that for a late integration theory it would be more detrimental when the two transposed letters are sent to different hemispheres (i.e., jug*de, where the * indicates the position of fixation) than when they are projected to the same hemisphere (e.g., ju*gde). The input jug* to the right hemisphere is as incompatible with the target word judge as the input jun*; similarly, the input *de to the left hemisphere is not more informative than the input *pe. In contrast, the input ju* is compatible with the target word judge, and the input *gde is more informative than the input *npe if letter positions are not coded in a strict manner (as suggested by the transposed letter priming effect). Contrary to the predictions of the late integration account but in line with the early integration account, Van der Haegen et al. (2009) found no extra drop in the priming when the participants were viewing between the two transposed letters compared to when they were viewing to the left or to the right of the transposed letters. There was an increase of priming as the distance between the transposed letters and the viewing position grew (arguably because letter position coding is less precise away from the viewing position), but there was no effect specific to the split of the transposed letters across the hemispheres.

Another attempt to test the late-integration account was made by McCormick, Davis, and Brysbaert (2010). Their starting point was the semantic competition effect for embedded subset words reported by Bowers, Davis, and Hanley (2005). Bowers et al. found that participants needed more time to indicate that the word warm did not refer to a body part than to indicate that the word gaunt did not refer to a body part, whereas the reverse pattern was obtained when participants were asked to indicate whether these words referred to a family relative. Bowers et al. (2005) had predicted this pattern of results on the basis of the semantic properties of the words embedded within the target stimuli. The meaning of the embedded word arm in warm was incongruent with the 'no' response to the question 'is this a body part?' Similarly, there was an incongruence between the meaning of the embedded word aunt in gaunt and the 'no' response to the question 'is this a relative?' The incongruence resulted in longer reaction times and more mistakes. McCormick et al. hypothesised that a late integration account would predict less interference from the embedded word when the embedded word was divided over the hemispheres (as in wa*rm and gau*nt) than when the embedded word was sent entirely to one hemisphere (as in w*arm and g*aunt). Again, however, they found no evidence for such a difference.

All in all, the evidence strongly points towards the early integration account of interhemispheric communication. This agrees with the critical role of the visual word form area as the gateway to visual word perception.

What contribution does the nondominant hemisphere make?

Although the evidence reviewed thus far strongly points to a model of visual word recognition in which the visual information is rapidly funnelled to the visual word form area from which further processing is initiated through interactions with the frontal language areas, there are some indications that the nondominant hemisphere is not completely left out of consideration. First, there usually is some concurrent activity in the homologue brain areas of the nondominant hemisphere each time the visual word form area or the frontal language areas are active (see Figure 7.1). Second, Cai et al. (2010) noticed that the nondominant homologue of the visual word form area became more active when words were presented vertically than when they were presented horizontally, as if assistance from the nondominant hemisphere was called upon to deal with the higher processing load. Third, Mohr, Pulvermuller, and Zaidel (1994a) and Mohr, Endrass, Hauk, and Pulvermuller (2007) reported that word processing improved if the same word was presented simultaneously in LVF and RVF than when the word was presented in RVF only. They interpreted this as evidence for cooperative interactions between word representations in the nondominant and the dominant hemisphere, possibly as the outcome of neural summation. The cooperation critically depends on interhemispheric transmission, as the gain of bilateral word presentation was not observed in a split-brain patient (Mohr, Pulvermuller, Rayman, & Zaidel, 1994b).

Other evidence for a contribution of the nondominant hemisphere came from Hillis, Newhart, Heidler, Barker, Herskovits, and Degaonkar (2005) who examined patients with acute injuries to the left visual word form area as a result of a stroke. They administered lexical tasks with spoken and written input and output, and identified the extent of brain damage with diffusion- and perfusion-weighted imaging. To their surprise, they did not find that damage to the visual word form area induced impairment of written word comprehension but lead to problems with naming or writing words, very similar to what has been observed in the nondominant hemisphere of split-brain patients. To account for their findings, Hillis et al. proposed that the visual word form area has two roles in reading: first, the computation of input-independent letter-sequences needed for visual word recognition and, second, the transfer of the input to output representations. They hypothesised that the nondominant homologue of the visual word form area can easily take over the first role, but not the second. Again, this points to a more dynamic organisation of the reading system than a simple unilateral stream of information processing.

Federmeier (2007) made a proposal along the same lines as Hillis et al. (2005). In her PARLO framework both hemispheres are capable of understanding words, but only the left hemisphere is able to predict upcoming words in sentences on the basis of interactions with the language production system. Because the right-hemisphere comprehension system lacks cross-talk between the word comprehension system and language production, it is more bottom-up, limited to the veridical maintenance of information processed thus far.

Suggestions that the nondominant hemisphere may be kept 'informed' along the stream of processing (and may occasionally be called to help in case of processing difficulties; e.g., Lindell, 2006) reminds us of Corballis and Beale's (1976) claim that the cerebral hemispheres keep each other up to date in order to maintain coherence. In Corballis and Beale's view, each time a hemisphere acquires new information, a copy of the memory trace is sent to the other brain half. It will be interesting to see whether further evidence for this idea can be found in language processing.

The importance of interhemispheric communication

The massive information exchange between the cerebral hemispheres involved in reading is likely to put demands on interhemispheric communication, certainly if all information is not initially sent to both brain halves in parallel as was believed by the traditional bilateral projection view. A highly relevant finding in this respect was published by Carreiras, Seghier, Baquero, Estevez, Lozano, Devlin, et al. (2009). These authors showed that learning to read results in a massive increase of white matter in the posterior part of the corpus callosum, the part related to visual information transfer from one hemisphere to the other. This was also true for illiterate adults learning to read, in line with the finding that the degree of myelination of axons is not fixed but depends on the use made of the connections.

The need for interhemispheric communication also raises the question of what happens when the communication is compromised. Indeed, the corpus callosum has been claimed to be part of the latest maturing network of the brain (Pujol, Vendrell, Junque, Martivilalta, & Capdevila, 1993) and a malfunctioning corpus callosum has been proposed as one of the factors that may contribute to difficulties in reading acquisition (Monaghan & Shillcock, 2008). Furthermore, the corpus callosum is not impervious to the deterioration of white matter in old age (Salat, Tuch, Greve, van der Kouwe, Hevelone, Zaleta, et al., 2005) and is known to be compromised in a number of diseases, such as HIV-1 infection (Wohlschlaeger, Wenger, Mehraein, & Weis, 2009). It will be interesting to see whether this has any consequences for reading speed.

Finally, there is evidence that the mechanisms of interhemispheric integration may differ between individuals. Chiarello, Welcome, Halderman, and Leonard (2009) examined the relationship between visual field asymmetries for lexical tasks and reading performance in a sample of 200 young adults. They found that participants with strong and consistent hand preferences performed better on word recognition tasks when they had large visual field asymmetries. The same relationship was not observed for mixed-handers, suggesting that the information integration across hemispheres in these participants may be achieved differently.

Conclusion

In this chapter we have seen that the anatomical divide between the left and the right brain half has implications for visual word recognition. In particular, it introduces the need for massive interhemispheric communication. Unlike what was believed in the traditional view, it looks increasingly likely that interhemispheric integration is already needed from the very first stages of word processing, when the letter information is combined to activate stored word representations. Taking into account these insights not only improves our understanding of the neurophysiological and cognitive mechanisms of reading, it also gives us new ideas to look at individual differences in reading.

- One hemisphere of the brain (usually the left) is more specialised in language processing than the other.
- This asymmetry has rarely been taken into account into models of visual word recognition, because researchers assumed that information from words in central vision is transmitted to both brain halves simultaneously, although it has been clear that there is a difference outside of central vision.
- Recent research has questioned the assumption of a bilaterally projecting fovea and shown that the fovea may very well be split, so that all information right of fixation is initially sent to the left hemisphere and all information left of fixation to the right hemisphere.
- Evidence for a split fovea includes the finding that persons with left-hemisphere language dominance show an advantage in viewing a word to the left of centre whereas individuals with right-hemisphere dominance show an advantage in viewing a word to the right of centre.
- Other evidence comes from the observation that effects which differ between the left and the right hemifield in peripheral vision – such as word length and disruption from cAsE aLtErNaTiOn – also do so in central vision.
- A split fovea implies that interhemispheric integration is needed to recognize written words when they are presented in central vision. At present, the evidence is strongest for an early integration account, according to which the information from both hemispheres is combined at an early stage.

References

Bourne, V.J. (2006). The divided visual field paradigm: Methodological considerations. *Laterality, 11,* 373–93.

Bowers, J.S., Davis, C.J., & Hanley, D.A. (2005). Automatic semantic activation of embedded words: Is there a 'hat' in 'that'? *Journal of Memory and Language, 52,* 131–143.

Bradshaw, J.L. & Nettleton, N.C. (1983). *Human cerebral asymmetry*. Englewood Cliffs, NJ: Prentice-Hall.

Bryden, M.P. (1982). *Laterality: Functional asymmetry in the intact brain*. New York: Academic Press.

Bryden, M.P., Hecaen, H., & De Agostini, M. (1983). Patterns of cerebral organization. *Brain and Language, 20,* 249–262.

Brysbaert, M. (1994). Interhemispheric transfer and the processing of foveally presented stimuli. *Behavioural Brain Research, 64,* 151–161.

Brysbaert, M. (2004). The importance of interhemispheric transfer for foveal vision: A factor that has been overlooked in theories of visual word recognition and object perception. *Brain and Language, 88,* 259–267.

Brysbaert, M. & Nazir, T.A. (2005). Visual constraints on written word recognition: Evidence from the optimal viewing position effect. *Journal of Research in Reading, 28,* 216–228.

Bunt, A.H. & Minckler, D.S. (1977). Foveal sparing: New anatomical evidence for bilateral representation of the central retina. *Archives of Ophthalmology, 95,* 1445–1447.

Bunt, A.H., Minckler, D.S., & Johanson, G.W. (1977). Demonstration of bilateral projection of the central retina of the monkey with horseradish peroxidase neuronography. *Journal of Comparative Neurology, 171,* 619–630.

Cai, Q., Lavidor, M., Brysbaert, M., Paulignan, Y., & Nazir, T.A. (2008). Cerebral lateralization of frontal lobe language processes and lateralization of the posterior visual word processing system. *Journal of Cognitive Neuroscience, 20,* 672–681.

Cai, Q., Paulignan, Y., Brysbaert, M., Ibarrola, D., & Nazir, T.A. (2010). The left ventral occipito-temporal response to words depends on language lateralization but not on visual familiarity. *Cerebral Cortex, 20,* 1153–1163.

Carreiras, M., Seghier, M.L., Baquero, S., Estevez, A., Lozano, A., Devlin, J.T., & Price, C.J. (2009). An anatomical signature for literacy. *Nature, 461,* 983–986.

Chiarello, C., Welcome, S.E., Halderman, L.K., & Leonard, C.M. (2009). Does degree of asymmetry relate to performance? An investigation of word recognition and reading in consistent and mixed handers. *Brain and Cognition, 69,* 521–530.

Cohen, L., Dehaene, S., Naccache, L., Lehericy, S., Dehaene-Lambertz, G., Henaff, M.A., & Michel, F. (2000). The visual word form area: Spatial and temporal characterization of an initial stage of reading in normal subjects and posterior split-brain patients. *Brain, 123,* 291–307.

Cohen, L., Lehericy, S., Chochon, F., Lemer, C., Rivaud, S., & Dehaene, S. (2002). Language-specific tuning of visual cortex functional properties of the Visual Word Form Area. *Brain, 125,* 1054–1069.

Corballis, M.C. & Beale, I.L. (1976). *The psychology of left and right*. Hillsdale, NJ: Erlbaum.

Cornellisen, P.L., Kringelbach, M.L., Ellis, A.W., Whitney, C., Holliday, I.E., & Hansen, P.C. (2009). Activation of the left inferior frontal gyrus in the first 200 ms of reading: Evidence from magnetoencephalography (MEG). *Plos One, 4,* Article e5359.

Ellis, A.W. & Brysbaert, M. (2010). Split fovea theory and the role of the two cerebral hemispheres in reading: A review of the evidence. *Neuropsychologia, 48,* 353–365.

Ellis, A.W., Brooks, J., & Lavidor, M. (2005). Evaluating a split fovea model of visual word recognition: Effects of case alternation in the two visual fields and in the left and right halves of words presented at the fovea. *Neuropsychologia, 43,* 1128–1137.

Faust, M., Kravetz, S., & Babkoff, H. (1993). Hemispheric-specialization or reading habits: Evidence from lexical decision research with Hebrew words and sentences. *Brain and Language, 44*, 254–263.

Federmeier, K.D. (2007). Thinking ahead: The role and roots of prediction in language comprehension. *Psychophysiology, 44*, 491–505.

Fendrich, R. & Gazzaniga, M.S. (1989). Evidence of foveal splitting in a commissurotomy patient. *Neuropsychologia, 27*, 273–281.

Fukuda, Y., Sawai, H., Watanabe, M., Wakakuwa, K., & Morigiwa, K. (1989). Nasotemporal overlap of crossed and uncrossed retinal ganglion-cell projections in the Japanese Monkey (Macaca-Fuscata). *Journal of Neuroscience, 9*, 2353–2373.

Gazzaniga, M.S. (1983). Right-hemisphere language following brain bisection: A 20-year perspective. *American Psychologist, 38*, 525–537.

Gold, B.T. & Rastle, K. (2007). Neural correlates of morphological decomposition during visual word recognition. *Journal of Cognitive Neuroscience, 19*, 1983–1993.

Harvey Jr, L.O. (1978). Single representation of the visual midline in humans. *Neuropsychologia, 16*, 601–610.

Haun, F. (1978). Functional dissociation of the hemispheres using foveal visual input, *Neuropsychologia, 16*, 725–733.

Heron, W. (1957). Perception as a function of retinal locus and attention. *American Journal of Psychology, 70*, 38–48.

Hillis, A.E., Newhart, M., Heidler, J., Barker, P., Herskovits, E., & Degaonkar, M. (2005). The roles of the 'visual word form area' in reading. *NeuroImage, 24*, 548–559.

Hsiao, J.H.W., Shillcock, R., & Lee, C.Y. (2007). Neural correlates of foveal splitting in reading: Evidence from an ERP study of Chinese character recognition. *Neuropsychologia, 45*, 1280–1292.

Hunter, Z.R. & Brysbaert, M. (2008). Visual half-field experiments are a good measure of cerebral language dominance if used properly: Evidence from fMRI. *Neuropsychologia, 46*, 316–325.

Hunter, Z.R., Brysbaert, M., & Knecht, S. (2007). Foveal word reading requires inter-hemispheric communication. *Journal of Cognitive Neuroscience, 19*, 1373–1387.

Ibrahim, R. & Eviatar, Z. (2009). Language status and hemispheric involvement in reading: Evidence from trilingual Arabic speakers tested in Arabic, Hebrew, and English. *Neuropsychology, 23*, 240–254.

Jansen, A., Deppe, M., Schwindt, W., Mohammadi, S., Sehlmeyer, C., & Knechts, S. (2006). Interhemispheric dissociation of language regions in a healthy subject. *Archives of Neurology, 63*, 1344–1346.

Jordan, T.R. & Paterson, K. (2009). Re-evaluating split-fovea processing in visual word recognition: A critical assessment of recent research. *Neuropsychologia, 47*, 2341–2353.

Jordan, T.R., Paterson, K., & Stachurski, M. (2008). Re-evaluating split-fovea processing in word recognition: Effects of retinal eccentricity on hemispheric dominance. *Neuropsychology, 22*, 738–745.

Knecht, S., Drager, B., Deppe, M., Bobe, L., Lohmann, H., Floel, A., Ringelstein, E.B., & Henningsen, H. (2000). Handedness and hemispheric language dominance in healthy humans. *Brain, 123*, 2512–2518.

Lavidor, M. & Walsh, V. (2004). The nature of foveal representation. *Nature Reviews Neuroscience, 5*, 729–735.

Lavidor, M., Ellis, A.W., Shillcock, R., & Bland, T. (2001). Evaluating a split processing model of visual word recognition: Effects of word length. *Cognitive Brain Research, 12*, 265–272.

Lavidor, M., Ellis, A.W., & Pansky, A. (2002). Case alternation and length effects in lateralized word recognition: Studies of English and Hebrew. *Brain and Cognition, 50,* 257–271.

Lavidor, M., Hayes, A., Shillock, R., & Ellis, A.W. (2004). Evaluating a split processing model of visual word recognition: Effects of orthographic neighborhood size. *Brain and Language, 88,* 312–320.

Leventhal, A.G., Ault, S.J., & Vitek, D.J. (1988). The nasotemporal division of primate retina: The neural bases of macular sparing and splitting. *Science, 240,* 66–67.

Lindell, A.K. (2006). In your right mind: Right hemisphere contributions to language processing and production. *Neuropsychology Review, 16,* 131–148.

Lindell, A.K. & Nicholls, M.E.R. (2003). Cortical representation of the fovea: Implications for visual half-field research. *Cortex, 39,* 111–117.

Lines, C.R. & Milner, A.D. (1983). Nasotemporal overlap in the human retina investigated by means of simple reaction time to lateralized light flash. *Experimental Brain Research, 50,* 166–172.

Loring, D.W., Measor, K.J., Lee, G.P., Murro, A.M., Smith, J.R., Flanigin, H.F., Gallagher, B.B., & King, D.W. (1990). Cerebral language lateralization: Evidence from intracarotid amobarbital testing. *Neuropsychologia, 28,* 831–838.

McCormick, S., Davis, C.J., & Brysbaert, M. (2010). Embedded words in visual word recognition: Does the left hemisphere see the rain in brain? *Journal of Experimental Psychology: Learning, Memory, and Cognition, 36,* 1256–1266.

McFadzean, R.M., Hadley, D.M., & Condon, B.C. (2002). The representation of the visual field in the occipital striate cortex. *Neuro-Ophthalmology, 27,* 55–78.

Marzi, C.A., Mancini, F., Sperandio, I., & Savazzi, S. (2009). Evidence of midline retinal nasotemporal overlap in healthy humans: A model for foveal sparing in hemianopia? *Neuropsychologia, 47,* 3007–3011.

Mishkin, M. & Forgays, D.G. (1952). Word recognition as a function of retinal locus. *Journal of Experimental Psychology, 43,* 43–48.

Mohr, B., Pulvermuller, F., & Zaidel, E. (1994a). Lexical decision after left, right, and bilateral presentation of function words, content words and non-words: Evidence for interhemispheric interaction. *Neuropsychologia, 32,* 105–124.

Mohr, B., Pulvermuller, F., Rayman, J., & Zaidel, E. (1994b). Interhemispheric cooperation during lexical processing is mediated by the corpus callosum: Evidence from the split-brain. *Neuroscience Letters, 181,* 17–21.

Mohr, B., Endrass, T., Hauk, O., & Pulvermuller, F. (2007). ERP correlates of the bilateral redundancy gain for words. *Neuropsychologia, 45,* 2114–2124.

Monaghan, P. & Shillcock, R. (2008). Hemispheric dissociation and dyslexia in a computation model of reading. *Brain and Language, 107,* 185–193.

Orbach, J. (1952). Retinal locus as a factor in the recognition of visually perceived words. *American Journal of Psychology, 65,* 555–562.

Perea, M. & Lupker, S.J. (2003). Does jugde prime COURT? Transposed-letter similarity effects in masked associative priming. *Memory & Cognition, 31,* 829–841.

Perea, M. & Lupker, S.J. (2004). Can CANISO activate CASINO? Transposed-letter similarity effects with nonadjacent letter positions. *Journal of Memory and Language, 51,* 231–246.

Pollatsek, A., Bolozky, S., Well, A.D., & Rayner, K. (1981). Asymmetries in the perceptual span for Israeli readers. *Brain and Language, 14,* 174–180.

Pujol, J., Vendrell, P., Junque, C., Martivilalta, J.L., & Capdevila, A. (1993). When does human brain development end: Evidence of corpus callosum growth up to adulthood. *Annals of Neurology, 34*, 71–75.

Pujol, J., Deus, J., Losilla, J.M., & Capdevila, A. (1999). Cerebral lateralization of language in normal left-handed people studied by functional MRI. *Neurology, 52*, 1038–1043.

Rayner, K. (1998). Eye movements in reading and information processing: 20 years of research. *Psychological Bulletin, 124*, 372–322.

Rayner, K., Well, A.D., Pollatsek, A., & Bertera, J.H. (1982). The availability of useful information to the right of fixation in reading. *Perception & Psychophysics, 31*, 537–550.

Reinhard, J. & Trauzettel-Klosinski, S. (2003). Nasotemporal overlap of retinal ganglion cells in humans: A functional study. *Investigative Ophthalmology & Visual Science, 44*, 1568–1572.

Salat, D.H., Tuch, D.S., Greve, D.N., van der Kouwe, A.J.W., Hevelone, N.D., Zaleta, A.K., Rosen, B.R., Fischl, B., Corkin, S., Rosas, H.D., & Dale, A.M. (2005). Age related alterations in white matter microstructure measured by diffusion tensor imaging. *Neurobiology of Aging, 26*, 1215–1227.

Shillcock, R., Ellison, T.M., & Monaghan, P. (2000). Eye-fixation behavior, lexical storage and visual word recognition in a split processing model. *Psychological Review, 107*, 824–851.

Stone, J., Leicester, L., & Sherman, S.M. (1973). The naso-temporal division of the monkey's retina. *Journal of Comparative Neurology, 150*, 333–348.

Tootell, R.B.H., Switkes, E., Silverman, M.S., & Hamilton, S.L. (1988). Functional anatomy of macaque striate cortex, 2: Retinotopic organization. *Journal of Neuroscience, 8*, 1531–1568.

Trauzettel-Klosinski, S. & Reinhard, J. (1998). The vertical field border in hemianopia and its significance for fixation and reading. *Investigative Ophthalmology & Visual Science, 39*, 2177–2186.

Van der Haegen, L. & Brysbaert, M. (2011). The mechanisms underlying the interhemispheric integration of information in foveal word recognition: Evidence for transcortical inhibition. *Brain and Language, 188*, 81–89.

Van der Haegen, L., Brysbaert, M., & Davis, C.J. (2009). How does interhemispheric communication in visual word recognition work? Deciding between early and late integration accounts of the split fovea theory. *Brain and Language, 108*, 112–121.

Van der Haegen, L., Cai, Q., Seurinck, R., & Brysbaert, M. (2011). Further fMRI validation of the visual half field technique as an indicator of language laterality: A large-group analysis. *Neuropsychologia, 49*, 2879–2888.

Whitney, C. (2001). How the brain encodes the order of letters in a printed word: The SERIOL model and selective literature review. *Psychonomic Bulletin & Review, 8*, 221–243.

Wohlschlaeger, J., Wenger, E., Mehraein, P., & Weis, S. (2009). White matter changes in HIV-1 infected brains: A combined gross anatomical and ultrastructural morphometric investigation of the corpus callosum. *Clinical Neurology and Neurosugery, 111*, 422–429.

Wyatt, H.J. (1978). Nasotemporal overlap and visual field sparing. *Investigative Ophthalmology and Visual Science, 17*, 1128–1130.

Zaidel, E. (1983). Language in the right-hemisphere, convergent perspectives: Response. *American Psychologist, 38*, 542–546.

8 The front end of visual word recognition

Jonathan Grainger and Stéphane Dufau

Letter-based word recognition: 'in the beginning was the word?'

At some point in the development of different writing systems, spaces were introduced between words in order to facilitate reading (note the counterexample of Chinese logographic script where the spacing is between characters, not words). In certain alphabetic scripts, spaces are also introduced between the individual letters in printed text, presumably also to facilitate reading.[1] The present chapter addresses issues related to reading printed words in such alphabetic scripts, with a specific focus on orthographic processing – that is, how information concerning letter identities and letter positions is processed.

One of the central questions guiding early research on visual word recognition concerned the extent to which the recognition process proceeds via the constituent letters of the word. Are printed words recognized via their constituent letters? Cattell's (1886) seminal work on the 'word superiority effect' suggested a negative response to that question. Indeed, Cattell found that the constituent letters of real words (e.g., silence) could be read aloud more rapidly than a random combination of the same letters (e.g., lesinec). In later research with improved methodology, Reicher (1969) and Wheeler (1970) confirmed the existence of a word superiority effect in conditions that controlled for confounds related to better memory for words than random combinations of letters, and guessing with word stimuli. Even when participants only have to identify a single letter, performance is superior for letters embedded in real words compared with nonsense strings of letters.

Early research on the word superiority effect led to the 'word shape' hypothesis, according to which some form of supra-letter or holistic information about a printed word (e.g., the word envelope generated by a specific combination of ascending, descending and neutral letters, Bouma, 1970) is used to identify the word. Having recognized a word using this type of word-specific information, one could then use spelling knowledge to infer the identities of the constituent letters. Such a procedure would not be available for nonword stimuli. However, this explanation of the word superiority effect ignores two major problems: one empirical, the other computational. First, at an empirical level, a word shape theory of word recognition cannot account for the standard finding that there is no observable advantage for reading lower case compared with upper case text (e.g., Paap, Newsome, & Noel, 1984; but see Perea & Rosa, 2002, for an exception). Since only lower case text carries shape information at the level of words rather than individual letters (via ascending and descending letters), reading lower case text should benefit from these extra cues to word identity.[2] Second, from a computational point of view, the word shape theory has to resolve the problem of shape invariance for each word – possibly with distinct representations for the same word in lowercase and uppercase format, and for certain fonts (e.g., Chauncey, Holcomb, & Grainger, 2008). Given that the average skilled reader knows something around 30,000 words (an estimate for British English: Crystal, 1987), the computation involved in solving shape invariance for each word is going to be a lot more costly than solving it for each letter of the alphabet. This point is illustrated in Figure 8.1.

So why are words easier to identify than their constituent letters even if word recognition proceeds via the constituent letters? One clear answer to this question was provided by McClelland and Rumelhart (1981) with their interactive-activation model (IAM) of context effects on letter perception. There are two important ingredients in the IAM, and either one of them alone can account for the word superiority effect in a letter-based account of word recognition. These are cascaded processing and interactive processing. Cascaded processing can account for the word superiority effect by having activation build up faster in

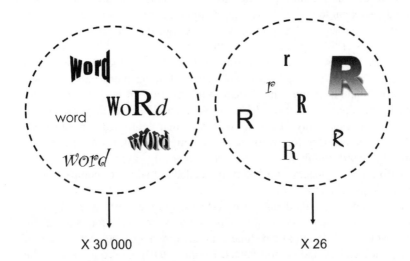

X 30 000   X 26

Figure 8.1 Solving shape invariance for letters and words. A solution based on whole-word representations would involve associating the different formats of a given word to an abstract representation of that word for each of the words in the vocabulary. Much more economical, a solution involving letter-based word recognition would only require shape-invariant representations for the 26 letters of the alphabet.

word representations than letter representations, even if the latter are the first to receive any bottom-up activation input. This can occur due to the greater amount of activation input at the word level through the convergence of inputs that are separated at the letter level. Grainger and Jacob's (1994) dual read-out model provided an account of the word superiority effect within the framework of a non-interactive version of the IAM. Superior identification of letters in words compared to letters in pseudowords is due to identification of the word enabling correct identification of its constituent letters via read-out from a whole-word orthographic representation in long-term memory. According to this non-interactive account of the word superiority effect, the pseudoword superiority effect (superior identification of letters in orthographically regular, pronounceable nonwords compared with irregular unpronounceable nonwords) is due to misperceiving the pseudoword as a real word (see Grainger & Jacobs, 2005, for a detailed discussion of this possibility).

There are other accounts of word and pseudoword superiority effects, including Massaro's 'fuzzy logical model of perception' (FLMP, Massaro & Cohen, 1994), and Paap, Newsome, McDonald, and Schvaneveldt's (1982) activation-verification model (AVM). In both of these accounts, word recognition is thought to be letter-based, and letter identification accuracy is determined by a combination of letter-level activity with other sources of information (word-level activity in AVM, and supra-letter orthographic constraints in FLMP). The difference with respect to accounts couched within the framework of the IAM is simply in terms of the mechanisms by which the different sources of information conjointly determine response output.

Of course, one cannot rule out the possibility that some form of global shape information or supra-letter information does influence visual word recognition for certain words under certain conditions. This might be expected, for example, with words that can be easily discriminated from other words on the basis of such information (e.g., long words with distinctive combinations of ascending

Figure 8.2 A picture of an animal (top) and a printed word (bottom) after filtering out the high spatial frequencies. Can you identify them?[3]

and descending letters), or when normal letter-level processing is perturbed as for example in some dyslexic readers (Lavidor, 2011).[4] On this point, it should be noted that global shape information has been proposed as a key ingredient of visual object recognition (Bar, Kassam, Ghuman, Boshyan, Schmidt, Dale, et al., 2006). The key idea here is that fast processing of low spatial frequencies (that carry gross shape information) enables the early activation of several hypotheses as to object identity, which are then used to modulate on-going slower processing of high spatial frequencies (that carry information about details). However, Figure 8.2 illustrates why the application of the Bar et al. (2006) model for visual object identification is not that straightforward with printed word stimuli (which stimulus can you recognize, the picture or the word?). Nevertheless, future research should provide a specific test of the role of low spatial frequency information in visual word recognition, focusing on those words that might benefit the most from such information (i.e., long words with informative patterns of ascending, descending, and neutral letters).

Furthermore, although the role of low spatial frequency information in visual word recognition awaits more extensive investigation, the arguments raised above against a key role for global shape information are equally valid for the information carried by low spatial frequencies. The key difference between words and objects is the amount of information about word/object identity that is carried by low spatial frequencies. One recent study provides a simple illustration of the greater difficulty in processing word stimuli as opposed to pictures of animals in peripheral vision, where the role of information carried by low spatial frequencies is exaggerated (Chanceaux, Vitu, Bendahman, Thorpe, & Grainger, 2011). This study built on Kirchner and Thorpe's (2006) demonstration that participants can accurately initiate a saccade to a scene containing an animal, presented left or right of fixation along with a contralateral scene not containing an animal, in as little as 120 ms post-stimulus onset. Chanceaux et al. used the same saccadic choice paradigm with five-letter words presented along with five-letter nonwords that were random consonant strings. Words and nonwords were presented randomly left or right of fixation at 6° eccentricity (from fixation to stimulus centre). The shortest accurate saccade latencies were 200 ms for words compared with 140 ms for animal detection. It should be noted that in a related study (Bendahman, Vitu, Thope, & Grainger, 2010), it was found that substituting the consonant strings with pronounceable pseudowords greatly increased the difficulty of the word detection task, and the fastest accurate saccade latencies were greater than 400 ms.

Although further experimentation is required to clarify the nature of these differences in processing times, these preliminary results do suggest that the information used to rapidly access higher-level representations of visual objects is not available when processing printed words. Nevertheless, the general idea of distinguishing fast coarse-grained processing from slower fine-grained processing is maintained in the model presented at the end of this chapter. However, in the account to be developed here, both pathways require information about details (letter identities), and therefore both involve processing of high spatial frequencies.

Letter identification: 'From pixels to pandemonium'

Given the evidence that a significant part of visual word recognition involves processing the individual letter identities in the word, the next obvious question to ask is what is known about letter perception. This is exactly the question asked by Grainger, Rey, and Dufau (2008) in a recent review article, and by Finkbeiner and Coltheart (2009) in their special issue dedicated to letter recognition. According to Grainger et al. (2008), Selfridge's seminal work (Selfridge, 1959; Selfridge & Neisser, 1960) laying the foundations for a cognitive theory of letter perception, is still one of the best bets around. In Selfridge's 'pandemonium' model, letter identification is achieved by hierarchically organized layers of feature and letter detectors. Support for such a hierarchical organization was provided at that time by neurophysiological studies of the cat visual cortex (Hubel & Wiesel, 1962), and over the years, a general consensus has developed in favor of a generic feature-based approach to letter perception. One key guiding principle here is that isolated letter perception is just a simplified case of visual object recognition (e.g., Pelli, Burns, Farrell, & Moore-Page, 2006). Therefore, our knowledge of visual object perception, much of which has been derived from neurophysiological studies of non-human primates, should help constrain our knowledge of letter perception in humans. This general principle is exemplified in the model presented in Figure 8.3. This figure shows a blueprint for a model of letter perception (Grainger et al., 2008) adapted from a classic account of object recognition (Riesenhuber & Poggio, 1999). What is the evidence in favor of such an approach, and what might be the nature of the sub-letter features involved in letter identification?

The confusion matrix is the traditional method used to hunt for features. In a typical experiment used to generate a confusion matrix, isolated letters are presented in data-limited conditions (brief exposures and/or low luminance and/or masking) and erroneous letter reports are noted. Error rate (e.g., reporting F when E was presented) is hypothesized to reflect visual similarity driven by shared features. An analysis of the pattern of letter confusions was therefore expected to reveal the set of features used to identify letters. There are more than 70 published studies on letter confusability, and some have formed the basis of concrete proposals of lists of features for letters of the Roman alphabet, mainly consisting of lines of different orientation and curvature (Gibson, 1969; Geyer & DeWald, 1973; Keren & Baggen, 1981).

One major drawback of standard letter confusion data is that the method used to degrade stimuli (in order to generate confusion errors) influences the nature of the confusions and furthermore confounds perceptual confusions with post-perceptual guessing. In one of the first studies to overcome this drawback, Podgorny and Garner (1979) used a same-different matching task and showed that the resulting discrimination time matrix for letters correlated well with judgments of perceptual similarity (see also Jacobs, Nazir, & Heller, 1989, for confusion matrices expressed as saccade latencies). Furthermore, having response time (RT) as the dependent measure avoids the problem of empty cells and provides a ratio scale that enables the application of more powerful metric analyses. More recently,

From features to letters

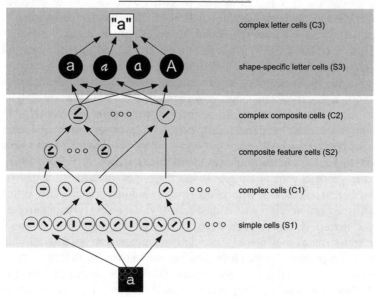

Figure 8.3 Adaptation of Riesenhuber and Poggio's (1999) model of object identification to the case of letter perception (Grainger et al., 2008). Information about
simple visual features (lines of different orientation at precise locations in the
visual field) extracted from the visual stimulus is progressively pooled across
different locations (complex cells) and feature combinations (composite cells)
as one moves up the processing hierarchy. Reprinted from *Trends in Cognitive Sciences*, Vol. 12, Jonathan Grainger, Arnaud Rey and Stéphane Dufau,
'Letter perception: from pixels to pandemonium,' pp. 381–387, © 2008, with
permission from Elsevier.

Courrieu, Farioli, and Grainger (2004) used a go/no-go variant of the same–different
matching task, with participants responding only when the two letters were different. The discrimination times were transformed into Euclidean distances, and a
principal component analysis of these distances revealed 25 dimensions, many of
which were clearly interpretable as elementary visual features.

Two more recent papers opened up a new perspective for research investigating feature-based letter perception. Pelli et al. (2006) measured contrast thresholds to Roman letters presented in different fonts, as well as letters and characters
from other languages. The authors expected letters to be identified optimally, like
a single feature (i.e., a spatial frequency channel or filter in a grating experiment).
This is what one would expect from a template-matching approach. To test this,
Pelli et al. measured efficiency of letter identification under varying viewing
conditions and found that efficiency was independent of stimulus duration, eccentricity, and size, but did vary across different alphabets and fonts. The sub-optimal
performance of human observers was therefore taken to reflect feature-based

letter identification, where identification of the whole is affected by the identification of each component feature. What is it that changes across alphabets and fonts that might be driving these changes in efficiency? Pelli et al. found one particular measure that correlated highly with letter identification efficiency. That was *perimetric complexity* – the square of the length of inside and outside perimeter, divided by ink area (for size invariance). In the absence of independent evidence concerning the nature of the features subtending letter identification, perimetric complexity provided a measure of visual complexity thought to be proportional to the number of features.

Another line of research has applied Gosselin and Schyns' 'bubbles' technique (2001) to explore the nature of the critical features for letter perception. The classification images obtained by Fiset, Blais, Ethier-Majcher, Arguin, Bubu, and Gosselin (2007) for 26 lowercase and 26 uppercase Roman letters in Arial font revealed several important pieces of evidence. First, on average only 32% of the printed area of uppercase and 24% of lowercase letters was used by observers to identify letters, and the greatest proportion of useful information was apparent in the two-to-four cycles per letter frequency band, in line with estimates from critical-band masking studies (Solomon & Pelli, 1994). Second, the analysis revealed that terminations were by far the most diagnostic piece of information for letter identification, with intersections and horizontal lines providing further significant sources of information for uppercase letters. For example, the letter W was mainly distinguished from other letters by the presence of two terminations, one in the upper left corner and the other in the upper right corner.

Today, it would seem that the next major phase of research in this field must involve systematic testing of computational models of letter perception with a range of empirical data obtained using a variety of paradigms. Indeed, the level of sophistication of computational modeling in this area (e.g., Hinton, 2007), plus the level of sophistication of the experimental paradigms that are available (e.g., Fiset et al., 2007), suggest that it should be possible to home-in on the model that provides the most accurate account of the data. An example of this general approach can be found in Rey, Dufau, Massol, and Grainger (2009), who used item-level event-related potentials (ERPs) to select between different versions of an interactive-activation model of letter perception. The ERPs to individual letters started to differ at around 150 ms post-stimulus onset. Simulations with several versions of an interactive-activation model of letter perception were fitted with these item-level ERP measures. The results were in favor of a model of letter perception that has feedforward excitatory connections from the feature to the letter levels, lateral inhibition at the letter level, excitatory feedback from the letter to the feature levels, but no inhibitory connections between the feature and letter levels.

Processing letters in strings: 'Adaptation to hyper-crowding'

In this section we will examine how skilled readers perform parallel independent letter processing, how this particular skill is learned during reading acquisition, and what factors influence the processing of letters in strings in skilled readers.

Assuming that letter-in-string perception involves basically the same mechanisms as isolated letter perception, then the model shown in Figure 8.3 can be thought of as a module of letter perception that, when duplicated and aligned to form a bank of letter detectors, will perform parallel independent letter processing. This general idea was implemented in Grainger and van Heuven's (2003) model of orthographic processing, shown in Figure 8.4. The key difference with respect to McClelland and Rumelhart's (1981) interactive activation model is that the positions of the different letters in a string are initially coded relative to eye fixation in the Grainger and van Heuven model, whereas the slot coding of the IAM applied a word-centered position code. According to Grainger and van Heuven, the very first phase of orthographic processing involves the mapping of visual features onto location-specific letter identities, where location is defined relative to eye fixation along the horizontal meridian (for horizontally aligned alphabetic scripts). They referred to this horizontally aligned bank of letter detectors as the 'alphabetic array'.

In the Grainger and van Heuven model, letter detectors in the alphabetic array signal the presence of a particular configuration of visual features at a given location on the horizontal meridian. Stimuli that are not aligned with the horizontal meridian require a transformation of retinotopic coordinates onto this special

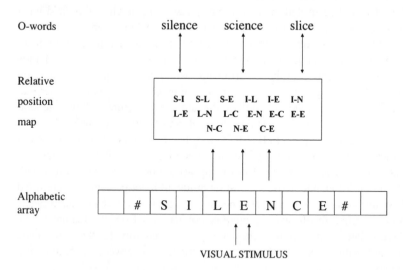

Figure 8.4 Grainger and van Heuven's model of orthographic processing. Location-specific letter detectors (alphabetic array) send information on to a sublexical, word-centered, orthographic code (relative position map), which in turn activates whole-word orthographic representations (O-words). The word-centered sublexical orthographic code is formed of location-invariant ordered combinations of contiguous and non-contiguous letters.

coordinate system for letter strings. This specialized mechanism for processing strings of letters is hypothesized to develop through exposure to print, and its specific organization will depend on the characteristics of the language of exposure. Setting up such a bank of letter detectors is likely to occur during the first phase of learning to read, once the beginning reader has mastered the alphabet, and painstakingly proceeds letter-by-letter through the word. Learning the spelling-to-sound correspondences that provide access to a whole-word phonological code could provide the beginning reader with the top-down support that would help the gradual transformation from letter-by-letter reading to parallel, independent letter processing (see Adelman, 2011, for an alternative account of orthographic processing that starts with parallel, retinotopic letter processing).

A different approach to early visuo-orthographic processing can be found in the work of Carol Whitney (Whitney, 2001, 2008; Whitney & Cornelissen, 2008). The defining characteristic of this approach is the sequential, beginning-to-end firing of letter detectors that is achieved via a monotonically decreasing gradient of activation imposed at the level of retinotopic feature processing. This is the essential starting point of the letter position coding mechanism of the SERIOL model. The strictly sequential beginning-to-end firing of letter detectors provides information about the order of the letters in the string (readers are referred to Whitney, 2008, for a detailed description of the mechanisms that enable ordered firing of letter detectors). One clear advantage of serial processing as implemented in the SERIOL model, compared with the parallel processing of letter identities such as proposed by Grainger and van Heuven (2003), is that serial letter processing provides a simple mechanism for generating ordered letter combinations given that order information is already specified. One key question then is what is the evidence for serial vs parallel letter processing?

Although Whitney (2008) describes a number of studies that arguably provide evidence in favor of serial letter processing, one recent study (Adelman, Marquis, & Sabatos-DeVito, 2010) has reported evidence in favor of parallel letter processing. These authors used the classic Reicher–Wheeler paradigm in order to examine variations in the identifiability of letters in a word as a function of: (1) their position in the word; and (2) stimulus duration. Participants saw briefly presented pattern-masked words of four letters in length, and were asked to choose between two alternatives to indicate which word they had seen (e.g., stimulus 'lung' – choice 'lung' or 'sung', which tests identification accuracy of the first letter). Results showed that performance rose above chance level with a minimal increase in exposure duration from 18 ms to 24 ms, and this occurred at the same timestep for all letter positions, in line with the predictions of parallel letter processing (see also Adelman, 2011).

Related to the issue of serial versus parallel letter processing, there is a long tradition of research investigating the visual factors that modulate the perceptibility of letters in strings. Luckily, much of this research can be summarized in the form of a single serial position function for letter-in-string processing that is M-shaped for speed and W-shaped for accuracy (see Figure 8.5). More precisely, the serial position function for letter stimuli is M-shaped for response times in the letter search

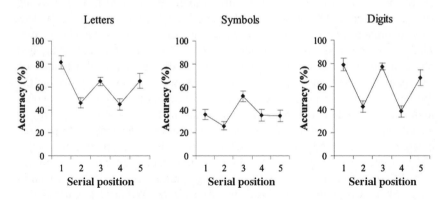

Figure 8.5 Serial positions functions from Tydgat and Grainger (2009, Experiment 5). Percent correct post-cued identification at the different positions in five-character arrays of random consonants, symbols, or digits. Participants were shown briefly presented strings of five characters followed by a pattern mask, and were asked to identify the character that was present in the string at a post-cued location. Tydgat, I. and Grainger, J. (2009). Serial position effects in the identification of letters, digits and symbols. Reprinted with permission from *Journal of Experimental Psychology: Human Perception and Performance, 35*, 480–498, published by American Psychological Association.

task (Hammond & Green, 1982; Ktori & Pitchford, 2008; Mason, 1975, 1982; Mason & Katz, 1976; Pitchford, Ledgeway, & Masterson, 2008), and W-shaped for studies using data-limited identification procedures (Averbach & Coriell, 1961; Butler, 1975; Butler & Merikle, 1973; Haber & Standing, 1969; Merikle, Coltheart, & Lowe, 1971a; Merikle, Lowe, & Coltheart, 1971b; Mewhort & Campbell, 1978; Schwantes, 1978; Stevens & Grainger, 2003; Wolford & Hollingsworth, 1974).

A popular account of the form of this serial position function for letter-in-string processing is that it reflects the combined influence of two factors: Visual acuity and lateral masking (crowding). Figure 8.6 shows the variation of visual acuity as a function of eccentricity along the horizontal meridian. What is most noticeable is the sharp drop in acuity within the 1–2° of the fovea, the area that will be involved in processing words that are fixated. Indeed, under standard reading conditions, a five-letter word is about 1 cm long and therefore spans about 1.4° of visual angle at a reading distance of 40 cm. This implies that for a centrally fixated word there is a very sharp, almost linear drop in acuity as one moves from the fixated letter to the outer letters (first and last letter) of the word. Furthermore, given that words up to about eight letters in length are typically read in a single fixation, this represents about 93% of English words that a skilled reader is likely to encounter (estimated from a token frequency word form count).[5]

The role of 'crowding' as a key factor in explaining the shape of serial position functions for letter-in-string processing is more controversial. The general idea is

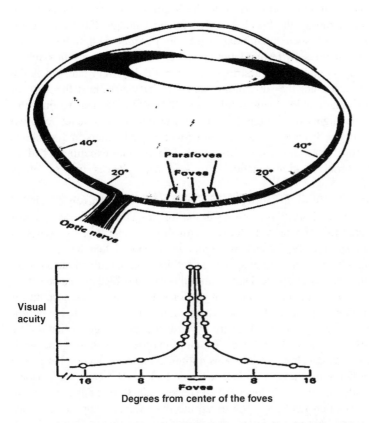

Figure 8.6 Variation in visual acuity along the horizontal meridian (from Figure 2.3 of Just, Marcel Adam; Carpenter, Patricia, *Psychology of Reading and Language Comprehension*, 1st Edition, © 1987. Reprinted by permission of Pearson Education, Inc., Upper Saddle River, NJ.).

that the advantage for outer letters (the first and last letter in the string) arises because of reduced crowding on these letters, since they are flanked by only one other letter (Bouma, 1970, 1973; Estes, 1972; Estes, Allmeyer, & Reder, 1976; Haber & Standing, 1969; Van der Heijden, 1992). However, this account fails to explain why strings of symbols do not produce the same serial position function as letters or digits (e.g., Mason, 1982; Tydgat & Grainger, 2009), since crowding is thought to act independently of stimulus type (Pelli & Tillman, 2008).

Tydgat and Grainger (2009) tested different possible accounts of these differences in serial position function as a function of stimulus type. One possibility is that reading-specific attentional factors are at play with alphabetic stimuli. There is a long tradition of research demonstrating attentional influences on the perception of letters and words (e.g., Heron, 1957; see Ducrot & Grainger, 2007, for a more recent study). On presentation of a centrally fixated string of letters, attention could be automatically drawn to the beginning of the stimulus, hence facilitating processing of the first letter. Tydgat and Grainger (2009) tested for the possible role of such attentional biases in generating stimulus-specific serial position functions, by testing letter targets embedded in strings of symbols and symbol targets embedded in strings of letters. They found that it was the nature of the target, not the surrounding context, that determined the form of the serial position function. This result also allowed Tydgat and Grainger to reject a role for higher-order units (i.e., letter clusters or supra-letter features) as the basis of the different serial position functions for letters and symbols. Finally, randomly intermixing letter and symbol trials in an experiment had no effect on the serial position function compared with blocked lists of letters and symbols.

On the basis of their results, Tydgat and Grainger (2009) tentatively concluded that the different serial position functions found for strings of letters and symbols might be related to differences in the way crowding affects these two types of stimulus. More specifically, Tydgat and Grainger proposed that the effects of crowding might be more limited in spatial extent for letter stimuli compared with symbol stimuli, such that a single flanking stimulus would suffice to generate close to maximum interference for symbols, but not for letters. This would account for the superior performance at the first and last positions for letter stimuli, but not for symbol stimuli. The key idea put forward by Tydgat and Grainger is that during reading acquisition, a specialized system develops in order to optimize processing of strings of letters. One key aspect of this optimization is a reduction in the size of integration fields associated with location-specific letter detectors that perform parallel letter identification (Grainger & van Heuven, 2003). It is this reduction in the size of integration fields, specific to stimuli that typically appear in strings (letters and digits), that results in less crowding for such stimuli compared with other types of visual stimuli such as symbols and geometric shapes. This follows from one standard account of crowding as integration of inappropriate feature information from neighboring stimuli during target identification (Levi, 2008; Pelli, Tillman, Freeman, Su, Berger, & Majaj, 2007). The larger the integration field involved in identifying a given target at a given location, the greater the number of features from neighboring stimuli that can interfere in target identification (see Grainger, Tydgat, & Isselé, 2010, for a concrete proposal).

Might crowding vary as a function of type of stimulus, contrary to what has been argued by Pelli and Tillman (2008) and others? Most prior research on crowding has focused on evaluating effects of certain variables such as eccentricity and size for a given type of target (see Levi, 2008, for review), and have not provided direct comparisons across different types of stimulus. Therefore, in order to test Tydgat and Grainger's (2009) prediction, Grainger et al. (2010) proceeded to compare effects of crowding on letters and symbols comparing the size of flanker interference effects and critical spacing for these two types of stimulus. The results were clear-cut, letter stimuli were shown to have smaller critical spacing values than symbol stimuli, and for a given eccentricity (corresponding to the eccentricity of the first and last positions of the centrally fixated strings tested by Tydgat and Grainger) symbols were more affected by the presence of a single flanking stimulus than were letters.

Why are letters less sensitive to crowding than symbols? The answer to this question is very likely related to the extensive experience that we have, as skilled readers, in processing strings of letters compared with strings of symbols. Tydgat and Grainger (2009) hypothesized that when children learn to read they develop a specialized system that is custom built to handle the very specific nature of written words (see McCandliss, Cohen, & Dehaene, 2003, for one version of this hypothesis). Most notably, this system would develop in order to optimize processing in the extremely crowded conditions that arise with printed words, compared with other visual objects that do not typically occur in such a cluttered environment. One way to achieve such optimization is to establish a bank of letter detectors that enable parallel independent identification of letters in a string (Dehaene, Cohen, Sigman, & Vinckier, 2005; Grainger, Granier, Farioli, Van Assche, & van Heuven, 2006; Grainger & van Heuven, 2003). Since these letter detectors are designed to identify a given letter at a relatively precise location in space, they do not require the relatively wide integration fields necessary to achieve location invariance in object recognition. A reduction in the integration field size of these letter detectors could be the mechanism responsible for the reduced effects of crowding found with letter stimuli compared with symbols.[6]

Initial support for the hypothesized reduction in crowding with letters as a function of exposure to print was provided by Atkinson, Anker, Evans, Hall, and Pimm-Smith (1988), who found greater crowding effects with letter targets and a combination of horizontal and vertical flankers in 3-year-old children compared with 5–7-year–old children. More recent research examining the development of reading fluency provides further support for this hypothesis. Kwon and Legge (2006) found that crowding effects were stronger in children than adults. Furthermore, Kwon, Legge, and Dubbels (2007) found a strong correlation between the development of reading speed and the size of the visual span (number of letters that can be identified without eye movements). Since Pelli et al. (2007) have shown that crowding is the critical factor determining the size of the visual span, one can again conclude that reduced crowding in letter strings is a key factor at play in the development of reading fluency. Finally, Williamson, Scolari, Jeong, Kim, and Awh (2009) found that crowding effects on the identification of single digit targets embedded in a display of Roman letters varied as a function of the native language of participants (English vs Korean, Chinese, or Japanese). Such language-dependent crowding effects were not apparent with non-alphanumeric stimuli. The pattern found by Williamson et al. might, however, be more a reflection of the improved encoding of letter distractors by English native speakers, since they actually observed greater rather than reduced crowding effects in the English native group. Indeed evidence for improved encoding of letter stimuli compared with symbol stimuli in a visual short-term memory paradigm (change detection) has recently been found by Ktori, Grainger, and Dufau (2011).

Furthermore, in line with the hypothesis of experience-dependent changes in the pattern of crowding effects, there is research showing that crowding can be modified by training. Huckauf and Nazir (2007) reported that training participants to identity targets surrounded by two flankers reduces the effects of crowding, but mostly for the specific stimuli, eccentricities, and spacing used during training. Their results suggested that more extensive training might be necessary to observe greater levels of transfer to untrained stimuli. This was done by Chung (2007), who trained observers to identify target letters flanked by two other letters with pre-test and post-test phases separated by 6000 training trials. The results of Chung's study showed that training produced a large improvement in letter identification accuracy accompanied by an equally large reduction in critical spacing (the inter-letter spacing allowing 50% correct target identification). However, given the huge exposure to letter strings of the average adult partici-pant in the above-cited studies, it seems unlikely that even extensive training as in Chung's study, is having the same influence as years of exposure to print. What is missing at present is a developmental investigation of crowding effects from pre-readers to skilled readers. We hypothesize that the integration fields of letter detectors decrease in size during the process of learning to read. Therefore, a measure of critical spacing for letter trigrams (e.g., Chung, 2007; Pelli et al., 2007) should reveal a gradual decrease in the size of integration fields as a function of reading age.

Finally, a recent study has shown that children diagnosed as dyslexic show a general deficit when processing letter strings compared with age-matched control children, but show the same serial position functions (Ziegler, Pech-Georgel, Dufau, & Grainger, 2010). This is evidence against visuo-attentional accounts of developmental dyslexia, and suggests that dyslexics have developed normal capacities for letter-in-string processing, being influenced by the same factors as normal readers. According to this account, the overall deficit in letter-in-string identification seen in dyslexic children would be due to their overall lower expo-sure to printed words in conditions where semantic access is successful, due to the impaired mapping of orthography onto phonology. This interpretation fits well with the general framework for orthographic processing to be developed in the final section of this chapter.

A dual-route approach to orthographic processing: 'Diagnosticity and chunking'

In the Grainger and van Heuven model of orthographic processing (Figure 8.4), the alphabetic array codes for the presence of a given letter at a given location relative to eye fixation along the horizontal meridian. It does not say where a given letter is relative to the other letters in the stimulus, since each letter is proc-essed independently of the others. Thus, processing at the level of the alphabetic array is insensitive to the orthographic regularity of letter strings. However, for the purposes of location-invariant word recognition, this location-specific map must be transformed into a 'word-centered' code such that letter identity is tied to within-word position (where a word is defined as a string of letters separated by spaces) independently of spatial location (cf. Caramazza & Hillis, 1990). In the final part of this chapter we introduce a dual-route account of orthographic processing that postulates the existence of two fundamentally different kinds of location-invariant, sublexical, orthographic code.

The starting point of this endeavor is the traditional dual-route model of reading aloud, that distinguishes between a lexical route and a sublexical route for transforming print to sound (Coltheart, this volume, Chapter 1; Coltheart, Curtis, Atkins, & Haller, 1993; Coltheart, Rastle, Perry, Langdon, & Ziegler, 2001). This general approach was adopted for silent word reading in the bi-modal interactive activation model (Diependaele, Ziegler, & Grainger, 2010; Grainger & Ferrand, 1994; Grainger, Diependaele, Spinelli, Ferrand, & Farioli, 2003; Grainger & Ziegler, 2008; Jacobs, Rey, Ziegler, & Grainger, 1998), and provides a localist implementation of the generic division of labor or triangle approach to visual word recognition in which there are two routes from orthography to semantics – a direct route, and an indirect route via phonology (Seidenberg & McClelland, 1989; Plaut, McClelland, Seidenberg, & Patterson, 1996). The bi-modal interactive activation model accounts for a wide range of phenomena associated with visual word recognition, and in particular, the rapid involvement of phonological codes in the process of silent word reading (Diependaele et al., 2010; see Grainger & Ziegler, 2008, for review).

With the focus on silent word reading, the general goal of our modeling efforts is to account for how, given the constraints on letter-in-string visibility, plus the temporal constraints imposed by reading rate (about 250 ms per word), the skilled reader optimizes uptake of information from the printed word stimulus in order to recover the appropriate semantic and syntactic information necessary for text comprehension. The dual-route approach acknowledges that two different types of constraint affect processing along the two routes. Both types of constraint are driven by the frequency with which different combinations of letters occur in printed words. On the one hand, frequency determines the probability with which a given combination of letters belongs to the word being read, as opposed to all other words. Letter combinations that are encountered less often in other words are more diagnostic of the identity of the word being processed. On the other hand, frequency of co-occurrence enables the formation of higher-order representations (chunking) in order to diminish the amount of information that is processed via data compression. Letter combinations that often occur together can be usefully grouped to form higher-level orthographic representations such as multi-letter graphemes (⟨TH⟩, ⟨CH⟩, ⟨AI⟩) and morphemes (ING, ER), and therefore facilitate the contact between orthographic representations and pre-existing phonological and morphological representations during the course of reading acquisition. This dual-route approach to orthographic processing is illustrated in Figure 8.7.

Fundamentally different types of orthographic processing are performed by these two routes, since they are geared to use frequency of occurrence in diametrically opposite ways. The two routes differ notably in terms of the level of precision with which letter position information is coded. In one route, a coarse-grained orthographic code is computed in order to rapidly home in on a unique word identity, and corresponding semantic representations (the fast track to semantics). Given variations in visibility across letters in a string, the key hypothesis here is that the best way to optimize performance is to adapt processing to the constraints

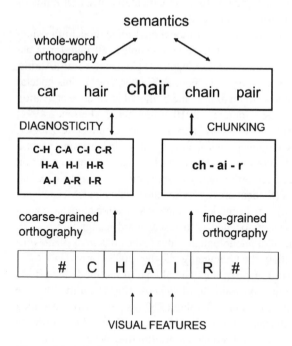

Figure 8.7 A dual-route approach to orthographic processing (Grainger & Ziegler, 2011). Starting from location-specific letter detectors, two fundamentally different types of location-invariant sublexical orthographic code are computed. A coarse-grained code optimizes the mapping of orthography to semantics by selecting letter combinations that are the most informative with respect to word identity, irrespective of letter contiguity. A fine-grained code optimizes processing via the chunking of frequently co-occurring contiguous letters.

imposed by variations in letter visibility and variations in the amount of information carried by different letter combinations. That is, to code for combinations of the most visible letters that best constrain word identity. This fits with the idea of coding for contiguous and non-contiguous letter combinations proposed in recent models of orthographic processing (so-called 'open-bigram' coding: Grainger & van Heuven, 2003; Grainger & Whitney, 2004; Whitney, 2001; see Dandurand, Grainger, Duñabeitia, & Granier, 2011, for further discussion, and Adelman, 2011, for a similar proposal). Empirical evidence in favor of this type of coarse orthographic coding has been obtained using the masked priming paradigm in the form of robust priming effects with transposed-letter primes (e.g., gadren-GARDEN: Perea & Lupker, 2004; Schoonbaert & Grainger, 2004), and subset and superset primes (e.g., grdn-GARDEN, gamrdsen-GARDEN: Grainger et al., 2006; Peresotti & Grainger, 1999; Welvaert, Farioli, & Grainger, 2008; Van Assche & Grainger, 2006). Not only does open-bigram coding provide a natural explanation for these empirical demonstrations of flexible orthographic processing, but when combined with the constraints of letter visibility and informativeness it can also account for more subtle variations in orthographic priming effects as a function of the position of orthographic overlap and the precise letters involved (e.g., consonants vs vowels; Dandurand et al., 2011).

There are alternative theoretical proposals that provide equally good accounts of the empirical evidence in favor of flexible orthographic processing. One such account, that merits some discussion here, is the SOLAR model (Davis, 2010). The mechanism for letter position coding implemented in the SOLAR model is an example of spatial coding (Grossberg, 1978), where the relative position of spatially distributed items is coded in terms of their relative activation level. This is best achieved when the items in the list form a monotonically increasing or decreasing set of activation values, referred to as an activation gradient. For the purposes of letter position coding, abstract context-independent letter detectors (one for each letter of the alphabet) are assigned an activation value as a function of their position in the string, with a certain degree of positional uncertainty modeled by a Gaussian function (similarly to an alternative account of letter position coding, the 'overlap model', Gomez, Ratcliff, & Perea, 2008). Input to word representations is determined by computing the match between the spatial code for the input and the stored spatial codes for known words (see Davis, 2010, and this volume, Chapter 9, for details). Davis (2010) showed that an implemented version of the SOLAR model provided an excellent fit to a large set of benchmark phenomena. Furthermore, Hannagan, Dupoux, and Christophe (2011) showed that the spatial coding scheme of the SOLAR model satisfied more priming constraints than alternative coding schemes, albeit with a greater number of free parameters.

The fact that precise within-word letter order information is computed in order to generate an activation gradient in the SOLAR model means that this model has the level of precision necessary for computing contiguous letter combinations such as those that occur in complex graphemes.[7] This level of precision is necessary for the transformation of a sublexical orthographic code into a phonological code, as postulated in various dual-route accounts of visual word recognition. How is this achieved in the context of our dual-route approach to orthographic processing?

On the right-hand side of Figure 8.7, a fine-grained orthographic code provides more precise information about the ordering of letters in the string. This fine-grained code enables the coding of multi-letter graphemes and their precise ordering in the string. These graphemes then activate the corresponding phonemes, which in turn lead to activation of the appropriate whole-word phonological representation and the corresponding semantic representations (see Perry, Ziegler, & Zorzi, 2007, for a specific implementation of a graphemic parser). However, the theoretical approach illustrated in Figure 8.7 suggests that the fine-grained orthographic processing route is not limited to the case of processing graphemic representations. Here we hypothesize that this route is more generally dedicated to precisely specifying the within-string positions of letter identities in order to facilitate the chunking of frequently co-occurring contiguous letter combinations, such as complex graphemes (⟨TH⟩, ⟨CH⟩, ⟨OO⟩, etc.) and small morphemes (i.e., affixes such as RE, ED, ER, ING, etc.). How then is letter position information coded in this orthographic processing route?

Applying a standard beginning-to-end slot code as in dual-route cascaded (DRC) models (Coltheart et al., 2001; Perry et al., 2007), is fine as far as phonology is concerned, but would not permit the chunking of suffixes. For example, the same suffix ER in the six-letter word FARMER would be coded by different letter units (L5, L6) than the ER in five-letter word MAKER (L4, L5). One solution would be to adopt slot-coding with both beginning and end anchor points, such as proposed by Jacobs et al. (1998), a variant of which has been adopted in recent work on letter position coding in written language production (Fischer-Baum, McCloskey, & Rapp, 2010). Fischer-Baum et al. propose that letter position is coded both from the beginning to the end, and from the end to the beginning of the string. This applies the same anchor points as in the Jacobs et al. scheme, but extends coding in both directions to cover all letters, such that each letter in the string is represented twice – with its location relative to word beginning on the one hand, and its position relative to the end of the word on the other. Fischer-Baum et al. showed that this type of coding provided a superior account of the patterns of spelling errors in two dysgraphic persons, compared with alternative letter position coding schemes.

Why would a human brain exposed to print adopt this dual-route approach to orthographic processing? As suggested by Grainger and Holcomb (2009), it is possible that this dual-route architecture emerges from the fact that visual word recognition is a mixture of two worlds – one whose main dimension is space – the world of visual objects, and the other whose main dimension is time – the world of spoken language. Skilled readers might therefore have learned to capitalize on this particularity, using structure in space in order to optimize the mapping of an orthographic form onto semantics, and using structure in time in order to optimize the mapping of an orthographic form onto phonology. However, even in the domain of spoken language one can draw a distinction between diagnosticity and chunking. Therefore, a more general answer to the above question would be that optimization of recognition processes (for any kind of object) involves extraction of diagnostic information on the one hand, and simplification of processing via data compression on the other. A dual-route approach follows naturally from this distinction to the extent that fundamentally different learning mechanism must be involved in learning these two types of code. The important consequence of this distinction for models of visual word recognition, is that we should not be looking for a single type of sublexical orthographic code, but different types of orthographic code that are developed to perform very different functions.

- In languages that use an alphabetic script to represent written language, printed words are recognized via their component letters. This does not mean that you need to identify each component letter before you can start to identify the word. As soon as information starts to accrue in feature and letter representations this is transferred to higher-levels in the manner of cascaded processing. This can explain why it is easier to identify a letter embedded in a real word as opposed to letters in nonwords, the so-called 'word superiority effect'.

- Word-shape information might play a role in certain specific conditions, but there is little evidence at present for generalized use of this type of information. It should be remembered that finding a difference in the ability to read text printed in MixEd cAsE versus homogeneous case does not necessarily imply a role for word shape information.

- The very first phase of orthographic processing proper involves the mapping of retinotopic features onto letter representations – most likely simultaneously for each letter position. This mapping process is constrained by two main factors: visual acuity and crowding. The combination of these two factors explains the typical W-shaped serial position function for letter-in-string identification, with highest accuracy at initial and final positions as well as for the letter that is fixated. Due to the sharp drop in visual acuity, accuracy becomes worse as one moves away from fixation, except for the first and last letter in the string, that suffer less crowding than the inner letters.

- Location-invariant word recognition requires a word-centered orthographic code, hence the hard problem of orthographic processing: how to enable the transition from retinotopic coordinates to word-centered coordinates for letter position coding. There is considerable evidence that this location-invariant word-centered orthographic code is robust to small chagnes in letter odrer and the inserstion and remval of lettrs. One way to achieve such flexibility is to code for ordered pairs of letters while ignoring to a certain extent whether these letters are adjacent or not. Alternatively one could assign an approximate position code to each individual letter.

- This proposed flexibility in orthographic processing contrasts with the level of precision that is required to make contact with pre-existing phonological and morphological representations during reading acquisition. Therefore, a complete account of orthographic processing must be able to simultaneously exhibit the kind flexibility revealed notably by research on orthographic priming, as well as being able to accurately code for the presence of the letter T immediately before the letter H in the grapheme <TH> or the E before the R in the suffix ER.

Notes

1 There has been very little research examining possible specificities of word recognition in cursive script (with connected letters), be it machine-generated or handwritten (see Barnhart & Goldinger, 2011, for a recent exception).

2   Note that finding a cost in reading mIXeD cAsE text compared with homogeneous case text (e.g., Pelli & Tillman, 2007) does not necessarily imply a role for word shape information. As convincingly demonstrated by Mayall, Humphreys, and Olson (1997), the cost is better explained by low-level perceptual grouping of same-case elements disrupting processing. Moreover, the demonstration of superior performance to lower case words compared with upper case words in Spanish (Perea & Rosa, 2002) could be due to letter case providing a good cue as to whether a letter is a vowel or a consonant (vowels do not have ascending or descending segments), plus the possibility that this could facilitate syllabification processes involved in reading Spanish words.

3   The animal is a member of the canine species, and the word is 'elephant'.

4   Familiar acronyms (e.g., IBM) have often been used as an example of shape-based identification. A study by Brysbaert, Speybroeck, and Vanderelst (2009) showed, however, that abstract letter identities are also a key part of the processing of such stimuli, in that priming effects were found to be independent of format (e.g., equivalent priming of the target 'books' by the primes isbn, iSbN, ISBN).

5   It should be noted that when reading text of average difficulty, skilled readers will typi-cally fixate the majority of words, skipping only short high-frequency words, and the majority of fixated words are only fixated once. Furthermore, the distribution of initial fixation positions (or landing sites) has a strong peak near the centre of the word (the preferred viewing position, Rayner, 1979).

6   A possible neurophysiological correlate of such developmental changes in orthographic processing is the N1 or N170 ERP component. Maurer , Brem, Kranz, Bucher, Benz, Halder, et al. (2006) measured N1 activity in kindergarten pre-readers and the same children after 2 years of reading instruction (Grade 2). The children were presented with words, pseudowords, and strings of symbols. They found a significant increase in N1 amplitude to word stimuli as a function of reading experience, and no such developmen-tal change for symbol strings. Furthermore, the difference in N1 amplitude for words and symbols correlated significantly with a measure of reading fluency in second grade.

7   One might legitimately wonder, however, why a more precise within-word position code would be abandoned in favor of a less precise code as the input for the lexical activation function? In the parallel open-bigram model, the increased flexibility is due to the mechanism used to transform the position code from retinotopic to word-centered coordinates.

References

Adelman, J.S. (2011). Letters in time and retinotopic space. *Psychological Review, 118*, 570–582.

Adelman, J.S., Marquis, S.J., & Sabatos-DeVito, M.G. (2010). Letters in words are read simultaneously, not in left-to-right sequence. *Psychological Science, 21*, 1799–1801.

Atkinson, J., Anker, S., Evans, C., Hall, R., & Pimm-Smith, E. (1988). Visual acuity test-ing of young children with the Cambridge Crowding Cards at 3 and 6 m. *Acta Opthalmologica, 66*, 505–508.

Averbach, E. & Coriell, A.S. (1961). Short-term memory in vision. *Bell Telephone Technical Journal, 40*, 19–31.

Bar, M., Kassam, K.S., Ghuman, A.S., Boshyan, J., Schmidt, A.M., Dale, A.M., Hamalainen, M.S., Marinkovic, K., Schacter, D.L., Rosen, B.R., & Halgren, E. (2006). Top-down facilitation of visual recognition. *Proceedings of the National Academy of Sciences, 103*, 449–454.

Barnhart, A.S. & Goldinger, S.D. (2011). Interpreting chicken-scratch: Lexical access with handwritten words. *Journal of Experimental Psychology: Human Perception and Performance, 36*, 906–923.

Bendahman, L. A., Vitu, F., and Grainger, J. (2010). Ultra-fast processing of printed words? *Perception*, *39* (ECVP Abstract Supplement), 147.

Bouma, H. (1970). Interaction effects in parafoveal letter recognition. *Nature*, *226*, 177–8.

Bouma, H. (1973). Visual interference in the parafoveal recognition of initial and final letters of words. *Vision Research*, *13*, 767–782.

Brysbaert, M., Speybroeck, S., & Vanderelst, D. (2009). Is there room for the BBC in the mental lexicon? On the recognition of acronyms. *Quarterly Journal of Experimental Psychology*, *62*, 1832–1842.

Butler, B.E. (1975). Selective attention and target search with brief visual displays. *Quarterly Journal of Experimental Psychology*, *27*, 467–477.

Butler, B.E. & Merikle, P.M. (1973). Selective masking and processing strategy. *Quarterly Journal of Experimental Psychology*, *25*, 542–548.

Caramazza, A. & Hillis, A. E. (1990). Spatial representation of words in the brain implied by studies of a unilateral neglect patient. *Nature*, *346*, 267–269.

Cattell, J. (1886). The time it takes to see and name objects. *Mind*, *11*, 53–65.

Chanceaux, M., Vitu, F., Bendahman, L., Thorpe, S., & Grainger, J. (2011). Word processing speed in peripheral vision measured with a saccadic choice task. *Vision Research*, *56*, 10–19.

Chauncey, K., Holcomb, P.J., & Grainger, J. (2008). Effects of stimulus font and size on masked repetition priming: An ERP investigation. *Language and Cognitive Processes*, *23*, 183–200.

Chung, S.T.L. (2007). Learning to identify crowded letters: Does it improve reading speed? *Vision Research*, *47*, 3150–3159.

Coltheart, M., Curtis, B., Atkins, P., & Haller, M. (1993). Models of reading aloud: Dual-route and parallel-distributed-processing approaches. *Psychological Review*, *100*, 589–608.

Coltheart, M., Rastle, K., Perry, C., Langdon, R., & Ziegler, J.C. (2001). DRC: A dual-route cascaded model of visual word recognition and reading aloud. *Psychological Review*, *108*, 204–256.

Courrieu, P., Farioli, F., & Grainger, J. (2004). Inverse discrimination time as a perceptual distance for alphabetic characters. *Visual Cognition*, *11*, 901–919.

Crystal, D. (1987). How many words? *English Today*, *12*, 11–14.

Dandurand, F., Grainger, J., Duñabeitia, J.A., & Granier, J.P. (2011). On coding non-contiguous letter combinations. *Frontiers in Cognitive Sciences*, *2*, 136. DOI: 10.3389/fpsyg.2011.00136.

Davis, C.J. (2010). The spatial coding model of visual word recognition. *Psychological Review*, *117*, 713–758.

Dehaene, S., Cohen, L., Sigman, M., & Vinckier, F. (2005). The neural code for written words: a proposal. *Trends in Cognitive Sciences*, *9*, 335–341.

Diependaele, K., Ziegler, J., & Grainger, J. (2010). Fast phonology and the bi-modal inter-active activation model. *European Journal of Cognitive Psychology*, *22*, 764–778.

Ducrot, S. & Grainger, J. (2007). Deployment of spatial attention to words in central and peripheral vision. *Perception & Psychophysics*, *69*, 578–590.

Estes, W.K. (1972). Interactions of signal and background variables in visual processing. *Perception & Psychophysics*, *12*, 278–286.

Estes, W.K., Allmeyer, D.H., & Reder, S.M. (1976). Serial position functions for letter identification at brief and extended exposure durations. *Perception & Psychophysics*, *19*, 1–15.

Finkbeiner, M. & Coltheart, M. (2009). Letter recognition: From perception to representation. *Cognitive Neuropsychology*, *26*(1), 1–6.

Fischer-Baum, S., McCloskey, M., & Rapp, B. (2010). Representation of letter position in spelling: Evidence from acquired dysgraphia. *Cognition, 115,* 466–490.

Fiset, D., Blais, C., Ethier-Majcher, C., Arguin, M., Bubu, D., & Gosselin, F. (2007). Features for uppercase and lowercase letter identification. *Psychological Science, 19,* 1161–1168.

Geyer, L.H. & DeWald, C.G. (1973). Feature lists and confusion matrices. *Perception & Psychophysics, 14,* 471–482.

Gibson, E.J. (1969). *Principles of perceptual learning and development.* New York: Appleton-Century-Crofts.

Gomez, P., Ratcliff, R., & Perea, M. (2008). The overlap model: A model of letter position coding. *Psychological Review, 115,* 577–601.

Gosselin, F. & Schyns, P.G. (2001). Bubbles: A technique to reveal the use of information in recognition. *Vision Research, 41,* 2261–2271.

Grainger, J. & Ferrand, L. (1994). Phonology and orthography in visual word recognition: Effects of masked homophone primes. *Journal of Memory and Language, 33,* 218–233.

Grainger, J. & Holcomb, P. J. (2009). Watching the word go by: on the time-course of component processes in visual word recognition. *Language and Linguistics Compass, 3,* 128–156.

Grainger, J. & Jacobs, A.M. (1994). A dual read-out model of word context effects in letter perception: Further investigations of the word superiority effect. *Journal of Experimental Psychology: Human Perception and Performance, 20,* 1158–1176.

Grainger, J. & Jacobs, A. (2005). Pseudoword context effects on letter perception: The role of word misperception. *European Journal of Cognitive Psychology, 17,* 289–318.

Grainger, J. & van Heuven, W. (2003). Modeling letter position coding in printed word perception. In P. Bonin (Ed.), *The Mental Lexicon* (pp. 1–24). New York: Nova Science Publishers.

Grainger, J. & Whitney, C. (2004). Does the huamn mind raed wrods as a wlohe? *Trends in Cognitive Sciences, 8,* 58–59.

Grainger, J. & Ziegler, J. (2008). Cross-code consistency effects in visual word recognition. In E.L. Grigorenko and A. Naples (Eds) *Single-word reading: Biological and behavioral perspectives* (pp. 129–157). Mahwah, NJ: Lawrence Erlbaum Associates.

Grainger, J., Diependaele, K., Spinelli, E., Ferrand, L., & Farioli, F. (2003). Masked repetition and phonological priming within and across modalities. *Journal of Experimental Psychology: Learning, Memory and Cognition, 29,* 1256–1269.

Grainger, J., Granier, J.P., Farioli, F., Van Assche, E., & van Heuven, W.J. (2006). Letter position information and printed word perception: the relative-position priming constraint. *Journal of Experimental Psychology: Human Perception and Performance, 32,* 865–884.

Grainger, J., Rey, A., & Dufau, S. (2008). Letter perception: From pixels to pandemonium. *Trends in Cognitive Sciences, 12,* 381–387.

Grainger, J., Tydgat, I., & Isselé, J. (2010). Crowding affects letters and symbols differently. *Journal of Experimental Psychology: Human Perception and Performance, 36,* 673–688.

Grossberg, S. (1978). A theory of human memory: Self-organization and performance of sensory-motor codes, maps, and plans. In R. Rosen & F. Snell (Eds) *Progress in Theoretical Biology* (pp. 233–374). New York: Academic Press.

Haber, R.N. & Standing, L. (1969). Location of errors with a poststimulus indicator. *Psychonomic Science, 17,* 345–346.

Hammond, E.J. & Green, D.W. (1982). Detecting targets in letter and non-letter arrays. *Canadian Journal of Psychology, 36*, 67–82.

Hannagan, T., Dupoux, E., & Christophe, A. (2011). Holographic string encoding. *Cognitive Science, 35*, 79–118.

Heron, W. (1957). Perception as a function of retinal locus and attention. *American Journal of Psychology, 70*, 38–48.

Hinton, G.E. (2007). Learning multiple layers of representation. *Trends in Cognitive Sciences, 11*, 428–434.

Hubel, D. & Wiesel, T. (1962). Receptive fields, binocular interaction and functional architecture in the cat's visual cortex. *Journal of Physiology of London, 160*, 106–154.

Huckauf, A. & Nazir, T.A. (2007). How odgcrnwi becomes crowding: Stimulus-specific learning reduces crowding. *Journal of Vision, 7(2):18*, 1–12.

Jacobs, A.M., Nazir, T.A., & Heller, O. (1989). Letter perception in peripheral vision: a temporal discrimination matrix using eye movements. *Perception & Psychophysics, 46*, 95–102.

Jacobs, A.M., Rey, A., Ziegler, J.C., & Grainger, J. (1998). MROM-P: An interactive activation, multiple read-out model of orthographic and phonological processes in visual word recognition. In J. Grainger & A.M. Jacobs (Eds), *Localist connectionist approaches to human cognition* (pp. 147–188). Mahwah, NJ: Erlbaum.

Just, M.A. & Carpenter, P.A. (1987). *The Psychology of Reading and Language Comprehension*. Newton, MA: Allyn and Bacon, Inc.

Keren, G. & Baggen, S. (1981). Recognition models of alphanumeric characters. *Perception & Psychophysics, 29*, 452–466.

Kirchner, H. & Thorpe, S.J. (2006). Ultra-rapid object detection with saccadic eye movements: visual processing speed revisited. *Vision Research, 46*, 1762–1776.

Ktori, M. & Pitchford, N.J. (2008). Effect of orthographic transparency on letter position encoding: A comparison of Greek and English monoscriptal and biscriptal readers. *Language and Cognitive Processes, 23*, 258–281.

Ktori, M., Grainger, J., & Dufau, S. (2012). Letter string processing and visual short-term memory. *Quarterly Journal of Experimental Psychology*, in press, Doi:10.1080/174702 18.2011.611889.

Kwon, M.Y. & Legge, G.E. (2006). Developmental changes in the size of the visual span for reading: effects of crowding. *Journal of Vision, 6*, 1003a (Abstract).

Kwon, M.Y., Legge, G.E., & Dubbels, B.R. (2007). Developmental changes in the visual span for reading. *Vision Research, 47*, 2889–2890.

Lavidor, M. (2010). Whole-word shape effect in dyslexia. *Journal of Research in Reading, 34*, 443–454.

Levi, D.M. (2008). Crowding – an essential bottleneck for object recognition: A mini-review. *Vision Research, 48*, 635–654.

McCandliss, B.D., Cohen, L., & Dehaene, S. (2003). The visual word form area: Expertise for reading in the fusiform gyrus. *Trends in Cognitive Sciences, 13*, 155–161.

McClelland, J.L. & Rumelhart, D.E. (1981). An interactive activation model of context effects in letter perception: Part 1. An account of basic findings. *Psychological Review, 88*, 375–407.

Mason, M. (1975). Reading ability and letter search time: Effects of orthographic structure defined by single-letter positional frequency. *Journal of Experimental Psychology, 104*, 146–166.

Mason, M. (1982). Recognition time for letters and nonletters: Effects of serial position, array size, and processing order. *Journal of Experimental Psychology: Human Perception and Performance, 8,* 724–738.

Mason, M. and Katz, L. (1976). Visual processing of nonlinguistic strings: Redundancy effects and reading ability. *Journal of Experimental Psychology, 105,* 338–348.

Massaro, D.W. & Cohen, M.M. (1994). Visual, orthographic, phonological, and lexical influences in reading. *Journal of Experimental Psychology: Human Perception and Performance, 20,* 1107–1128.

Maurer, U., Brem, S., Kranz, F., Bucher, K., Benz, R., Halder, P., Steinhausen, H.C., & Brandeis, D. (2006). Coarse neural tuning for print peaks when children learn to read. *NeuroImage, 33,* 749–758.

Mayall, K., Humphreys, G. W., & Olson, A. (1997). Disruption to word or letter processing? The origins of case-mixing effects. *Journal of Experimental Psychology: Learning, Memory, and Cognition, 23,* 1275–1286.

Merikle, P.M., Coltheart, M., & Lowe, D.G. (1971a). On the selective effects of a patterned masking stimulus. *Canadian Journal of Psychology, 25,* 264–279.

Merikle, P.M., Lowe, D.G., & Coltheart, M. (1971b). Familiarity and method of report as determinants of tachistoscopic performance. *Canadian Journal of Psychology, 25,* 167–174.

Mewhort, D.J.K. & Campbell, A.J. (1978). Processing spatial information and the selective-masking effect. *Perception & Psychophysics, 24,* 93–101.

Paap, K., Newsome, S.L., McDonald, J.E., & Schvaneveldt, R.W. (1982). An activation-verification model for letter and word recognition: The word superiority effect. *Psychological Review, 89,* 573–594.

Paap, K.R., Newsome, S.L., & Noel, R.W. (1984). Word shape's in poor shape for the race to the lexicon. *Journal of Experimental Psychology: Human Perception and Performance, 10,* 413–428.

Pelli, D.G. & Tillman, K.A. (2007). Parts, wholes, and context in reading: A triple dissociation. *PLoS ONE, 2(8):* e680. doi:10.1371/journal.pone.0000680

Pelli, D.G. & Tillman, K.A. (2008). The uncrowded window of object recognition. *Nature Neuroscience, 11,* 1129–1135.

Pelli, D.G., Burns, C.W., Farrell, B., & Moore-Page, D.C. (2006). Feature detection and letter identification. *Vision Research, 46,* 4646–4674.

Pelli, D.G., Tillman, K.A., Freeman, J., Su, M., Berger, T.D., & Majaj, N.J. (2007). Crowding and eccentricity determine reading rate. *Journal of Vision, 7(2):20,* 1–36.

Perea, M. & Lupker, S.J. (2004). Can caniso activate casino? Transposed-letter similarity effects with nonadjacent letter positions. *Journal of Memory and Language, 51,* 231–246.

Perea, M. & Rosa, E. (2002). Does 'whole-word shape' play a role in visual word recognition? *Perception & Psychophysics, 64,* 785–794.

Peressotti, F. & Grainger, J. (1999). The role of letter identity and letter position in orthographic priming. *Perception & Psychophysics, 61,* 691–706.

Perry, C., Ziegler, J.C., & Zorzi, M. (2007). Nested incremental modeling in the development of computational theories: The CDP+ model of reading aloud. *Psychological Review, 114,* 273–315.

Pitchford, N.J., Ledgeway, T., & Masterson, J. (2008). Effect of orthographic processes in letter position encoding. *Journal of Research in Reading: Special Issue – Orthographic Processes in Reading, 31,* 97–116.

Plaut, D.C., McClelland, J.L., Seidenberg, M.S., & Patterson, K. (1996). Understanding normal and impaired word reading: Computational principles in quasi-regular domains. *Psychological Review, 103*, 56–115.

Podgorny, P. & Garner, W. (1979). Reaction time as a measure of inter- and intraobject visual similarity: Letters of the alphabet. *Perception & Psychophysics, 26*, 37–52.

Rayner, K. (1979). Eye guidance in reading: Fixation location within words. *Perception, 8*, 21–30.

Reicher, G.M. (1969). Perceptual recognition as a function of meaningfulness of stimulus material. *Journal of Experimental Psychology, 81*, 275–280.

Rey, A., Dufau, S., Massol, S., & Grainger, J. (2009). Testing computational models of letter perception with item-level ERPs. *Cognitive Neuropsychology, 26*, 7–22.

Riesenhuber, M. & Poggio, T. (1999). Hierarchical models of object recognition in cortex. *Nature Neuroscience, 2*, 1019–1025.

Schoonbaert, S. & Grainger, J. (2004). Letter position coding in printed word perception: Effects of repeated and transposed letters. *Language and Cognitive Processes, 19*, 333–367.

Schwantes, F.M. (1978). Stimulus position functions in tachistoscopic identification tasks: Scanning, rehearsal, and order of report. *Perception & Psychophysics, 23*, 219–226.

Seidenberg, M.S. & McClelland, J.L. (1989). A distributed, developmental model of word recognition and naming. *Psychological Review, 96*, 523–568.

Selfridge, O.G. (1959). Pandemonium: A paradigm for learning. In D. V. Blake & A. M. Uttley (Eds), *Proceedings of the Symposium on Mechanisation of Thought Processes* (pp. 511–529). London: H. M. Stationery Office.

Selfridge, O.G. & Neisser, U. (1960). Pattern recognition by machine. *Scientific American, 20*, 60–68.

Solomon, J.A. & Pelli, D.G. (1994). The visual filter mediating letter identification. *Nature, 369*, 395–397.

Stevens, M. & Grainger, J. (2003). Letter visibility and the viewing position effect in visual word recognition. *Perception & Psychophysics, 65*, 133–151.

Tydgat, I. & Grainger, J. (2009). Serial position effects in the identification of letters, digits and symbols. *Journal of Experimental Psychology: Human Perception and Performance, 35*, 480–498.

Van Assche, E. & Grainger, J. (2006). A study of relative-position priming with superset primes. *Journal of Experimental Psychology: Learning, Memory, and Cognition, 32*, 399–415.

Van der Heijden, A.H.C. (1992). *Selective attention in vision*. London: Routledge.

Welvaert, M., Farioli, F., & Grainger, J. (2008). Graded effects of number of inserted letters in superset priming. *Experimental Psychology, 55*, 54–63.

Wheeler, D. (1970). Processes in word recognition. *Cognitive Psychology, 1*, 59–85.

Whitney, C. (2001). How the brain encodes the order of letters in a printed word: the SERIOL model and selective literature review. *Psychonomic Bulletin and Review, 8*, 221–243.

Whitney, C. (2008). Supporting the serial in the SERIOL model. *Language and Cognitive Processes, 23*, 824–865.

Whitney, C. & Cornelissen, P. (2008). SERIOL reading. *Language and Cognitive Processes, 23*, 143–164.

Williamson, K., Scolari, M., Jeong, S., Kim, M.S., & Awh, E. (2009). Experience-dependent changes in the topography of visual crowding. *Journal of Vision, 9*, 1–9.

Wolford, G. & Hollingsworth, S. (1974). Retinal location and string position as important variables in visual information processing. *Perception & Psychophysics*, *16*, 437–442.

Ziegler, J.C., Pech-Georgel, C., Dufau, S., & Grainger, J. (2010). Rapid processing of letters, digits, and symbols: What purely visual-attentional deficit in developmental dyslexia? *Developmental Science*, *13*, 8–14.

9 The orthographic similarity of printed words

Colin J. Davis

An inescapable feature of alphabetic languages, in which a relatively small alphabet is used to represent tens or hundreds of thousands of words, is that the spelling of a given word is often similar to that of many other words. This orthographic similarity requires the visual word identification system to make rather fine discriminations, so as to recognise, for example, that "the thickset man" is not the same as "the thickest man". Ordinarily, the word identification system succeeds in selecting the word that best matches the visual input, implying that letter identity and position can be coded quite precisely. However, as we shall see, there is ample evidence that the process of visual word identification involves active processing of not only the best-matching word, but also of the close "neighbours" of that word. In this chapter, I consider the following questions concerning orthographic similarity: (a) What constitutes an orthographic neighour?; (b) How should we measure the similarity of a given pair of letter strings?; (c) What are the implications of this similarity? (i.e., is similarity to another word a hindrance or a help to identification, or does it not affect identification at all?); and finally, (d) What effect does the density of a word's orthographic neighbourhood have on its identification? The answers to these questions have important implication for models of visual word identification and for our understanding of the mechanisms and representations underlying skilled reading.

Initial formulation of the orthographic similarity neighbourhood

The concepts of orthographic neighbours and of an orthographic similarity neighbourhood were introduced by Landauer and Streeter (1973). They defined these terms as follows:

> *A similarity neighborhood* will be defined as the set of words in the language from which a given stimulus word is indistinguishable after a specified loss of information about the stimulus word. The similarity neighborhood of a word thus always includes the word itself. Words other than the stimulus belonging to a neighborhood will be called *neighbors*.

(p. 120)

More specifically, Landauer and Streeter focussed on what they called one-letter substitution neighbours: words that could be formed by replacing a single letter of the stimulus. For example, the neighbours of WORD include CORD, WARD, WOOD, and WORK. The neighbourhood size of a stimulus was defined to be the count of such neighbours (plus the stimulus word itself, in their formulation). Landauer and Streeter's (1973) interest in similarity neighbourhoods was mostly linguistic; they wished to discover whether there was any difference between common and rare words with respect to their similarity neighbourhoods. They concluded that there was in fact, such a difference, in that "common words are more like other common words, and rare words more like other rare words than they are like each other. Moreover, common words are similar to more other words than are rare words" (p. 129). Landauer and Streeter's analysis was based on a relatively small sample of four-letter words: 50 high-frequency words and 50 low-frequency words. Nowadays, of course, with the ready availability of reliable word frequency counts, software to automate the counting of neighbours (e.g., Davis, 2005), and computers to do the calculations, such analyses are much easier to perform. Although the results of these analyses show a weak correlation that is in the same direction as that observed by Landauer and Streeter, it is fair to say that the size of a word's neighbourhood has relatively little relationship to its frequency. However, in the years since Landauer and Streeter defined the idea of an orthographic neighbourhood, a question that has provoked considerable interest is whether the size of a word's neighbourhood affects the speed with which the word can be identified.

The first psychological investigation of the effect of neighbourhood size was reported by Coltheart, Davelaar, Jonasson, and Besner (1977). They followed Landauer and Streeter (1973) in counting the number of single-letter substitution neighbours of a stimulus, a metric that has come to be referred to as Coltheart's *N*, or simply *N*. Coltheart et al. conducted a lexical decision experiment in which they manipulated *N* for both the word and the nonword stimuli. They found that *N* had no effect on *Yes* responses, but had a large inhibitory effect on *No* responses, i.e., participants took longer to reject nonwords with many neighbours than to reject nonwords with few neighbours. As we shall see later on, the former (null) result has been challenged by subsequent research (e.g., Andrews, 1989, 1992). However, the inhibitory effect of *N* for nonwords has been replicated consistently (e.g., Andrews, 1989; Forster & Shen, 1996). Coltheart et al. took this result to indicate that the orthographic neighbours of a stimulus are activated during processing, and that this lexical activation interferes with the production of a *No* response.

Expanding the similarity neighbourhood

A key feature of the definition of the orthographic similarity neighbourhood used by Landauer and Streeter (1973) and Coltheart et al. (1977) is the assumption that the neighbours of a letter string are those words that can be formed by substituting a single letter. However, subsequent research has shown that this way of defining the similarity neighbourhood is too narrow. For example, consider a nonword like GADREN. According to the definition used by Landauer and Streeter (1973) and Coltheart et al. (1977), this nonword has no lexical neighbours. Nevertheless, it is probably apparent to most readers that GADREN is very similar to a word in their lexicon, namely, the word GARDEN, which can be formed by transposing two of the letters of GADREN. Words that share this type of similarity relationship are referred to as *transposition neighbours*.

To investigate the orthographic similarity of transposition neighbours, Chambers (1979) exploited a phenomenon that I will refer to as the *near-word effect*: nonwords that are orthographically similar to real words are more difficult to reject in a lexical decision task than are matched control nonwords. One advantage of this methodology is that it involves a speeded task in which participants are not encouraged to generate words, and in which activating the orthographically similar word would produce a response conflict – any cost of similarity to a real word implies that the participant could not help but retrieve this word (whether or not it was consciously retrieved). Another general advantage of experiments based on the near-word effect is related to the fact that the stimuli are nonwords, and are therefore considerably easier to match than are word stimuli. Variables such as word frequency, familiarity, age-of-acquisition, imageability, spelling-sound consistency – all of which affect the speed with which words are processed in various tasks – have no bearing on nonwords. Furthermore, the set of available nonwords is much greater than the pool of letter strings that happen to be words. For these reasons, the near-word effect provides a very useful laboratory tool, and one that many experimenters have taken advantage of in the last few decades.

One experiment reported by Chambers (1979) compared lexical decision latencies for nonwords like GADREN with matched control nonwords like GALBEN. When the letter transposition affected the interior letters of the word (as in GARDEN-GADREN) the difference between nonwords with transposition neighbours and controls was around 100 ms in mean reaction time and 12% in accuracy. When the letter transposition affected the initial letters the inhibitory effect of transposition neighbours was approximately 50 ms (there was no effect on accuracy). These very large inhibitory effects imply that the transposition neighbours were accessed/activated when participants responded to nonwords like GADREN, and that this made it relatively difficult to correctly respond *No*. Because the critical comparison was with control nonwords in which two letters were replaced (rather than transposed), we can conclude that transposing adjacent letters is less disruptive to the perception of a word than substituting two letters. Chambers (1979) interpreted the inhibitory effects in terms of a search model of visual word identification (e.g., Forster, 1976). According to such a model, word identification involves a serial search through a frequency-ordered lexicon. When searching for a near-word like GADREN, it is likely that the word GARDEN will be accessed at some point during the search. Performing a lexical check of this entry against the input stimulus will delay the search process, which would explain the inhibitory effect of orthographic similarity on response latency.

Furthermore, this lexical check may sometimes incorrectly conclude that the lexical entry is a match to the stimulus, which would explain the effect of orthographic similarity on response accuracy (with the absence of such an effect for transpositions affecting the initial letters presumably indicating the relative importance of initial letters in the matching process).

In another experiment, Chambers (1979) directly compared transposition neighbours with single substitution neighbours (i.e., neighbours of the form counted by the *N* metric). She found that nonwords with internal transposition neighbours (e.g., LIIMT) took significantly longer to classify than nonwords with internal substitution neighbours (e.g., LIRIT), but that the effect went in the opposite direction for initial and final transpositions/substitutions (e.g., VISTI was responded to more rapidly than VISIN). The comparison of transposition and substitution neighbours here is not ideal, because letter transposition is more likely than letter substitution to create illegal letter strings, which can be rejected as nonwords more rapidly than legal letter strings, other things being equal (Rubenstein, Lewis, & Rubenstein 1971).

Nevertheless, these data do appear to demonstrate that internal transposition neighbours are closer in similarity space than are internal substitution neighbours, and also agree with Bruner and O'Dowd's (1958) results in suggesting that exterior letter transpositions are more disruptive to word perception than interior transpositions.

The inhibitory effect of transposition neighbours on lexical decisions to nonwords has been replicated many times, and has been extended in various ways. O'Connor and Forster (1981; see also Andrews, 1996 and Perea, Rosa, & Gómez, 2005) showed that the speed and accuracy of *No* responses depends on the frequency of the transposition neighbour. For example, participants were slower to classify nonwords like MOHTER (derived from the high frequency word MOTHER) than nonwords like BOHTER (derived from the low frequency word BOTHER). This finding clearly points to the specific lexical locus of the inhibitory effect, i.e., nonwords like GADREN and MOHTER are difficult because of their similarity to their transposition neighbours, and not because of some more general similarity to words. Davis and Andrews (2001) showed that the magnitude of the inhibitory effect increases as a function of stimulus length (e.g., there is a very large effect for nonwords like BACLONY, but little or no effect for nonwords like CRAD). Perea and Lupker (2004) showed that the inhibitory effect of transposition neighbours is also observed when the transposition involves nonadjacent letters. For example, nonwords like CANISO (derived from CASINO) take longer to reject than matched control nonwords like CAVIRO. Interestingly, both Perea and Lupker (2004), using Spanish stimuli, and Lupker, Perea, and Davis (2008), using English stimuli, found that this transposition neighbour effect was restricted to the case where the transposed letters were consonants (e.g., inhibitory effects were obtained for AMINAL but not for ANAMIL). This finding may reflect some difference in the coding of consonants and vowels, but could also simply reflect the fact that consonants provide greater lexical constraint than vowels (e.g., AN-M-L is more constraining than A-I-AL).

The idea that words can still be identified when some of their letters are transposed and that exterior letter transpositions are more disruptive to word perception than interior transpositions is now most commonly associated with the infamous Cmabrigde email, which asserts that, "Aoccdrnig to a rscheearch at Cmabrigde Uinervtisy, it deosn't mttaer in waht oredr the ltteers in a wrod are, the olny iprmoatnt tihng is taht the frist and lsat ltteer be at the rghit pclae". The research in question is apocryphal, but the email is, in part, correct. It exaggerates the facts of the matter somewhat – clearly letter order is important, or we would not be able to distinguish words like TRIAL and TRAIL. Furthermore, it is probably quite difficult to read IPRMOATNT as IMPORTANT, without the aid of context ("the olny iprmoatnt thing is that"). Even when sentence context is provided, and the transpositions are restricted to adjacent letters, there is a cost of jumbling letter order. This was nicely demonstrated by Rayner, White, Johnson, and Liversedge (2006), who tracked participants' eyes while they silently read sentences of jumbled text. Although text with transposed letters is considerably easier to read than text with substituted letters (Rayner & Kaiser, 1975), participants took longer to read transposed text than normal text: their average fixation durations were longer and their eyes made a greater number of regressions within the text. Still, in agreement with the Cmabrigde email (and Chambers, 1979) the cost was greater for exterior than for interior letter transpositions.

To summarise the above findings, the similarity neighbourhood of a letter string is based not only on words formed via letter substitutions but also those formed via letter transpositions. Indeed, there is some evidence that such transposition neighbours are closer in similarity space than are substitution neighbours. It can be concluded that it takes some time to resolve letter position uncertainty, often more time than is required to resolve uncertainty regarding the identity of the letters.

Orthographic input coding schemes

Evidence that transposition neighbours are within the similarity neighbourhood (i.e., that they are relatively more similar than double substitution neighbours, and perhaps more similar than single substitution neighbours) is problematic for what has been the standard approach to encoding letter identity and order information. According to this approach, there are separate letter units for different letter positions, e.g., a unit that codes G in position 1, and a separate unit that code G in position 2, etc. This position-specific coding model explains how readers are able to distinguish anagrams like GARDEN and DANGER (which activate different sets of units, other than the A in position 2 and the E in position 5). However, it does not explain why GADREN is more similar to GARDEN than is GALBEN, because in both cases there are exactly four common position-specific letter units (i.e., the G, A, E, and N). The similarity of transposition neighbours is one of the empirical observations that has driven the search for new orthographic input coding schemes. A full discussion of such schemes is beyond the scope of this chapter, but below I briefly outline the two main alternatives to position-specific coding (for a more incremental approach, in which the position-specific coding model is supplemented with the assumption of letter position uncertainty, see Gomez, Ratcliff, & Perea, 2008).

Open-bigram coding

The key idea underlying open-bigram coding schemes is that letter position is encoded with respect to nearby (not necessarily contiguous) letters. In these schemes, a letter string is coded in terms of all of the ordered letter pairs that it contains (Grainger & Van Heuven, 2003; Schoonbaert & Grainger, 2004; Whitney & Berndt, 1999; Whitney, 2001). For example, the word SLAT would be coded by the set {SL, SA, ST, LA, LT, AT}, while its transposition neighbour SALT would be coded by the set {SA, SL, ST, AL, AT, LT}. The only bigram that differs these two sets is that which codes for the transposed letters; the remaining five open-bigrams are identical (the order in which the open bigrams is listed is arbitrary). This high degree of overlap indicates the ability of this type of scheme to explain the orthographic similarity of transposition neighbours.

A number of different versions of open-bigram coding have been proposed. These variations differ according to (a) whether open bigrams are coded by discrete or continuous activities, (b) whether continuous activities are used to encode contiguity information or serial position information, or both, (c) the maximum number of letters that may intervene between the letters of an open bigram, (d) whether open bigrams are activated for the reversed order of the letters, and (e) whether exterior letters have any special status. Some of these variations have been falsified by experiments on orthographical similarity. For example, the discrete open bigram model allows for no way of coding letter contiguity, e.g., the SO open-bigram is activated to the same extent by SOAP and STOP, even though its letters are contiguous in the former case and non-contiguous in the latter case. Davis and Bowers (2006) falsified this model by showing that substitution neighbours like STOP and SHOP are more similar than neighbours once-removed like STOP and SOAP.

Spatial coding

The key idea of spatial coding is that the same letter units can encode letters in different serial positions, i.e., these units are not tied to specific letter positions. Position information is represented by dynamically assigning a position code to active letter units. The relative order of the letters in a string is coded by the relative magnitude of the values in the position vector. This type of coding implies that each possible letter string is coded by a unique spatial pattern, hence the term spatial coding. Letter strings that share common letters are coded by relatively similar spatial codes, even if the common letters are found in different serial positions. Word detectors are assumed to compute their input by calculating the match between two spatial codes: (1) the spatial code corresponding to the word represented by this detector, and (2) the spatial orthographic code corresponding to the input stimulus. A match score is calculated by evaluating the degree of pattern overlap amongst these two spatial codes. It should be noted that the calculation does not rely on a standard dot-product, i.e., it is not the case that later letters (which are coded by smaller values) play a less important role in the match calculation. Furthermore, a letter that is common to the two codes contributes to the match calculation even if it occurs in different serial positions in the input stimulus and the word coded by the word detector. A program for computing these match values (as well as the match values for other orthographic coding schemes) can be downloaded from this website: http://www.pc.rhul.ac.uk/staff/c. davis/Utilities/

In summary, the specific similarity of two-letter strings depends on the nature of the orthographic input coding scheme. The standard approach, based on position-specific coding, explains the similarity of substitution neighbours, but doesn't explain why transposition neighbours are more similar than double substitution neighbours. The chief alternatives to the standard approach are open-bigram coding and spatial coding. Attempts to adjudicate between these alternatives are the subject of much ongoing research (e.g., Davis, 2010; Davis & Bowers, 2006; Grainger, 2008; Whitney, 2008).

A further expansion of the similarity neighbourhood

So far, our discussion of the orthographic similarity neighbourhood has been restricted to words that are formed by substituting or transposing letters. These sorts of orthographic disruptions preserve the length of the original letter string. But what about words that have very similar spellings to the original string, but which differ in length? Are such words part of the neighbourhood, e.g., is BEACH in the similarity neighbourhood of BLEACH? Perhaps surprisingly, the standard approach to orthographic input coding would say no. By their very nature, letter additions or deletions must shift the position of the letters in a string. According to a strict position-specific coding model, then, BEACH and BLEACH share only one common letter – the B in position one. By contrast, the correspondence in the absolute position of overlapping letters is not critical for newer orthographic input coding schemes like spatial coding and open-bigram coding. Thus, one of the implications of these schemes is that the orthographic similarity neighbourhood should also include words that are formed via letter additions or deletions (addition and deletion neighbours respectively). Researchers once again turned to the nonword interference paradigm to test this prediction.

Schoonbaert and Grainger (2004) compared nonwords that had addition neighbours (e.g., MIRCLE, derived from MIRACLE) with control nonwords; the two sets of nonwords were matched with respect to number of substitution neighbours. They found that the nonwords with addition neighbours took around 70 ms longer to reject in a lexical decision task, and were associated with an error rate of around 10%, compared to a 1% error rate for control nonwords. Interestingly, the size of the inhibitory effect was unaffected by whether the deleted letter occurred elsewhere within the word (e.g., deleting the letter A had equivalent effects in BALNCE and MIRCLE, even though there is an A in BALNCE). This finding is consistent with spatial coding (where the multiple occurrences of repeated letters are effectively treated as distinct letters), but appears problematic for open-bigram coding. Even after the letter deletion, BALNCE continues to include an AN open bigram, and thus the deletion should have less effect than deleting a nonrepeated letter would be expected to have (e.g., compare the effect of deleting the A in MIRACLE, which does eliminate the AC open bigram).

The similarity of deletion neighbours was investigated by Davis and Taft (2005). A noteworthy feature of their nonword interference experiment was the way in which the nonword conditions were matched with respect to their onsets and bodies; in this way, the viability of a sublexical account of any differences between conditions can be minimised. To achieve this matching, quadruplets of stimuli were constructed based on the combination of two onsets and two word bodies. For example, nonwords like PREAL and GLEAF (which have the deletion neighbours REAL and LEAF) were compared with nonwords like GLEAL and PREAF (which have no deletion neighbours). The results showed a significant inhibitory effect of deletion neighbours, although this effect (of 20 ms) was rather smaller than the inhibitory effects Schoonbaert and Grainger (2004) observed for nonwords with addition neighbours.

There are a number of factors that may explain the much greater interference effects in Schoonbaert and Grainger (2004)'s addition neighbour experiment compared with Davis and Taft's (2005) deletion neighbour experiment. The most important of these is the position of the added/deleted letter. There is good evidence that deleting or adding an interior letter has a less detrimental effect on word perception than deleting/adding an initial letter (Davis, Perea, & Acha, 2009). This evidence is consistent with that obtained for the effects of letter transpositions, and with other evidence concerning the importance of initial letters in visual word identification. Adding or deleting a final letter appears to have an effect that is intermediate between that for interior and initial letters. For example, it would seem that the nonword GARDE is closer in similarity space to the word GARDEN than is the nonword ARDEN, but that the nonword GADEN is closer still. This ordering is theoretically important for comparing orthographic input coding schemes. Not only is it incompatible with strict position-specific coding, but (in the absence of additional assumptions) it is also incompatible with newer models of orthographic input coding. For example, according to the open-bigram coding scheme proposed by Schoonbaert and Grainger (2004), interior letters can participate in twice as many open-bigrams as exterior letters, and thus deleting an interior letter should be more disruptive than deleting the final letter, not less. One way to capture the observed pattern of data is to assume that exterior letters have some sort of special status, and this is the approach that has been taken in refinements of the SERIOL model (Whitney, 2008) and the spatial coding model (Davis, 2010).

Another question of interest is whether deletions and additions have equivalent effects. For example, are MIRCLE and MIROACLE equally similar to the word MIRACLE? On the one hand, MIROACLE contains all of the letters of MIRACLE, whereas MIRCLE is missing one letter. On the other hand, MIROACLE contains a letter that is inconsistent with MIRACLE, whereas MIRCLE does not contain any letters inconsistent with this word. In practice, it is difficult to provide a completely satisfactory answer to this question, as there other factors that are inevitably confounded in such a comparison, notably stimulus length. Notwithstanding this qualification, the available data suggest that nonwords with addition neighbours (like MIRCLE) are more difficult to reject than nonwords with deletion neighbours (like MIROACLE) (Davis et al., 2009). One interpretation of such a pattern is that incompatible letters have a dampening effect on lexical activation, e.g., that the presence of the letter O in MIROACLE somehow reduces the extent to which activity accumulates in the lexical representation of MIRACLE.

The results summarised in this section suggest that the similarity neighbourhood is not tightly restricted to words of the same length as the input stimulus. Addition and deletion neighbours give rise to large near-word effects, implying that the lexical representations of these neighbours are accessed or activated during the identification process. This has some important theoretical implications (Davis et al., 2009), and also, by further highlighting the limitations of the N metric (which only counts substitution neighbours), some important methodological implications. Some alternatives to the N metric are discussed below.

Effects of specific orthographic similarity on identification of words

Although the near-word effect has been invaluable for asking questions about the nature of the orthographic similarity neighbourhood, the fact that it is specific to nonword stimuli limits the conclusions that can be drawn from this phenomenon. One question that it cannot answer is: What effect does orthographic similarity have on word identification; is perception of a word helped or hindered by the existence of a close orthographic neighbour?

What do models predict?

Before considering the evidence, it is interesting to consider the theoretical predictions arising from different models of visual word identification. These predictions span the full range of possible outcomes, i.e., facilitation, inhibition, or no effect. There are at least two theoretical models that predict an inhibitory effect of orthographic similarity to a close neighbour. One such model is the classic search model (e.g., Forster, 1976). As noted earlier, this model can explain the near-word effect by assuming that the search process is delayed by orthographically similar words, due to the necessity of checking close-matching lexical entries against the input stimulus more carefully. Such an account would predict inhibitory effects of orthographic similarity for both word and nonword stimuli. An important aspect of this prediction is that the inhibitory effect should be restricted to neighbours that are higher in frequency than the correct word. For example, when attempting to identify the word PREFECT, the search process should be delayed by the prior check that is necessary for the near match PERFECT. By contrast, identification of the word PERFECT should not be affected by its similarity to PREFECT, because the serial search process is expected to terminate after accessing the correct match PERFECT (and before the lexical entry for PREFECT can be accessed).

Another theoretical framework that predicts an inhibitory effect of ortho-graphic similarity to a close neighbour is the competitive network framework. The most well-known example of a competitive network model of visual word identification is the interactive activation (IA) model (McClelland & Rumelhart, 1981); other models in this framework that have explicitly simulated inhibitory neighbour effects have been discussed by Davis (1999, 2010) and Grainger and Jacobs (1996). According to such models, visual word identification involves competition between lexical representations – it is this competition that underlies the lexical selection process that chooses the learned representation that best matches the input stimulus. For example, the stimulus PREFECT will initially result in lexical activity in both the PREFECT and PERFECT word nodes, but lateral inhibition between these nodes will ultimately enable the PREFECT node to suppress the activity of the PERFECT word node. Like the search model, competitive network models predict an interaction between orthographic similar-ity and relative word frequency, i.e., inhibitory effects should be greater when the similar word is of higher frequency than the word to be identified (e.g., Jacobs & Grainger, 1992). However, unlike the search model, it need not be the case that inhibitory effects are restricted only to neighbouring words of higher frequency.

A very different prediction is made by parallel distributed processing (PDP) models of visual word recognition (e.g., Plaut, McClelland, Seidenberg, & Patterson, 1996; Seidenberg & McClelland, 1989). These models do not include localist lexical representations for words; instead, all lexical knowledge is encoded with the distributed pattern of connections between nodes. Over the course of training these connections are modified, so that words and sublexical patterns that been encountered very frequently will be better represented in the model's weights. Words that are orthographically similar will tend to share many connections, and thus training on one word tends to strengthen connections that are relevant not only to that word but also to orthographically similar words. This aspect of PDP models suggests that orthographic similarity should exert a facilita-tory effect on visual word recognition. Sears, Hino, and Lupker (1999a) reported simulations of two influential PDP models (the Seidenberg & McClelland, 1989 model and the Plaut et al., 1996 model) and confirmed that both models predict a facilitatory effect of having a higher frequency orthographic neighbour.

Another possible theoretical prediction is that orthographic similarity to a close neighbour will have no effect on visual word identification. There are at least two types of model that make this prediction. The first is the classic logogen model of visual word identification (Morton, 1969). Like the interactive activation model, this model assumes the existence of word detectors (logogens) that accumulate evidence until the point at which one logogen exceeds its response threshold. Unlike the interactive activation model (and other competitive network models), there is no interaction between logogens. That is, activation in a logogen for the word PERFECT has no impact on the activity in the logogen for the word PREFECT. This model could potentially predict an effect of orthographic similarity on accuracy, particularly for noisy stimuli, but it does not predict any effect of orthographic similarity on reaction time.

A modified version of the serial search model has also been proposed that predicts no effect of orthographic similarity on word identification (Forster, 1989). In this version of the model there is a first pass through the lexicon that flags near-matches – orthographically similar entries that are not exact matches. These flagged entries only become relevant if an exact match is not found, and thus this model predicts an inhibitory effect of orthographic similarity for nonword stimuli, but no effect for word stimuli.

What does the evidence say?

A variety of methodologies has been used in an attempt to answer the question of what effect neighbours have on visual word identification. The most frequently used approach has been to examine responses to word stimuli in the lexical decision task. A second approach has been to measure the speed (and accuracy) with which words can be read aloud. Yet another methodological approach is to embed such words within sentences, and measure the duration of readers' fixations. A practical difficulty with all of these methodological approaches is that they require a between-stimulus comparison: words that have orthographic neighbours must be compared with control words that do not. As noted already, matching different sets of words is fraught with problems (e.g., Cutler, 1981; Forster & Shen, 1996).

Nevertheless, there is a large literature of experiments that adopt this approach, and the evidence concerning the effects of specific orthographic similarity now paints a fairly clear picture. Close neighbours do exert an influence on visual word identification, and this influence is inhibitory. This effect is modulated by the relative word frequency of the two words – the inhibitory effect is clearest when the neighbour is higher in frequency than the word to be identified. An early example of such an effect was reported by Chambers (1979), who found that words with transposition neighbours (e.g., PREFECT, with the transposition neighbour PERFECT) took longer to classify as words than control words. Andrews (1996) reported a similar inhibitory effect of transposition neighbours on the accuracy of speeded word naming: words with higher frequency transposition neighbours were incorrectly named on 14% of trials latency, compared with 4% for control words; furthermore, most of the errors were productions of the higher frequency neighbour (e.g., participants would say SILVER instead of SLIVER). More recently, Acha and Perea (2008) reported an inhibitory effect in a silent reading experiment. Readers spent longer fixating on (and made more regressions to) words with higher frequency transposition neighbours than they did for matched control words.

Similar inhibitory findings have been reported for addition and deletion neighbours. Thus, words with higher frequency deletion neighbours (e.g., COMET, which has the neighbour COME) took longer to be classified in a lexical decision experiment reported by Davis and Taft (2005), and this result was replicated with Spanish stimuli by Davis et al. (2009). Likewise, words with higher frequency addition neighbours (e.g., WIDOW, which has the neighbour WINDOW) took longer to be classified in a lexical decision experiment reported by Davis et al. (2009); once again, this result was obtained for both English and Spanish stimuli. Davis et al. (2009) also reported a silent reading experiment that showed an inhibitory effect of addition and deletion neighbours, paralleling the findings of Perea and Acha (2008) for transposition neighbours.

Inhibitory effects of higher frequency neighbours have also been reported for substitution neighbours. The original study examining this issue was reported by Grainger, O'Regan, Jacobs, and Segui (1989), who found that both lexical decision latencies and fixation durations were longer for words with a higher frequency substitution neighbour. These effects have been replicated many times by different investigators and in different languages. The effect in lexical decision was replicated by Carreiras, Perea, and Grainger (1997), Grainger (1990), Grainger and Jacobs (1996), Huntsman and Lima (1996), Perea and Pollatsek (1998). The inhibitory effect in silent reading has been replicated and extended by Perea and Pollatsek (1998) and Pollatsek, Perea, and Binder (1999).

Although there is very considerable evidence for an inhibitory neighbour frequency effect, it should be noted that some studies have not observed this effect, or have found effects that are marginal (e.g., Forster & Shen, 1996; Sears, Hino, & Lupker 1995). Johnson (2009) noted some problems with the matching of stimuli in the latter studies. Of course, it is equally possible that studies that have observed inhibitory effects are subject to problems with stimulus matching. Clearly, it would be advantageous to be able to point to a source of evidence that was not subject to potential confounds related to stimulus matching. This requires replacing the standard between-stimulus methodology with some form of within-stimulus approach, i.e., one in which a word is compared with itself.

Two experiments that have attempted to provide such evidence are worth noting. The first was by Zagar and Mathey (2000). They exploited the fact that accents in French are shown only on lowercase letters, and hence some French words have substitution neighbours when they are printed in uppercase (e.g., DEFI has the higher frequency neighbour DEMI), but not when they are printed in lowercase (i.e., demi is not a single substitution neighbour of défi). In a lexical decision task, Zagar and Mathey found that such words took longer to classify when they were presented in uppercase than when presented in lowercase. This effect of case was not present for words whose neighbourhood was unchanged by case manipulation, and so it seems reasonable to conclude that the effect was due to the neighbours (which were of higher frequency than the target words).

Another within-stimulus approach to manipulating the existence of a neighbour was demonstrated by Bowers, Davis, and Hanley (2005). In this experiment, the critical manipulation was achieved by introducing new words into participants' lexicons. For example, participants were trained on novel words like BANARA, a neighbour of the word BANANA. Following training, participants were asked to perform a semantic categorisation task in which they had to classify words as referring either to natural entities (e.g., BANANA) or to (wo) manmade artefacts (e.g., CRADLE). Training was counterbalanced, so that each participant learned 20 new words, 10 of which were neighbours of the critical words from the Natural category (e.g., BANARA) and 10 which were neighbours of the critical words from the Artefact category (e.g., CRAGLE). Each critical word gained a neighbour for half the participants and remained lexical hermits for the other half of the participants. The results of the experiment showed that words that had gained neighbours were categorised significantly more slowly than words that had not.

In summary, the evidence from both between-stimulus and within-stimulus methodologies strongly supports the conclusion that the specific similarity of a word to close neighbours has an inhibitory effect on word identification. This conclusion is consistent with competitive network models of visual word identification such as the IA model and its variants. According to such models, close orthographic neighbours are automatically activated during word identification, and these candidates compete with each other in order to select the best-fitting lexical representation. An alternative theoretical account that could explain inhibitory effects of close orthographic neighbours is offered by a classic serial search model in which near-matches slow down the search process. On the other hand, the inhibitory effect of specific similarity to a close orthographic neighbour is problematic for other theoretical approaches such as the logogen model and, in particular, PDP models (which predict an opposite, facilitatory effect of orthographic similarity).

Effects of general orthographic similarity on identification of words

Our focus so far has been on the effects of specific orthographic similarity between two words (or between a word and a nonword). A separate question, which has also been the subject of extensive research, concerns what effect general orthographic similarity has on visual word identification. That is, is the speed and/or accuracy of word identification affected by whether the word is situated in a dense or a sparse orthographic neighbourhood? Neighbourhood density is typically measured using Landauer and Streeter's (1973) N metric. It can also be measured in various different ways. Yarkoni, Balota, and Yap (2008) proposed an alternative metric, called OLD20, which computes the average Levenshtein distance of the closest 20 neighbours. Loth and Davis (2012) describe a highly correlated measure that measures orthographic typicality using a hidden Markov model algorithm. Both of these metrics have advantages over the N metric (including the capacity to explain more of the variance in lexical decision latency). However, for present purposes it is not critical exactly how neighbourhood density is measured: irrespective of the exact metric, words with many neighbours have high neighbourhood density, high orthographic typicality, and low values of the OLD20 metric. Our central concern is what impact this general orthographic similarity to words in the language has on word identification.

Although competitive network models and the classic serial search model make similar predictions concerning the effects of similarity to a specific orthographic neighbour, they make different predictions concerning the effects of similarity to many neighbours. The search model predicts a linear inhibitory effect of the number of (higher frequency) neighbours, because each of these neighbours must be checked and rejected. As Coltheart et al. (1977) noted, the null effect of N on the latency of *Yes* responses in the LDT is inconsistent with this prediction.

Intuitively, it might seem that competitive network models should make the same prediction: if similarity to one neighbour is inhibitory, presumably similarity to many neighbours should be especially inhibitory? However, this inference is incorrect. In competitive networks models, there is a nonlinear relationship between number of neighbours and lexical competition. Lateral inhibition has a strong tendency to normalise (or conserve) the total activity across a field. For this reason, competitive network models predict essentially no difference between the inhibitory effect of several neighbours and very many neighbours: the predicted inhibitory effect of neighbourhood size is steep between 0 and 1, but is approximately flat for two or more neighbours (see Davis, 2003). Thus, the null effect of N (i.e., no difference between words with few neighbours and word with many neighbours) reported by Coltheart et al. (1977) is perfectly consistent with such models, as shown by Jacobs and Grainger (1992). Likewise, such models are also consistent with studies that have found that the inhibitory effect of having several higher frequency neighbours is no greater than that of having only one higher frequency neighbour (e.g., Grainger, 1990; Grainger, O'Regan, Jacobs, & Segui, 1989; Grainger & Jacobs, 1996; Huntsman & Lima, 1996; Perea & Pollatsek, 1998).

However, competitive network models are challenged by Andrews' (1989) finding of a facilitatory effect of N for low frequency words, an effect that has frequently been replicated in the years since (e.g., Andrews, 1992; Forster & Shen, 1996, etc.). Andrews (1989) suggested that the facilitatory effect of N could be accommodated by an IA-type model as a consequence of feedback from the orthographic lexicon to the letter level. However, although a weak facilitatory effect may be obtained for nonword stimuli, simulations of the IA model have failed to find a way in which facilitatory effects of N on *Yes* responses could arise via top-down feedback (Jacobs & Grainger, 1992; see also Reynolds & Besner, 2002, Simulation 8).

One possible explanation for the facilitatory effect of N in lexical decision responses to words is suggested by data from Andrews (1989). The facilitatory effect in Experiment 1 from Andrews (1989) was not significant in the analysis over items. In Experiment 2, the same word stimuli were tested, but the nonwords were replaced by a different set of nonwords that were much less wordlike. The word stimuli in the latter experiment showed a much larger facilitatory effect of N that was not significant in the analysis over items. Andrews (1989, p. 807) concluded that N effects "are somewhat obscured when the discrimination required for lexical classification is made more difficult by the inclusion of highly wordlike nonwords". Similar effects of nonword context have been observed by other researchers (Carreiras et al., 1997; Grainger & Jacobs, 1996; Johnson & Pugh, 1994). A likely explanation of this interaction between neighbourhood size and nonword context is that the use of "easy" (less wordlike) nonwords encourages a decision strategy that makes *Yes* responses on the basis of information other than the unique identification of the word (e.g., Balota & Chumbley, 1984; Davis, 1999, 2010; Grainger & Jacobs, 1996). Grainger & Jacobs (1996) implemented this idea by assuming that there are two distinct thresholds that, when exceeded, can trigger a *Yes* response: a threshold based on the local activity of individual word nodes and another threshold based on the overall (global) activity of the orthographic lexicon. They showed that such a model predicted a facilitatory effect of N when the global threshold was set relatively low, a setting which is appropriate when the nonwords are relatively unwordlike, and thus do not generate strong lexical activity. When the nonwords are more wordlike it is necessary to set the global threshold higher to avoid false positives (i.e., *Yes* responses to nonwords). With this setting, Grainger and Jacobs (1996) obtained a null effect of N.

The possibility that participants in lexical decision tasks sometimes use global lexical activity as a cue to lexical status provides a plausible account of the interaction between neighbourhood size and nonword context, and of the facilitatory N effect found in several experiments (e.g., Andrews, 1989; Sears et al., 1995) and the absence of N effects in many other experiments (e.g., Carreiras et al., 1997; Coltheart et al., 1977; Grainger & Jacobs, 1996; Johnson & Pugh, 1994). However, as Andrews (1997) noted, it seems unlikely that this possibility can explain all of the observations of facilitatory N effects, which include several experiments in which the neighbourhood characteristics of the nonwords were matched with those of the words (e.g., Andrews, 1992; Forster & Shen, 1996). In some cases, the results of these experiments may not be robust (see Keeulers, Lacey, Rastle, and Brysbaert, 2012, for failures to replicate facilitatory N effects when "virtual experiments" are tested with a megadatabase of lexical decision latencies). Another possibility that deserves serious consideration, though, is that some of the facilitatory effects of N that have been reported reflect confounds with other variables. In particular, neighbourhood size is positively correlated with imageability and negatively correlated with age-of-acquisition (Stadthagen-Gonzalez & Davis, 2006). That is, large-N words tend to be learned earlier than small-N words (based on AoA ratings made by adults; for developmental evidence, see Storkel, 2004), and tend to be richer in imageability. Although imageability and AoA are known to have large effects on lexical decision latency (e.g., Balota, Cortese, Sergent-Marshall, Spieler, & Yap, 2004; Brysbaert &

Ghyselinck, 2006; Cortese & Khanna, 2008; Keeulers et al., 2012; Stadthagen-Gonzalez, Bowers, & Damian, 2004; Whaley, 1978), as well as reading time (Juhasz & Rayner, 2003), published experiments on *N* effects have not controlled for their effects, and manipulations of *N* have typically been confounded with AoA and/or imageability. The stimuli from Andrews (1992) are a case in point: the low frequency small-*N* and large-*N* words differ significantly with respect to both AoA and imageability, $p < 0.0005$ and $p < 0.05$ respectively, based on the norms collected by Cortese & Khanna, 2008 and Cortese & Fugett, 2004). Confounds with these variables also provide a likely explanation of the phonological neighbourhood size effect reported by Yates, Locker and Simpson (2004). In a number of unpublished experiments, Jeff Bowers and I (Davis & Bowers, in preparation) have failed to find any evidence for an *N* effect on *Yes* responses when AoA and imageability are both controlled.

Effects of neighbourhood size in other tasks

The possibility that facilitatory effects of *N* in the LDT reflect a response strategy that is specific to this task (and that does not require unique word identification) has led researchers to investigate *N* effects in other tasks. One task that clearly necessitates unique lexical identification is semantic categorisation. That is, in order to say that *watch* does not refer to a type of animal, one must presumably have identified the word *watch*. Experiments that have examined *N* effects in semantic categorisation have reported mixed findings. On the one hand, nonsignificant effects of neighbourhood size were reported by Forster and Shen (1996), Forster and Hector (2002), and Carreiras et al. (1997). On the other hand, Sears, Lupker, and Hino (1999b) observed a facilitatory *N* effect on semantic categorisation latency. However, the latter result is subject to the same confound between *N* and AoA noted above (a *t*-test on the AoA values associated with the words in the large and small *N* conditions was highly significant, $p < 0.0005$). On balance, it seems safest to conclude that neighbourhood size does not affect semantic categorisation.

   Another task that has been used to assess neighbourhood size effects is the perceptual identification task, in which participants are asked to identify words that have been degraded in some way (e.g., by the addition of visual noise, or by very brief, masked presentation). When participants are restricted to a single identification response, this task has typically shown inhibitory effects of neighbourhood size (Carreiras et al., 1997; Snodgrass & Minzer, 1993; Grainger & Jacobs, 1996). Grainger and Jacobs (1996) found that this inhibitory effect was restricted to the situation where the large-N condition included several high-frequency neighbours, and presented simulations of their M-ROM model that showed that it correctly predicted this pattern of results. Nevertheless, as Andrews (1997) pointed out, there are problems involved in drawing inferences from identification of visually degraded stimuli, because the strategies that participants use to resolve partial information may differ from the selection mechanisms underlying identification of undegraded stimuli.

A further task that researchers have used to examine the effects of neighbourhood size is speeded word naming. This task has usually shown facilitatory *N* effects (Andrews, 1989, 1992; Grainger, 1990, Peereman & Content, 1995; Sears et al., 1995). However, as Peereman and Content (1995) noted, this effect need not reflect an influence of N on lexical identification. Rather, it may reflect an influence of N on the mapping from orthography to phonology. Two observations provide support for this claim. First, Peereman and Content (1995) found that facilitatory effects of N were numerically larger for nonwords than for words. Second, they found that the facilitatory effect depended on what they referred to as phonographic neighbours: those which are both orthographic and phonological neighbours (e.g., ROUGH and TOUGH are phonographic neighbours, but ROUGH and COUGH are not, because they are orthographic but not phonological neighbours). Adelman and Brown (2007) provided further support for the importance of phonographic, as opposed to orthographic neighbours on word naming. Regressions on four separate sets of megastudy data showed unique facilitatory effects of phonographic *N* in the absence of unique facilitatory orthographic *N* effects. One interpretation of this result is that *N* effects in naming reflect feedback between phonology and orthography; the activation of phonographic neighbours facilitates the computation of phonology, whereas the activation of so-called "enemies" (like ROUGH and COUGH) may exert a weak inhibitory effect on the computation of phonology.

In summary, several studies have observed a facilitatory effect of neighbourhood size. In lexical decision experiments, this may reflect the way in which participants make decisions, i.e., they may use neighbourhood size as an index of lexical status. Data from the semantic categorisation task, which provides a more unambiguous measure of lexical identification, do not support the claim that neighbourhood size has a facilitatory effect on identification itself. Facilitatory effects have also been observed in speeded naming tasks, but these effects may reflect neighbourhood influences on the conversion of orthography to phonology (Adelman & Brown, 2007). Finally, a problem that has affected many investigations of neighbourhood size effects is that this variable is correlated with other variables that influence word identification, notably AoA and imageability. It will be important for future investigations to control these variables more carefully.

In conclusion, research over the last four decades has considerably advanced our understanding of orthographic similarity – how it should be measured and what influence it has on word identification. Starting from a rather simple approximation of how orthographic similarity should be measured we have seen the emergence of more complex metrics that take into consideration letter position uncertainty, serial position effects, and the effects of word length; these metrics result in a better fit to the data. Both theory and data require that we count the number of words in the similarity neighbourhood in a more inclusive way than early approaches. Finally, we need to distinguish between the effects of close neighbours and the effect of overall neighbourhood density. Close neighbours have an inhibitory effect on word identification, especially when they are of higher frequency. The effect of neighbourhood density remains somewhat controversial, but data are converging on the conclusion that (beyond densities of one or two words in the surrounding neighbourhood) there is no effect of neighbourhood density on word identification per se, although there may be task-specific effects on lexical decision and reading aloud. Such task-specific effects are a reminder that there remains more to be gained from methodologies that could provide converging data, such as eye tracking and ERP measurements during silent reading (e.g., Carreiras, Vergara, & Perea, 2007; Holcomb, Grainger, & O'Rourke, 2002).

- Orthographic similarity can be measured in different ways. A full count of a word's neighbours should include words formed by letter substitutions, transpositions, additions, or deletions.
- Close orthographic neighbours have an inhibitory effect on the time that it takes to identify a word.
- A word's general orthographic similarity to other words (as measured by its neighbourhood density) has often been reported to exert a facilitatory effect, but this effect may reflect task-specific processes rather than word identification per se.

References

Acha, J. & Perea, M. (2008). The effect of neighborhood frequency in reading: Evidence with transposed-letter neighbors. *Cognition, 108*, 290–300.

Adelman, J.S. & Brown, G.D.A. (2007). Phonographic neighbors, not orthographic neighbors, determine word naming latencies. *Psychonomic Bulletin & Review, 14*, 455–459.

Andrews, S. (1989). Frequency and neighborhood effects on lexical access: Activation or search? *Journal of Experimental Psychology: Learning, Memory, and Cognition, 15*, 802–814.

Andrews, S. (1992). Neighbourhood effects on lexical access: Lexical similarity or orthographic redundancy? *Journal of Experimental Psychology: Learning, Memory and Cognition, 18*, 234–254.

Andrews, S. (1996). Lexical retrieval and selection processes: Effects of transposed-letter confusability. *Journal of Memory and Language, 35*, 775–800.

Andrews, S. (1997). The effect of orthographic similarity on lexical retrieval: Resolving neighborhood conflicts. *Psychonomic Bulletin and Review, 4*, 439–461.

Balota, D.A. & Chumbley, J.I. (1984). Are lexical decisions a good measure of lexical access? The role of word frequency in the neglected decision stage. *Journal of Experimental Psychology: Human Perception and Performance, 10*, 340–357.

Balota, D.A., Cortese, M.J., Sergent-Marshall, S.D., Spieler, D.H., & Yap, M.J. (2004). Visual word recognition of single-syllable words. *Journal of Experimental Psychology: General, 133*, 283–316.

Bowers, J.S., Davis, C.J., & Hanley, D.A. (2005). Interfering neighbours: The impact of novel word learning on the identification of visually similar words. *Cognition, 97*, 45–54.

Bruner, J.S. & O'Dowd, D. (1958). A note on the informativeness of parts of words. *Language and Speech, 1,* 98–101.

Brysbaert, M. & Ghyselinck, M. (2006). The effect of age of acquisition: Partly frequency-related, partly frequency-independent. *Visual Cognition, 13,* 992–1011.

Carreiras, M., Perea, M., & Grainger, J. (1997). Effects of orthographic neighborhood in visual word recognition: Cross-task comparisons. *Journal of Experimental Psychology: Learning, Memory, and Cognition, 23,* 857–871.

Carreiras, M., Vergara, M., & Perea, M. (2007). ERP correlates of transposed-letter similarity effects: Are consonants processed differently from vowels? *Neuroscience Letters, 419,* 219–224.

Chambers, S.M. (1979). Letter and order information in lexical access. *Journal of Verbal Learning and Verbal Behavior, 18,* 225–241.

Coltheart, M., Davelaar, E., Jonasson, J.T., & Besner, D. (1977). Access to the internal lexicon. In S. Dornic (Ed.), *Attention and performance VI* (pp. 535–555). New York: Academic Press.

Cortese, M.J. & Fugett, A. (2004). Imageability ratings for 3,000 monosyllabic words. *Behavior Research Methods, Instruments, and Computers, 36,* 384–387.

Cortese, M.J. & Khanna, M.M. (2008). Age of acquisition ratings for 3,000 monosyllabic words. *Behavior Research Methods, 40,* 791–794.

Cutler, A. (1981). Making up materials is a confounded nuisance: or Will we be able to run any psycholinguistic experiments at all in 1990? *Cognition, 10,* 65–70.

Davis, C.J. (1999). The self-organising lexical acquisition and recognition (SOLAR) model of visual word recognition. Doctoral dissertation, University of New South Wales.

Davis, C.J. (2003). Factors underlying masked priming effects in competitive network models of visual word recognition In S. Kinoshita & S. J. Lupker (Eds), *Masked Priming: The State of the Art.* Philadelphia: Psychology Press.

Davis, C.J. (2005). N-Watch: A program for deriving neighborhood size and other psycholinguistic statistics. *Behavior Research Methods, 37,* 65–70.

Davis, C.J. (2010). The spatial coding model of visual word identification. *Psychological Review, 117,* 713–58.

Davis, C.J. & Andrews, S. (2001). Inhibitory effects of transposed-letter similarity for words and non-words of different lengths. *Australian Journal of Psychology, 53,* 50.

Davis, C.J. & Bowers, J. S. (2006). Contrasting five different theories of letter position coding: Evidence from orthographic similarity effects. *Journal of Experimental Psychology-Human Perception and Performance, 32,* 535–557.

Davis, C.J. & Taft, M. (2005). More words in the neighborhood: Interference in lexical decision due to deletion neighbors. *Psychonomic Bulletin & Review, 12,* 904–910.

Davis, C.J., Perea, M., & Acha, J. (2009). Re(de)fining the orthographic neighbourhood: The role of addition and deletion neighbours in lexical decision and reading. *Journal of Experimental Psychology: Human Perception and Performance, 35,* 1550–1570.

Forster, K.I. (1976). Accessing the mental lexicon. In E.C.J. Walker & R.J. Wales (Eds), *New approaches to language mechanisms* (pp. 257–287). Amsterdam: North-Holland.

Forster, K.I. (1989). Basic issues in lexical processing. In W.Marslen-Wilson (Ed.), *Lexical representation and process* (pp. 75–107).Cambridge, MA: M.I.T. Press.

Forster, K.I. & Hector, J. (2002). Cascaded versus noncascaded models of lexical and semantic processing: the *turple* effect. *Memory and Cognition, 30,* 1106–1116.

Forster, K.I. & Shen, D. (1996). No enemies in the neighborhood: Absence of inhibitory neighborhood effects in lexical decision and semantic categorization. *Journal of Experimental Psychology: Learning, Memory, and Cognition, 22,* 696–713.

Gomez, P., Ratcliff, R., & Perea, M. (2008). The overlap model: A model of letter position coding. *Psychological Review, 115,* 577–600.

Grainger, J. (1990). Word frequency and neighbourhood frequency effects in lexical decision and naming. *Journal of Memory and Language, 29,* 228–244.

Grainger, J. (2008). Cracking the orthographic code: An introduction. *Language and Cognitive Processes, 23,* 1–35.

Grainger, J. & Jacobs, A.M. (1996). Orthographic processing in visual word recognition: A multiple read-out model. *Psychological Review, 103,* 518–565.

Grainger, J. & van Heuven, W.J.B. (2003). Modeling letter position coding in printed word perception. In P. Bonin (Ed.), *The mental lexicon* (pp. 1–23). New York: Nova Science.

Grainger, J., O'Regan, J.K., Jacobs, A.M., & Segui, J. (1989). On the role of competing word units in visual word recognition: The neighbourhood frequency effect. *Perception & Psychophysics, 51,* 49–56.

Holcomb, P.J., Grainger, J., & O'Rourke, T. (2002). An electrophysiology study of the effects of orthographic neighborhood size on printed word perception. *Journal of Cognitive Neuroscience, 14,* 938–950.

Huntsman, L.A. & Lima, S.D. (1996). Orthographic neighborhood structure and lexical access. *Journal of Psycholinguistic Research, 25,* 417–429.

Jacobs, A.M. & Grainger, J. (1992). Testing a semistochastic variant of the interactive activation model in different word recognition experiments. *Journal of Experimental Psychology: Human Perception and Performance, 18,* 1174–1188.

Johnson, N.F. & Pugh, K.R. (1994). A cohort model of visual word recognition. *Cognitive Psychology, 26,* 240–346.

Johnson, R.L. (2009). The quiet clam is quite calm: Transposed-letter neighborhood effects on eye movements during reading. *Journal of Experimental Psychology: Learning, Memory, and Cognition, 35,* 943–969.

Juhasz, B.J. & Rayner, K (2003) Investigating the effects of a set of intercorrelated variables on eye fixation durations in reading. *Journal of Experimental Psychology: Learning Memory and Cognition, 29,* 1312–1318.

Keuleers, E., Lacey, P., Rastle, K., & Brysbaert, M. (2012). The British Lexicon Project: Lexical decision data for 28,730 monosyllabic and disyllabic English words. *Behavior Research Methods, 44,* 287–304.

Landauer, T. & Streeter, L.A. (1973). Structural differences between common and rare words: Failure of equivalence assumptions for theories of word recognition. *Journal of Verbal Learning and Verbal Behavior, 12,* 119–131.

Loth, S. & Davis, C.J. (2012). *A new measure of orthographic typicality.* Manuscript in preparation.

Lupker, S.J., Perea, M., & Davis, C. J. (2008). Transposed-letter effects: Consonants, vowels and letter frequency. *Language and Cognitive Processes, 23,* 93–116.

McClelland, J.L. & Rumelhart, D.E. (1981). An interactive activation model of context effects in letter perception: Part I. An account of basic findings. *Psychological Review, 88,* 375–407.

Morton, J. (1969). Interaction of information in word recognition. *Psychological Review, 76,* 165–178.

O'Connor, R.E. & Forster, K.I. (1981). Criterion bias and search sequence bias in word recognition. *Memory and Cognition, 9*, 78–92.

Peereman, R. & Content, A. (1995). Neighborhood size effect in naming: Lexical activation or sublexical correspondences? *Journal of Experimental Psychology: Learning, Memory, and Cognition, 21*, 409–421.

Perea, M. & Lupker, S.J. (2004). Can CANISO activate CASINO? Transposed-letter similarity effects with nonadjacent letter positions. *Journal of Memory and Language, 51*, 231–246.

Perea, M. & Pollatsek, A. (1998). The effects of neighborhood frequency in reading and lexical decision. *Journal of Experimental Psychology: Human Perception and Performance, 24*, 767–779.

Perea, M., Rosa, E., & Gómez, C. (2005). The frequency effect for pseudowords in the lexical decision task. *Perception and Psychophysics, 67*, 301–314.

Plaut, D.C., McClelland, J.L., Seidenberg, M.S., & Patterson, K. (1996). Understanding normal and impaired word reading: Computational principles in quasi-regular domains. *Psychological Review, 103*, 56–115.

Pollatsek, A., Perea, M., & Binder, K. (1999). The effects of neighborhood size in reading and lexical decision. *Journal of Experimental Psychology: Human Perception and Performance, 25*, 1142–1158.

Rayner, K. & Kaiser, J.S. (1975). Reading mutilated text. *Journal of Educational. Psychology, 67*, 301–306.

Rayner, K., White, S.J., Johnson, R.L., & Liversedge, S.P. (2006). Raeding wrods with jubmled lettres. *Psychological Science, 17*, 192–193.

Reynolds, M. & Besner, D. (2002). Neighbourhood density effects in reading aloud: New insights from simulations with the DRC model. *Canadian Journal of Experimental Psychology, 56*, 310–318.

Rubenstein, H., Lewis, S.S., & Rubenstein, M.A. (1971). Evidence for phonemic recoding in visual word recognition. *Journal of Verbal Learning and Verbal Behavior, 10*, 645–657.

Schoonbaert, S. & Grainger, J. (2004). Letter position coding in printed word perception: Effects of repeated and transposed letters. *Language & Cognitive Processes, 19*, 333–367.

Sears, C.R., Hino, Y., & Lupker, S.J. (1995). Neighborhood size and neighborhood frequency effects in word recognition. *Journal of Experimental Psychology: Human Perception and Performance, 21*, 876–900.

Sears, C.R., Hino, Y., & Lupker, S.J. (1999a). Orthographic neighbourhood effects in parallel distributed processing models. *Canadian Journal of Experimental Psychology, 53*, 220–230.

Sears, C.R., Lupker, S.J., & Hino, Y. (1999b). Orthographic neighborhood effects in perceptual identification and semantic categorization tasks. *Perception & Psychophysics, 61*, 1537–1554.

Seidenberg, M.S. & McClelland, J.L. (1989). A distributed, developmental model of word recognition and naming. *Psychological Review, 96*, 523–568.

Snodgrass, J.G. & Mintzer, M. (1993). Neighborhood effects in visual word recognition: Facilitatory or inhibitory? *Memory & Cognition, 21*, 247–266.

Stadthagen-Gonzalez, H. & Davis, C.J. (2006). The Bristol norms for age of acquisition, imageability and familiarity. *Behavior Research Methods, 38*, 598–605.

Stadthagen-Gonzales, H., Bowers, J.S., & Damian, M.F. (2004). Age-of-acquisition effects in visual word recognition: Evidence from expert vocabularies. *Cognition, 93*, B11–B26.

Storkel, H.L. (2004). Do children acquire dense neighborhoods? *Applied Psycholinguistics*, *25*, 201–221.

Whaley, C.P. (1978). Word-nonword classification time. *Journal of Verbal Learning and Verbal Behavior*, *17*, 143–154.

Whitney, C. (2001). How the brain encodes the order of letters in a printed word: The SERIOL model and selective literature review. *Psychonomic Bulletin and Review*, *8*, 221–243.

Whitney, C. & Berndt, R.S. (1999). A new model of letter string encoding: Simulating right neglect dyslexia. In J.A. Reggia, E. Ruppin, & D. Glanzman (Eds), *Progress in Brain Research* (Vol 121, pp. 143–163). Amsterdam: Elsevier.

Whitney, C. (2008). A comparison of the SERIOL and SOLAR theories of letter-position encoding. *Brain & Language*, *107*, 170–178.

Yates, M., Locker, L. Jr, & Simpson, G.B. (2004). The influence of phonological neighborhood on visual word perception. *Psychonomic Bulletin and Review*, *11*, 452–457.

Yarkoni, T., Balota, D.A., & Yap, M.J. (2008). Moving Beyond Coltheart's N: A New Measure of Orthographic Similarity. *Psychonomic Bulletin & Review*, *15*, 971–979.

Zagar, D. & Mathey, S. (2000). When words with higher-frequency neighbours become words with no higher-frequency neighbour (or how to undress the neighbourhood frequency effect). In A. Kennedy, R. Radach, D. Heller, & J. Pynte (Eds), *Reading as a perceptual process* (pp. 23–46). Oxford: Elsevier.

10 Phonology

An early and integral role in identifying words

Laura K. Halderman, Jane Ashby, and Charles A. Perfetti

Huey (1908), in his classic volume on the science and teaching of reading, reported clear evidence that the sounds of spoken language are part of reading: '…Of nearly thirty adults who were thus tested, the large majority found inner speech in some form to be a part of their ordinary reading. Purely visual reading was not established by any of the readers, …' (p. 119).

It took a while for later views on reading to come around to this conclusion. After a period in which the role of phonology was seen as, at most, a secondary and optional part of reading, Huey's conclusion now holds a privileged place in explanations of reading. In this chapter, we explain how the research has come to force a very strong conclusion: that the 'sounds' of words, both their phonemes and their larger, prosodic constituents (stress, syllabic structures), are an integral (and early) part of word identification. Phonology doesn't merely affect word identification, it fundamentally constrains and shapes it.

Of course, Huey was not talking about phonology in this specific sense, but rather the form of inner speech, a trailing echo of the print, formed into prosodic contours – the voice in the head. A contribution of modern research has been to decompose the phonology of reading into two related but different components. Huey's inner speech is one. Word identification is another. Baddeley and Lewis (1981) showed that these two components could be partially independent. In particular, it could be false that phonology produced word identification and true that there is a tendency for readers to have the trailing echo. This distinction corresponds approximately to the question of whether phonology is 'pre-lexical' or 'post-lexical', although it is not identical to it. It is the word identification question that is at issue in this chapter. Does phonology constrain the identification of words, or is it a product of identification? Is its role fundamental (shaping identification) or incidental (providing an output that can optionally fill the role identified by Huey)?

In what follows, we review research on these questions that affirms one part of what Frost (1998) termed the 'strong phonological hypothesis' – that phonology is an automatic part of word identification. However, we consider evidence that causes some reconsideration of what this hypothesis claimed about pre-lexical phonology – that it is 'minimal' in its content and that the full phonological form is retrieved from the lexicon rather than activated by pre-lexical processes. Certainly, the final phonological form has to be affected by the lexical entry including its morphosyntax; otherwise, whether RECORD receives first or second syllable stress remains undetermined. However, we review evidence indicating that a broad range of phonological content is activated very early during word identification. Our review suggests a stronger role for phonology than the role proposed by the 'strong phonological hypothesis': a role that is early and integral to word identification.

We begin by evaluating phonological processing in different writing systems, because the question of a general role for phonology cannot be exclusively based upon alphabetic writing systems. We then discuss behavioral and neurophysiological evidence from reading research in alphabetic systems on the time course of phonological representation in skilled reading. Finally we review evidence about the content of these phonological representations.

Phonology's universal role

For alphabetic writing, reading procedures can operate on letters or graphemes by activating their corresponding phonemes. English, however, is an alphabetic system with a complex and inconsistent mapping to phonology. Other alphabetic orthographies, e.g., Finnish, Welsh, and Serbo-Croatian, are built on a more consistent mapping of graphemes to phonemes. The variability in the mapping of graphemes to phonemes in alphabetic writing has led to hypotheses about corresponding variations in word reading (e.g., Share, 2008). The orthographic depth hypothesis (Katz & Frost, 1992) aimed to explain how variation in the way different writing systems encode speech (i.e., more or less transparently) can affect word reading processes, especially the relative dependence of word reading on sublexical phonological procedures compared with lexical procedures. Beyond alphabetic writing, the universal phonological principle (Perfetti, Zhang, & Berent, 1992) claimed that reading engages phonology at the earliest moment and smallest unit allowed by the writing system. More recently, Ziegler and Goswami (2005) hypothesized that readers process phonology according to the grain size of the orthography, with readers of German utilizing one grain size and readers of English using multiple grain sizes. Each of these related ideas – orthographic depth, universal phonology, and grain size – has been the object of experimental research. The generalization seems to be that although the orthographic structure of a writing system affects the phonological information that readers process, all alphabetic writing – from inconsistent English and French to highly consistent Finnish and Welsh – is read using phonological processes to identify words. Even in Hebrew, an alphabetic orthography that does not visually represent most vowels, both phonological and orthographic effects are found with as little as 14 ms of target word exposure (Frost & Yogev, 2001).

The point of high contrast with alphabetic writing is the morpho-syllabic (or logographic) systems represented by Chinese and the Japanese Kanji. If word reading occurs without phonology, Chinese is where one should find it. A review of the first burst of research (1990s) on the role of phonology in reading Chinese concluded that phonology provided an early source of constraint in reading Chinese characters, just as it does in reading words in alphabetic writing (Tan & Perfetti, 1998). This conclusion was based on many of the behavioral and eye-tracking paradigms that were used in alphabetic studies reviewed in the next section. These include brief exposure combined with masking (Tan, Hoosain, & Siok, 1996), primed perceptual identification experiments (Perfetti & Zhang, 1991), semantic decision experiments (Perfetti & Zhang, 1995; Xu, Pollatsek, & Potter, 1999), eye-tracking studies of parafoveal viewing (Liu, Inhoff, Ye, & Wu, 2002; Pollatesek, Tan, & Rayner, 2000; Tsai, Lee, Tzeng, Hung, & Yen, 2004), and ERP studies (Liu, Perfetti, & Hart, 2003), all of which have provided evidence for phonological processing in Chinese. Important too for the conclusion that phonology is general is the result that phonology is seen in the identification of high- as well as low-frequency Chinese words (Zhang, Perfetti, & Yang, 1999).

Along with the evidence for universal phonology came hypotheses about differences in its implementation across writing systems. Two key differences in Chinese are the dependence of phonology on whole-character orthography in general (although radical effects can be found for less frequent characters) and the unit of phonology activated (syllabic rather than phonemic). The onset of phonology in character reading is synchronized to character identification in a specific sense: phonological (syllable level) information is activated at the moment that the character's orthographic representation of the character is sufficient to distinguish it from perceptually similar (and partially activated) characters (Perfetti & Tan, 1998). This contrasts with the simultaneous rise of phonemic activation with letters prior to lexical access in alphabetic writing. Still, similarities in the process of phonological activation across the two writing systems can be captured by statistical learning models (Yang, McCandliss, Shu, & Zevin, 2009) as well as by the lexical constituency model (Perfetti & Tan, 1998; Perfetti, Liu, & Tan, 2005). The latter model proposes the idea of constituency: that words have graphic, phonological, and morphological constituents that constitute the word identity. All constituents become available when a graphic input initiates the identification process, although the detailed timing or connection strengths of the constituents vary with circumstances within a language (e.g., frequency, consistency) and across writing systems (phonemes, syllables).

We turn now to evidence from alphabetic reading, where there is sufficient research to show a detailed, yet complex picture of phonology's early role in word recognition.

Phonology's early role in alphabetic reading

Behavioral evidence

Behavioral evidence supports early phonological processing that arises immediately from visual contact with a letter string in skilled alphabetic reading. This early phonology may be approximately automatic as well, even if strategic influences can sometimes alter its expression in specific tasks. When phonology interferes with performance on a task (e.g., semantic categorization with homophonic foils), this is evidence that phonology is at least difficult to suppress (Van Orden, Johnston, & Hale, 1988).

Tasks' demands are critical to consider in reviews of phonological effects. For example, naming and lexical decisions, the bread-and-butter tasks of word recognition research, differ in whether they require phonology to perform the task. Naming does, lexical decision does not. Accordingly, one might take lexical decision to be the more appropriate task to reveal early phonology, as it avoids the articulatory processes that mandate phonological processing. Indeed, lexical decision studies have found longer reaction times for homophones, suggesting that phonology is accessed and a conflict arises when one phonological form activates more than one orthographic form (MADE, MAID) in the lexicon (Pexman, Lupker, & Jared, 2001). However, because lexical decisions involve *discriminating* between letter strings that are words and letter strings that are not, they are susceptible to strategies that control decision-making processes. These strategies can vary with the properties of the real words and the foils used in the experiments.

Other non-articulatory tasks also provide evidence for phonological processing in word identification. In semantic categorization tasks, subjects are more likely to accept pseudohomophones (e.g., ROZE) and homophones (e.g., ROWS) as members of the category FLOWER because these have the same phonological form as a correct category member (ROSE) (Van Orden et al., 1988; Jared & Seidenberg, 1991). Here, phonology is generated and leads to poorer performance in a task that on the surface, doesn't require the activation of phonology. This effect, however, is limited to low-frequency items sharing phonology with low-frequency exemplars.

Although naming tasks, because they require phonology, cannot provide completely persuasive evidence for the phonological processes that occur in silent reading, tasks such as mediated priming present interesting findings. Mediated priming experiments exploit the phonological relationships between words that are not presented in the experiment. The mediation effect requires activation of the mediating prime's pronunciation even though the word itself has not been presented. For example, the presentation of the prime SOFA delays the naming of TOUCH even though the two words are unrelated. This is because SOFA activates the semantically-related word COUCH, whose pronunciation is inconsistent with that of TOUCH, thus slowing the pronunciation of TOUCH (Farrar, Van Orden, & Hamouz, 2001). By contrast, when the mediator prime (COUCH) and the target (e.g., POUCH) share the same phonology for the orthographic body, then the prime facilitates identification.

Despite compelling evidence in several non-naming tasks, one does find inconsistent effects of phonology. Some studies find evidence for phonology's role in recognizing high-frequency words whereas other studies report phonological effects restricted to low-frequency words. Some studies suggest that access to meaning is mediated by phonology, whereas other studies do not. Such loose ends, along with differences among tasks, help sustain the debate about the role of phonology.

Phonological effects can depend on the degree of strategic processing encouraged by a task. For example, many of the tasks involve priming, with manipulations of the prime's orthography and phonology. A pseudohomophone (TODE) or homophone (TOWED) prime can facilitate the positive lexical decision to a word (TOAD) compared with an orthographic control prime (TODS, TOLD) (Drieghe & Brysbaert, 2002). But these priming effects turn out to be dependent on prime durations. Drieghe and Brysbaert (2002) report pseudohomophone priming effects at both short and long prime durations, but homophone priming at short prime durations only. This suggests that a short time-window is needed to observe automatic phonological processing. Drieghe and Brysbaert concluded phonology is activated automatically, however, strategic processes (e.g., spelling verification) can influence or minimize phonology's role in lexical decision.

To generalize this observation, the more room for strategic processing, the less likely it is that phonological effects will appear. Indeed, Berent and Perfetti (1995) concluded that methods that allow unlimited exposure to a target word encourage strategic processing and produce inconsistent phonological effects. In contrast, methods that limit exposure and/or interrupt processing tend to tap early (perhaps automatic) processes that are less subject to strategic control. Although all standard behavioral tasks are subject to strategies, studies that limit exposure may give a clearer picture on the earliness of phonology. Accordingly, we take a closer look at such studies.

Studies of brief exposure with masking

Restricting the availability of visual information available through a brief exposure can reveal early phonological processes. When information is presented so quickly that participants are not aware of it, strategic processing is suppressed and more automatic effects appear in word recognition. There are a number of variations on this basic idea that use perceptual identification (i.e., what word did you see?), lexical decisions, and even naming combined with a masking procedure that limits exposure. An important paper by Rastle and Brysbaert (2006) reviewed and critiqued these paradigms in a meta-analysis of previous research. In addition, they provided new data as well as computer simulations that modeled reading data to help clarify what has been learned about masked phonological priming to date. We illustrate here, two of the paradigms studied, perceptual identification with backward masking and lexical decisions with masked priming.

Backward masking limits the duration of the target word by immediately masking it with a letter string whose relation to the target varies in terms of orthographic and phonological similarity (see Figure 10.1 for an example). The logic is that the mask interrupts target processing and reduces the probability of word identification. Unidentified words nonetheless have their component letters and (by hypothesis) phonemes activated. If the nonword mask can reinstate these orthographic and phonological units of the word, it reduces the deleterious effects of the mask, resulting in higher identification accuracy than with masks with no shared letters or phonemes. In the case of phonology, if readers do activate the

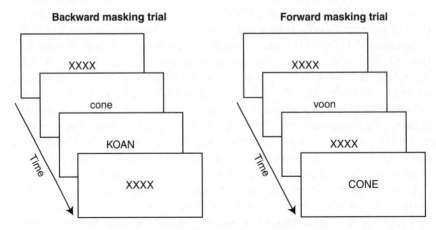

Figure 10.1 The left side shows an example of a backward masking trial using a phonologically similar nonword mask. A trial begins with a forward pattern mask
(e.g., XXXX) that is followed by the target (e.g., crew). A nonword mask
immediately follows the target and can be related to the target phonologically
(e.g., KROO), orthographically (e.g., CRAE), both (e.g., CRUE) or unrelated
baseline condition (e.g., GILF). A trial ends with another pattern mask. The
right shows an example of a masked priming trial using an orthographic control nonword mask. In both cases, the targets and nonword masks or primes
are presented very briefly (i.e., 14–66 ms each).

phonology of words within the brief target presentation before complete identification occurs, then phonological similarity between the target and nonword will
benefit recognition. Some backward masking experiments have used controls to
minimize the impact of guessing such as including trials with no target words
(Perfetti, Bell, & Delaney, 1988). The results from backward masking experiments generally show the predicted pattern – more accurate target identification
following phonologically similar nonword masks compared to orthographically
similar masks when the target words were presented for 35–55 ms (Perfetti &
Bell, 1991; Perfetti et al., 1988; Tan & Perfetti, 1999; Verstaen, Humphreys,
Olson, & d'Ydewalle, 1995; Xu & Perfetti, 1999). With shorter target durations,
phonological and orthographic effects tend to be equivalent.

These studies were taken as support for the hypothesis that phonology is
activated early and automatically during word identification. However, the backward masking method has been subject to the criticism that, despite controls for
guessing, the identification procedure allows guessing to play a role (e.g., Rastle
& Brysbaert, 2006). Related controversies arose around strategic effects controlled by stimulus conditions such as a low proportion of related trials or using
homophones as targets (Brysbaert & Praet, 1992; Verstaen et al., 1995; Xu &
Perfetti, 1999). Our conclusion is that the studies using this paradigm produced
evidence for phonological facilitation effects in identification that go beyond

strategic effects. This conclusion also applies to related paradigms using masked presentation, including priming studies.

In masked-priming studies, nonword primes are presented briefly (<50 ms) before a target word. The participant identifies the word or makes a lexical decision depending on the experiment. The prime improves performance when it is similar to the target orthographically and/or phonologically. For example, Ferrand and Grainger (1994) found both orthographic and phonological priming effects in lexical decision, with phonological priming requiring slightly longer exposures to produce effects (25 ms or more). Perfetti and Bell (1991) reported similar results with perceptual identification instead of lexical decisions. This lag between orthography and phonology is not usually found in backward masking. Phonological effects are delayed relative to the orthographic effects in forward masking because the first stimulus is a nonword, and it may take more time to compute the phonology of an unknown string. In backward masking, the initial stimulus is a word, whose phonology may become more quickly stabilized from top-down lexical influences.

These backward masking and masked priming studies represent two of the four methods from published results that were the object of a meta-analysis by Rastle and Brysbaert (2006). (See Table 10.1 for the phonological effect sizes that they report.) They concluded that each paradigm produced reliable but small effects of phonology on word recognition, whether measured by backward–masking perceptual identification, masked-priming lexical decision, or masked-priming with naming.

However, Rastle and Brysbaert (2006) were critical of the procedures and controls typically used in these experiments, and raised the question of whether there really was evidence for phonological effects. Specifically focusing on lexical decisions with masked priming, they carried out two new experiments that controlled for the problems they identified. Rastle and Brysbaert found clear evidence for phonological priming effects on lexical decisions. Similar to the meta-analysis data, words (GROW) preceded by phonologically similar primes (GROE) were recognized 13 ms faster on average than words in the orthographic control condition (GROY). Phonological facilitation was also found in their second experiment, even though using phonology here would have made the task

Table 10.1 Average phonological facilitation beyond orthographic facilitation and average effect sizes reported in Rastle and Brysbaert's (2006) meta-analysis

Methodology	Phonological facilitation	Effect size(r)
Forward masked perceptual identification	9.11%**	0.240
Backward masked perceptual identification	3.89%**	0.193
Forward masked naming	10 ms**	0.312
Forward masked lexical decision	10 ms*	0.204

$*p < 0.05$, $**p < 0.01$

more difficult. Therefore, the behavioral evidence supports claims of early phonological processing that begins immediately with the viewing of a word. Whereas strategic effects may play a role in the inconsistent findings of phonology in word identification, the evidence in favor of early, automatic phonological effects stands up to careful scrutiny.

In the next section, we present evidence from eye movement experiments. As eye movements are measured online during silent reading, rather than being a post-reading measure such as lexical decision time, they are considered to be relatively free from strategic effects.

Evidence from eye movements

Eye movements provide a fairly direct window on word recognition processes that affect fixation duration and fixation location. We say 'direct' because measurements are taken during silent reading without any additional task demands that could encourage strategic processes. Because when and where the eyes move during reading is driven mainly by automatic word recognition processes; fixation times are a sensitive measure of word processing variables (Rayner, 1998; Rayner, Pollatsek, Ashby, & Clifton, 2012).

Eye movements have a high spatial (within half a letter) and temporal (1000 samples per second) resolution that allows experimenters to unobtrusively manipulate what text readers see and when they see it by changing the display during reading (Rayner, 1975). Two types of display changes are relevant to understanding phonological processing in word identification – the fast-priming paradigm and the parafoveal preview paradigm. These paradigms enable researchers to manipulate variables during the initial moments of word recognition.

Fast-priming experiments provide information about word recognition once a word is fixated. In this procedure, a consonant string is displayed in the location of a target word that is embedded in a sentence (Sereno & Rayner, 1992). When the eyes saccade across an invisible boundary to the left of the target, a display change presents a prime for the first 20–45 ms of the fixation at the target location. The prime is then masked by the target word that appears during fixation. Rayner et al. (1995) presented skilled readers with sentences such as *The bird prefers beech trees for nesting*, with BEECH being the target word. At the 36-ms prime duration, targets preceded by homophone primes (BEACH) were read faster (i.e. produced shorter fixation times) than targets preceded by visually similar primes (BENCH), indicating that 36-ms primes can engage phonological processes during silent reading.

Lee, Rayner, & Pollatsek, (1999) used fast-priming to examine the relative time course to uptake orthographic, phonological, and semantic information in word recognition. Phonological primes in the 29–35 ms range facilitated word recognition, whereas semantic priming appeared at the 32-ms duration only. Thus, the Lee et al. data indicate that the foveal uptake of phonological information happens at least as quickly as the uptake of semantic information, contrary to the wide-spread perception that phonological processing is slow (Coltheart,

Rastle, Perry, Langdon, & Ziegler, 2001). This conclusion is consistent with the results of isolated word paradigms that compare the timing of semantic and phonological effects (e.g., Tan & Perfetti, 1999).

Whereas most content words are identified foveally during a fixation, readers also begin extracting information parafoveally before actually fixating the word (Dodge, 1907). Readers typically recognize words 40–50 ms faster with parafoveal preview than when preview is denied (Rayner, 2009; Rayner, Liversedge, & White, 2006). The parafoveal preview paradigm manipulates the relation of parafoveal information to the upcoming word. If readers process the information parafoveally, then congruent previews will facilitate recognition once the word is fixated. Thus, parafoveal preview studies measure effects of the initial information that skilled readers process during word recognition and provide singular insights into early lexical access processes.

The paradigm works as follows: A fixation cross on the far left side of the screen dissolves into a sentence display that initially includes the preview string (see sentence 1). Readers begin reading the sentence, with asterisks indicating hypothetical fixation points. They process the preview (either BALL or BAIL) parafoveally when they fixate the word just left of the target region (WON'T). During the saccade into the target region, the eyes cross an invisible boundary that triggers the display change (see sentence 2). The target word (BAWL) displays before the eyes begin the fixation, making the change very difficult to detect and the text appears completely normal in most cases.

1. *   *   *   *
  He claims he won't | ball/bail if his team loses.

2.   * $\longrightarrow$
  He claims he won't | bawl if his team loses.

Pollatsek, Lesch, Morris, & Rayner (1992) conducted the initial parafoveal preview study of phonological processing using such materials. Shorter first-fixation durations in the homophone preview condition (BALL) as compared to the orthographic control condition (BAIL) indicated that readers use phonological information parafoveally to facilitate word recognition. The data provide evidence for phonological priming that converges with that found in masked priming paradigms reviewed in the previous section (e.g., Rastle & Brysbaert, 2006). Parafoveal phonological effects have been found in several other languages as well, including Chinese and French (Miellet & Sparrow, 2004; Pollatsek et al., 2000). The preview studies make several contributions to the question of phonology in word reading. First, because readers have no way of knowing which word is the 'target', the findings suggest that skilled readers routinely assemble phonological information during word identification in the course of silent reading. Second, these studies discovered that skilled readers engage phonological processes automatically in the initial parafoveal phase of word recognition, even before a word is consciously perceived.

Thus, eye movement evidence extends the findings of many isolated word experiments to word recognition in context by indicating that skilled readers routinely activate phonological information during silent reading. The fact that the critical word (on which measurement is taken) is not visibly marked as different compared to the rest of the sentence means that the reader uses standard reading processes rather than some special strategic process. Another sense of 'routine' is that phonological processes apply not only to a subset of unfamiliar words, but to words in general. Experiments using several paradigms have demonstrated phonological effects for low, moderate, and high frequency words (Ashby, 2006; Ashby, Treiman, Kessler, & Rayner, 2006; Miellet & Sparrow, 2004; McCutchen & Perfetti, 1982; Newman, Jared, & Haigh (in press); Perfetti et al., 1992; Rayner, Sereno, Lesch, & Pollatsek, 1995). Such general effects are expected given the automaticity of parafoveal processing, which gains phonological information about a word before its frequency is determined.

The eye movement data also suggest that parafoveal phonological processing may contribute to the rate of skilled reading (Ashby et al., 2006; Ashby & Rayner, 2004; Fitzsimmons & Drieghe, 2011; Pollatsek et al., 1992). This leads to the interesting conclusion that automatic phonological processing may be a principal contributor to reading fluency, contrary to the assumption that speed depends on by-passing phonology. This would be consistent with observations of individual differences in reading skill. For example, preliminary research indicates that skilled readers benefit from parafoveal phonological information, but less skilled readers do not (Chase, Rayner, & Well, 2005). Also, remediated dyslexic readers who develop normal accuracy often remain slow readers, and slow reading is characteristic of dyslexia in any writing system (Rawson, 1995; Shaywitz & Shaywitz, 2008). The connection between phonology and fluency also helps to explain why phonological processing persists across reading development. Early readers intentionally employ phonological coding to accurately read words they haven't seen before, and skilled readers activate phonology parafoveally to speed word recognition.

The eye movement research leaves some unanswered questions about the time course of phonological processing. Subtracting the lag time needed to execute a saccade from the mean fixation duration, Rayner et al. (1995) estimated that phonological information is processed within the first 200–250 ms of reading a word in the fast-priming paradigm. However, it is difficult to narrow down that time window with eye movement measures because brief prime durations do not necessarily indicate when phonological processes operate. Prime duration simply indicates how long phonological information must be presented for uptake into the cognitive system in order for congruency effects to manifest at some future point in time (Rayner, Liversedge, White, & Vergilino-Perez, 2003). Nor can parafoveal preview experiments indicate the time course of phonological processing. Although the previewed information gets into the cognitive system sometime before a word is fixated, we cannot determine when readers compute phonological congruency. We turn now to event-related potentials (ERP) and magnetoencephalography (MEG) studies that can illuminate the time course of phonological processes.

Neurophysiological evidence from ERP and MEG studies

ERP studies

Event-related potentials contribute unique information about on-line reading processes as they unfold over time, capturing changes in brain electrical potentials recorded at the scalp during reading. Because ERPs measure the electrical potentials from brain activity, rather than the hand or eye movements that result from the sum of such activity, they are a sensitive indicator of the cognitive processes engaged during word recognition. Several ERP studies have found lexical and semantic effects in the first 200 ms of word recognition (e.g., Pulvermüller, Lutzenberger, & Birmbaumer, 1995; Sereno, Rayner, & Postner, 1998). In contrast, the majority of ERP experiments have not registered phonological effects until later in word recognition, or between 260–450 ms following word onset (Kutas & Van Petten, 1990; Kramer & Donchin, 1987; Rugg, 1984; Rugg & Barrett, 1987). These relatively late phonological effects provide evidence for post-lexical phonological processing during explicit tasks, such as deciding whether two words rhyme or have the same meaning. However, neurophysiological evidence of phonological processing prior to 200 ms is now beginning to accumulate.

Several studies have demonstrated early phonological effects in word recognition using the masked priming paradigm we discussed above. Using a four-field paradigm that displayed a mask between the prime and target, Grainger, Kiyonaga, and Holcomb (2006) were the first to combine masked priming and ERPs to examine the time course of orthographic and phonological code activation in word recognition. When words such as BRAIN were preceded by pseudo-homophone primes (BRANE), Grainger et al. found the magnitude of the N250 to be reduced, compared with an orthographic control condition (BRAIN followed by BRANT). This phonological N250 effect leaves open the question about the timing of phonological processing relative to semantic processing, as the effect occurred later than the lexical-semantic effects observed within 100–200 ms of word onset (Pulvermüller, 2001).

Ashby and colleagues conducted two ERP masked-priming studies in order to investigate the nature of phonological priming and its time course in word recognition. Because visual information can affect early ERPs, both studies used a visually matched design in which the prime and target letter overlap were identical in the phonological and control conditions so that phonological congruency depended strictly on the pairing of prime and target. To minimize task effects, participants read words silently and made semantic categorization judgments about filler items during the EEG recording. The first study examined the time course of sub-phonemic feature processing. Ashby, Sanders, and Kingston (2009) measured the ERPs elicited by words (e.g., FAT and FAD) that were preceded by nonword primes that were congruent (fak-FAT) or incongruent (faz-FAT) in terms of a sub-phonemic feature (voicing) of the final consonant. In this example, the prime-target pair fak-FAT is congruent, because both final consonants are unvoiced, whereas faz-FAT is incongruent because faz has voiced final consonant and FAT does not. In faz-FAD, however, both have a voiced final consonant so this pair is congruent. In both experiments, phonological congruency effects appeared around 80 ms, reducing the magnitude of the first peak in the waveform (N1) elicited by the target. In a second study, Ashby (2010) examined the time course of phonological processing at the syllable level. This study measured the ERPs elicited by words with either two or three phonemes in the initial syllable (e.g., PONY [po] and PONDER [pon]). These target words were preceded by partial word primes that were congruent or incongruent with the initial syllable of the target (PO## or PON# before PONY and PO#### or PON### before PONDER). In both experiments, a syllable congruency effect appeared: targets in the congruent conditions elicited a reduced N1 compared to targets in the incongruent conditions, with the effect appearing as early as 100 ms after target onset.

Taken together, the phonological congruency effects reported in Ashby (2010) and Ashby et al. (2009) indicate that skilled readers process both suprasegmental and sub-phonemic information quite quickly. The replicated effects in each study appeared on or before the N1, coincident with the timing of the semantic effects reviewed in Pulvermüller (2001). The observed effect of two very different types of phonological congruency on the magnitude of the N1 demonstrates the wide range of phonological information that is activated within 100 ms of seeing a word.

Magnetoencephalography studies

MEG studies, which measure the magnetic fields generated when large numbers of neurons fire, provide both spatial and temporal data about brain activity patterns. Accordingly, MEG studies of word reading can track the time course of phonology in relation to the brain's reading network. Of particular interest for the interplay of orthography and phonology are a posterior circuit that includes the infero-temporal (IT) area that responds to visually presented words and word-like stimuli (often referred to as the Visual Word Form Area) and an anterior circuit that includes the inferior-frontal gyrus (IFG), which is involved in linguistic processing. Studies using time frequency analysis show very early involvement of the left IFG (Broca's area) in word reading (Cornelissen, Kringelbach, Ellis, Whitney, Holliday, & Hansen, 2009; Pammer et al., 2004; Wheat, Cornelissen, Frost, & Hansen, 2010). For example, Pammer et al. (2004) manipulated lexical status by using words and anagrams (e.g., HOUSE/HOSUE). Pammer et al. found that the anterior (IFG) and posterior (IT) circuits became active in tandem for words but not for anagrams. The IT area also responded to anagrams, but in a somewhat later time window.

Finding concurrent activity in the IT and IFG areas contrasts with the intuition that words are initially processed primarily orthographically, and that phonological processes enter later. Were that the case, activation should appear earlier in IT than in IFG (Simos, Breier, Fletcher, Foorman, Mouzaki, & Papanicolaou, 2001). Pammer's measurement of concurrent activity in the IT and the IFG areas during word recognition was replicated when readers processed word-like letter strings, as opposed to consonant-only strings and faces (Cornelissen et al., 2009). They found visual areas active at 110 ms followed by concurrent activity in the IFG at 125 ms and IT at 145 ms for words. Early involvement of the left IFG was also observed recently in a masked priming naming study by Wheat et al. (2010) that compared pseudohomophone primes (BREIN) with orthographic (BROIN) and unrelated (LOPUS) control primes. Activation in the IFG occurred most strongly for pseudohomophone primes at approximately 100 ms post-stimulus onset. These results closely tie the activation of the IFG to the phonological processes of word reading by demonstrating that pseudohomophone primes lead to better target recognition, clarifying the role of the IFG in word reading tasks. In addition to the early phonological activation, all of these studies found left temporal-parietal activation at 200–400 ms post-stimulus, which suggests that phonology continues to be involved as lexical processes unfold.

These recent MEG studies suggest an early role for phonology in visual word recognition by showing frontal area activation associated with phonological processing that is conjoined temporally with activation in posterior areas that support visual processing of words and word-like stimuli (see Figure 10.2). The data from MEG studies using frequency analyses, masked-priming ERP experiments, and the most sensitive behavioral and eye-tracking paradigms converge on the conclusion that phonology plays an early, if not automatic, role in identifying words during reading. However, this converging information on the time course of phonology does not specify what kinds of phonological information are

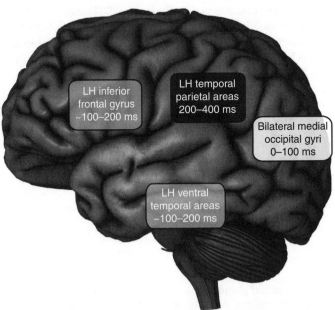

Figure 10.2 The left hemisphere reading network with approximate time estimates of activation onset, summarized from the time-frequency MEG analyses.

accessed during the initial moments of word recognition. In the next section, we review work that begins to specify the characteristics of these early phonological representations.

The contents of phonology

Berent and Perfetti (1995) pointed out that while research had focused on whether phonology played a role in visual word recognition, little attention was paid to the nature of the phonological information. Linguistic theories have established that the phonological representations of speech are structured, containing multiple layers of phonological information that include features, phoneme segments, skeletal structure, syllables, and lexical stress (e.g., Clements & Keyser, 1983) (see Figure 10.3). Potentially, the phonological representations used in reading may be as fully complex as the representations used to process spoken language. Results from behavioral and neurophysiological studies using diverse paradigms now indicate that the representations in reading are linguistically structured and include several layers of phonological information.

Berent and Perfetti (1995) originally proposed that phonological content was multi-linear at the level of consonants and vowels. Results from their perceptual identification masking experiments indicated that consonants and vowels are processed in two temporal streams; a rapid, automatic cycle that assembled consonant phonemes and a slower more controlled cycle that assembled vowel phonemes. Although other paradigms produced mixed results (e.g., Lukatela & Turvey, 2000), separate roles for consonants and vowels were supported by fast-priming eye tracking studies (Lee, Rayner, & Pollatsek, 2001) and ERP studies (Carreiras, Vergara , & Perea, 2009). Separate consonant–vowel cycles would be consistent with the distinctive roles of consonants and vowels in speech recognition, where consonants have a special role in lexical identification (Bonatti, Peña, Nespor, & Mehler, 2005).

Of course, a serial process in reading aloud that produces a co-articulated sequence of phonemes is necessary eventually, so the Dual Route Model (Coltheart et al., 2001) correctly predicts linear position effects in naming.

Information	Representation			
	PONY			
Lexical stress	1	0		
Syllables	σ	σ		
Skeleton	c	v	c	v
Segments	/p/	/o/	/n/	/i/
Features	***	****	***	****

Figure 10.3 The multiple layers of phonological information (e.g., Clements & Keyser, 1983) that skilled readers typically activate en route to word recognition, based on evidence from behavioral, eye-movement, and neurophysiological experiments that tap automatic phonological processes.

However, the activation of structured phonological information about syllables, consonant–vowel planes, and sub-phonemic features may also shape the early processes of word recognition during silent reading.

Parafoveal preview experiments indicate that readers may integrate these phonological layers automatically to facilitate word recognition. Ashby et al. (2006) found that skilled readers processed parafoveal rime information (i.e., the vowel plus the final consonant) to bias the activation of phonological vowels. Mean fixation durations were shorter when the consonant that followed orthographically ambiguous vowels, such as *oo* in *book* or *hoot*, activated vowel phonemes that were congruent with the target, suggesting that readers either represent rime information outright or use final consonant information to constrain the activation of possible vowel phonemes early in word recognition.

Several eye movement studies indicate that readers process initial syllable information parafoveally during silent reading. In the initial preview experiment, Ashby and Rayner (2004) found that readers recognized words faster when the parafoveal syllable information was congruent with the target than when it was not. Target words with consonant–vowel (CV) initial syllables (DE•MAND) or consonant–vowel–consonant (CVC) initial syllables (LAN•TERN) were preceded by primes that exactly matched their initial syllable (DE#### or LAN####) or contained one letter more or less (DEM### or LA#####). The syllable congruency effect in silent reading was replicated in later studies presenting targets matched on initial trigram (e.g., PONY and PONDER) in a preview lexical decision experiment and in a masked-priming ERP study (Ashby, 2010; Ashby & Martin, 2008). Experiments in Spanish, German, and Chinese have also found syllable effects in visual word recognition (Carreiras, Alvarez, & de Vega, 1993; Carreiras & Perea, 2002; Chen, Lin, & Ferrand, 2003; Hutzler, Conrad, & Jacobs, 2005). Together, these eye movement studies indicate that skilled readers in many languages activate suprasegmental syllable information during word recognition, whether or not the writing system makes syllables explicit.

A recent eye movement study suggests that readers may use phonological syllable information in determining whether to fixate a word. Fitzsimmons and Drieghe (2011) presented sentences containing one-syllable (e.g., GRAIN) or two-syllable (e.g., CARGO) five-letter words. During silent reading, readers were more likely to skip the one-syllable target words than the two-syllable targets. This pattern indicates that readers extracted the number of syllables from the parafoveal word early enough to influence the decision of where to move their eyes next. The Fitzsimmons and Drieghe finding converges with Ashby and Clifton (2005), which reported more fixations on words with two-stressed syllables than words with only a single stressed syllable. Therefore, it appears that skilled readers use phonological information to determine where to look next as well as to facilitate word identification.

Although there is more to learn about the range and structure of the phonological content that is part of word recognition, the data suggest that skilled readers have access to multi-layer phonological representations during word recognition. These representations are complex in that they can include several phonological layers – skeletal information about consonants and vowels, rimes, and initial syllables, but also subphonemic information (Ashby et al., 2009) that may reflect immediate activation of phonological production codes, such as voicing. During silent reading, skilled readers may use structured phonological representations to organize the available parafoveal information for easy integration with foveal information. Alternatively, readers may simply uptake any phonological information that is tagged as being informative of a particular aspect of a phonological word. Either way, it is possible that the activation of a full phonological representation influences where as well as when to move the eyes (Ashby & Clifton, 2005).

Conclusion

The extent to which phonology is a part of word reading has been subject to a range of views, evidence, and counter-evidence. Dissents pivot largely on such dichotomies as pre-lexical vs post-lexical, automatic vs optional (or controlled), and mediating meaning or incidental to it. Our review has referred to the dissents occasionally, but has largely focused on the conclusions we think can be reached by attending to studies with methods that are sensitive to what occurs *during* word identification. We conclude (a) that phonology is part of word reading universally across writing systems, even if its implementation does importantly depend on the details of the writing system, and (b) that phonology is an early and routine part of word identification in alphabetic reading, based on converging evidence from brief exposure behavioral methods, eye movements, ERPs, and MEGs.

Whether such phonology is always 'pre-lexical' is a question we did not explicitly answer, partly because we are not convinced that there is a single magic moment of 'access' to one specific piece of information (an orthographic-only word entry) as opposed to constituents that are made rapidly available over multiple moments (Perfetti et al., 1988; see also Balota, 1994), and partly because we think it is not the most interesting question to ask. Another question we did not answer is whether phonology 'mediates' word meaning. Early phonology – even phonology prior to meaning – does not allow the conclusion that meaning results because of the phonology (Lesch & Pollatsek, 1993; Tan & Perfetti, 1997, 1998). Instead, along with Van Orden and Goldinger (1994), we conceive of phonology as immediately stabilizing the identity of the word, leading to a specific and usually valid perceptual identification (a function that might also be supported by meaning or morpho-syntactic constituents). It is this identification of a word as a linguistic object that is the central recurring event in reading, brought about by a tight coupling of perceptual and phonological processes. Phonology appears to contribute to increased stability during the initial parafoveal processing of words, thereby playing a key role in faster word recognition and improved reading fluency.

Converging evidence for the early role of complex phonological information in word recognition suggests that theories that assign an optional or only late-occurring role to phonology are insufficient. Moreover, the evidence also forces a reconsideration of theories that assign a strong role to phonology. While the strong phonological theory (Frost, 1998) captured the pervasiveness of phonology in reading, its assumption of minimality may be too weak. Some evidence suggests a stronger phonological theory is needed, one that specifies a multi-layered phonological structure that affects word recognition.

The evidence that supports this stronger phonological theory also suggests that phonology facilitates skilled word recognition *in general*, not merely for low frequency words or consistently spelled words, or for that matter, not only for alphabetic reading. The neurophysiological data showing synchronous activity of orthographic and linguistic cortical areas make a strong case against the view that phonology is a sluggish tag-along in word reading. Instead, rapid and automatic phonological processes occur early in word recognition, contributing to the stability of word identification and promoting fluent reading.

- Phonology plays an early and integral role in word recognition, stabilizing the identity of a word so that accurate perceptual identification occurs. This early role of phonology is supported by evidence from:
  - o Behavioral experiments combining brief presentation and visual masking which reduce strategic effects and provide a window into early word recognition processes. These methods have demonstrated phonological facilitation with as little as 25–35 ms of stimulus presentation.
  - o Eye movement studies show effects of phonology on a similar time scale. These studies have also shown that the phonology of words is automatically activated while words are just outside of fixation in the parafoveal region.
  - o ERP studies that show readers are accessing sub-phonemic and syllable information within 80–100 ms of seeing a word.
  - o MEG studies which show concurrent activation in posterior areas that process the visual characteristics of words and anterior areas important for phonological and linguistic processing of words. These areas are active at only 100–200 ms post stimulus presentation.
- Recent work has begun to specify the nature of the phonological representations that are activated early in word recognition. It appears that readers are activating multi-layer representations that can include information about consonants and vowels, final rimes, syllables, and sub-phonemic features.
- Phonology's role in word recognition is universal across the world's orthographies. From shallow and deep alphabetic orthographies to logographic orthographies like Chinese, phonology provides an early constraint on identification.

References

Ashby, J. (2006). Prosody in skilled silent reading: Evidence from eye movements. *Journal of Research in Reading, 29*, 318–333.

Ashby, J. (2010). Phonology is fundamental in skilled reading: Evidence from ERPs. *Psychonomic Bulletin & Review, 17*, 95–100.

Ashby, J. & Clifton Jr, C. (2005). The prosodic property of lexical stress affects eye movements during silent reading. *Cognition, 96*, B89–B100.

Ashby, J. & Martin, A. E. (2008). Prosodic phonological representations early in visual word recognition. *Journal of Experimental Psychology: Human Perception & Performance, 34*, 224–236.

Ashby, J. & Rayner, K. (2004). Representing syllable information during silent reading: Evidence from eye movements. *Language and Cognitive Processes, 19*, 391–426.

Ashby, J., Treiman, R., Kessler, B., & Rayner, K. (2006). Vowel processing during silent reading: Evidence from eye movements. *Journal of Experimental Psychology: Learning, Memory, and Cognition, 32*, 416–424.

Ashby, J., Sanders, L. D., & Kingston, J. (2009). Skilled readers begin processing phonological features by 80 msec: Evidence from ERPs. *Biological Psychology, 80*, 84–94.

Baddeley, A. D. & Lewis, V. J. (1981). Inner active processes in reading: The inner voice, the inner ear and the inner eye. In A. M. Lesgold & C. A. Perfetti (Eds), *Interactive processes in reading* (pp. 107–129). Hillsdale, NJ: Erlbaum.

Balota, D. A. (1994). Visual word recognition: The journey from features to meaning. In M. A. Gernsbacher (Ed.), *Handbook of psycholinguistics* (pp. 303–358). New York: Academic Press.

Berent, I. & Perfetti, C. A. (1995). A rose is a REEZ: The two-cycles model of phonology assembly in English. *Psychological Review, 102*, 146–84.

Bonatti, L. L., Peña, M., Nespor, M., & Mehler, J. (2005). Linguistic constraints on statistical computations: The role of consonants and vowels in continuous speech processing. *Psychological Science, 16*, 451–459.

Brysbaert, M. & Praet, C. (1992). Reading isolated words: No evidence for automatic incorporation of the phonetic code. *Psychological Research, 54*, 91–102.

Carreiras, M. & Perea, M. (2002). Masked priming effects with syllabic neighbors in a lexical decision task. *Journal of Experimental Psychology: Human Perception & Performance, 28*, 1228–1242.

Carreiras, M., Alvarez, C. J., & de Vega, M. (1993). Syllable frequency and visual word recognition in Spanish. *Journal of Memory & Language, 32*, 766–780.

Carreiras, M., Vergara, M., & Perea, M. (2009). ERP correlates of transposed-letter priming effects: The role of vowels versus consonants. *Psychophysiology, 46*, 34–42.

Chase, K. H., Rayner, K., & Well, A. D. (2005). Eye movements and phonological preview benefit: Effects of reading skill. *Canadian Journal of Experimental Psychology, 59*, 209–217.

Chen, J.-Y., Lin, W. C., & Ferrand, L. (2003). Masked priming of the syllable in Mandarin Chinese speech production. *Chinese Journal of Psychology, 45*, 107–120.

Clements, G. N. & Keyser, S. J. (1983). *CV phonology. A generative theory of the syllable*. Cambridge: MIT Press.

Coltheart, M., Rastle, K., Perry, C., Langdon, R., & Ziegler, J. (2001). DRC: A dual route cascaded model of visual word recognition and reading aloud. *Psychological Review, 108*, 204–256.

Cornelissen, P. L., Kringelbach, M. L., Ellis, A. W., Whitney, C., Holliday, I. E., & Hansen, P. C. (2009). Activation of the left inferior frontal gyrus in the first 200 ms of reading: Evidence from magnetoencephalography (MEG). *PLoS ONE, 4*, e5359.

Dodge, R. (1907). Studies from the psychological laboratory of Wesleyan University: An experimental study of visual fixation. *Psychological Monographs, 84*, 1–95.

Drieghe, D. & Brysbaert, M. (2002). Strategic effects in associative priming with words, homophones, and pseudohomophones. *Journal of Experimental Psychology: Learning, Memory, and Cognition, 28*, 951–961.

Farrar, W. T., Van Orden, G. C., & Hamouz, V. (2001). When SOFA primes TOUCH: Interdependence of spelling, sound, and meaning in 'semantically mediated' phonological priming. *Memory and Cognition, 29*, 530–539.

Ferrand, L. & Grainger, J. (1994). Effects of orthography are independent of phonology in masked form priming. *Quarterly Journal of Experimental Psychology, 47A*, 365–382.

Fitzsimmons, G. & Drieghe, D. (2011). The influence of number of syllables on word skipping during reading. *Psychonomic Bulletin & Review, 18*, 736–741.

Frost, R. (1998). Toward a strong phonological theory of visual word recognition: True issues and false trails. *Psychological Bulletin, 123*, 71–99.

Frost, R. & Yogev, O. (2001). Orthographic and phonological computation in visual word recognition: Evidence from backward masking in Hebrew. *Psychonomic Bulletin & Review, 8*, 524–530.

Grainger, J., Kiyonaga, K., & Holcomb, P. J. (2006). The time course of orthographic and phonological code activation. *Psychological Science, 17*, 1021–1026.

Huey, E. B. (1908) *The psychology and pedagogy of reading.* New York: Macmillan.

Hutzler, F., Conrad, M., & Jacobs, A. M. (2005). Effects of syllable frequency in lexical decision and naming: An eye-movement study. *Brain & Language, 92*, 138–152.

Jared, D. & Seidenberg, M. S. (1991). Does word identification proceed from spelling to sound to meaning? *Journal of Experimental Psychology: General, 120*, 358–364.

Katz, L. & Frost, R. (1992). Reading in different orthographies: The orthographic depth hypothesis. In R. Frost & L. Katz (Eds), *Orthography, phonology, morphology, and meaning* (pp. 67–84). Amsterdam: Elsevier North Holland Press.

Kramer, A. F. & Donchin, E. (1987). Brain potentials as indices of orthographic and phonological interaction during word matching. *Journal of Experimental Psychology: Learning, Memory, and Cognition, 13*, 76–86.

Kutas, M. & Van Petten, C. (1990). Electrophysiological perspectives on comprehending written language. In P. M. Rossini & F. Mauguiere (Eds), *New trends and advanced techniques in clinical nehrophysiology (EEG Suppl. 41)* (pp. 12–16). Tilburg, Germany: Tilburg University Press.

Lee, H., Rayner, K., & Pollatsek, A. (1999). The time course of phonological, semantic, and orthographic coding in reading: Evidence from the fast priming technique. *Psychometric Bulletin & Review, 5*, 624–634.

Lee, H., Rayner, K., & Pollatsek, A. (2001). The relative contribution of consonants and vowels to word identification during reading. *Journal of Memory and Language, 44*, 189–205.

Lesch, M. F. & Pollatsek, A. (1993). Automatic access of semantic information by phonological codes in visual word recognition. *Journal of Experimental Psychology: Learning, Memory, and Cognition, 19*, 285–294.

Liu, W., Inhoff, A. W., Ye, Y., & Wu, C. (2002). Use of parafoveally visible characters during the reading of Chinese sentences. *Journal of Experimental Psychology: Human Perception & Performance, 28*, 1213–1227.

Liu, Y., Perfetti, C. A., & Hart, L. (2003). ERP evidence for the time course of graphic, phonological, and semantic information in Chinese meaning and pronunciation decisions. *Journal of Experimental Psychology: Learning, Memory, and Cognition, 29,* 1231–1247.

Lukatela, G. & Turvey, T. (2000). An evaluation of the two-cycles model of phonology assembly. *Journal of Memory and Language, 42,* 183–207.

McCutchen, D. & Perfetti, C. A. (1982). The visual tongue-twister effect: Phonological activation in silent reading. *Journal of Verbal Learning & Verbal Behavior, 21,* 672–687.

Miellet, S. & Sparrow, L. (2004). Phonological codes are assembled before word fixation: Evidence from boundary paradigm in sentence reading. *Brain & Language, 90,* 299–310.

Newman, R. L., Jared, D., & Haigh, C.A. (in press). Does phonology play a role when skilled readers read high-frequency words? Evidence from ERPs. *Language and Cognitive Processes.*

Pammer, K., Hansen, P. C., Kringelback, M. L., Holliday, I., Barnes, G., Hillebrand, A., Singh, K. D., & Cornelissen, P. L. (2004). Visual word recognition: The first half second. *NeuroImage, 22,* 1819–1825.

Perfetti, C. A. & Bell, L. (1991). Phonemic activation during the first 40 ms of word identification: Evidence from backward masking and masked priming. *Journal of Memory and Language, 30,* 473–85.

Perfetti, C. A. & Tan, L. H. (1998). The time course of graphic, phonological, and semantic activation in Chinese character identification. *Journal of Experimental Psychology: Learning, Memory, and Cognition, 24,* 101–118.

Perfetti, C. A. & Zhang, S. (1991). Phonological processes in reading Chinese characters. *Journal of Experimental Psychology: Learning, Memory, and Cognition, 17,* 633–643.

Perfetti, C. A. & Zhang, S. (1995). Very early phonological activation in Chinese reading. *Journal of Experimental Psychology: Learning, Memory, and Cognition, 21,* 24–33.

Perfetti, C. A., Bell, L., & Delaney, S. (1988). Automatic phonetic activation in silent word reading: Evidence from backward masking. *Journal of Memory and Language, 27,* 59–70.

Perfetti, C. A., Zhang, S., & Berent, I. (1992). Reading in English and Chinese: Evidence for a 'universal' phonological principle. In R. Frost & L Katz (Eds), *Orthography, phonology, morphology, and meaning* (pp. 227–248). Amsterdam: North-Holland.

Perfetti, C. A., Liu, Y., & Tan, L. H. (2005). The Lexical Constituency Model: Some implications of research on Chinese for general theories of reading. *Psychological Review, 12,* 43–59.

Pexman, P. M., Lupker, S. J., & Jared, D. (2001). Homophone effects in lexical decision. *Journal of Experimental Psychology: Learning, Memory & Cognition, 27,* 59–70.

Pollatsek, A., Lesch, M., Morris, R. K., & Rayner, K. (1992). Phonological codes are used in integrating information across saccades in word identification and reading. *Journal of Experimental Psychology: Human Perception and Performance, 18,* 148–162.

Pollatsek, A., Tan, L. H., & Rayner, K. (2000). The role of phonological codes in integrating information across saccadic eye movements in Chinese character identification. *Journal of Experimental Psychology: Human Perception and Performance, 26,* 607–633.

Pulvermüller, F. (2001). Brain reflections of words and their meaning. *Trends in Cognitive Sciences, 5*, 517–524.

Pulvermüller, F., Lutzenberger, W., & Birmbaumer, N. (1995). Electrocortical distinction of vocabulary types. *Electroencephalography and Clinical Neurophysiology, 94*, 357–370.

Rastle, K. & Brysbaert, M. (2006). Masked phonological priming effects in English: Are they real? Do they matter? *Cognitive Psychology, 53*, 97–145.

Rawson, M. B. (1995). *Dyslexia over the lifespan: A 55 year longitudinal study.* Cambridge: Educators Publishing Services.

Rayner, K. (1975). The perceptual span and peripheral cues in reading. *Cognitive Psychology, 7*, 65–81.

Rayner, K. (1998). Eye movements in reading and information processing: Twenty years of research. *Psychological Bulletin, 124*, 372–422.

Rayner, K. (2009). The 35th Sir Frederick Bartlett Lecture: Eye movements and attention during reading scene perception and visual search. *Quarterly Journal of Experimental Psychology, 62*, 1457–1506.

Rayner, K., Sereno, S. C., Lesch, M. F., & Pollatsek, A. (1995). Phonological codes are automatically activated during reading: Evidence from an eye movement priming paradigm. *Psychological Science, 6*, 26–32.

Rayner, K., Liversedge, S. P., White, S. J., & Vergilino-Perez, D. (2003). Reading disappearing text: Cognitive control of eye movements. *Psychological Science, 14*, 385–389.

Rayner, K., Liversedge, S. P., & White, S. J. (2006). Eye movements when reading disappearing text: The importance of the word to the right of fixation. *Vision Research, 46*, 310–323.

Rayner, K., Pollatsek, A., Ashby, J., & Clifton, C. E. (2012). *Psychology of reading.* New York Psychology Press.

Rugg, M. D. (1984). Event-related potentials in phonological matching tasks. *Brain and Language, 23*, 225–240.

Rugg, M. D. & Barrett, S. E. (1987). Event-related potentials and the interaction between orthographic and phonological information in a rhyme-judgment task. *Brain and Language, 32*, 336–361.

Sereno, S. C. & Rayner, K. (1992). Fast priming during eye fixations in reading. *Journal of Experimental Psychology: Human Perception and Performance, 18*, 173–184.

Sereno, S. C., Rayner, K., & Postner, M. I. (1998). Establishing a time-line of word recognition: Evidence from eye movements and event-related potentials. *NeuroReport, 9*, 2195–2200.

Share, D. L. (2008). On the anglocentricities of current reading research and practice: The perils of overreliance on an outlier orthography. *Psychological Bulletin, 134*, 584–615.

Shaywitz, S. E. & Shaywitz, B. A. (2008). Paying attention to reading: the neurobiology of reading and dyslexia. *Development and Psychopathology, 20*, 1329–1349.

Simos, P. G., Breier, J. I., Fletcher, J. M., Foorman, B. R., Mouzaki, A., & Papanicolaou, A. C. (2001). Age-related changes in regional brain activation durating phonological decoding and printed word recognition. *Developmental Neuropsychology, 19*, 191–210.

Tan, L. H. & Perfetti, C. A. (1997). Visual Chinese character recognition: Does phonological information mediate access to meaning? *Journal of Memory and Language, 37*, 41–57.

Tan, L. H. & Perfetti, C. A. (1998). Phonological codes as early sources of constraint in Chinese word identification: A review of current discoveries and theoretical accounts. In 'Cognitive processing of Chinese and Japanese' special issue. *Reading and Writing: An Interdisciplinary Journal, 10*, 165–200. [Reprinted in C. K. Leong & K. Tamaoka (Eds), *Cognitive Processes of the Chinese and the Japanese languages.* Series in Neuropsychology and Cognition, R. Joshi, Series Editor. Boston: Kluwer Academic Publishers, 1998.]

Tan, L. H. & Perfetti, C. A. (1999). Phonological and associative inhibition in the early stages of English word identification: Evidence from backward masking. *Journal of Experimental Psychology: Human Perception and Performance, 25*, 382–393.

Tan, L. H., Hoosain, R., & Siok, W. W. T. (1996). Activation of phonological codes before access to character meaning in written Chinese. *Journal of Experimental Psychology: Learning, Memory and Cognition, 22*, 865–882.

Tsai, J. L., Lee, C. Y., Tzeng, O. J. L., Hung, D. L., & Yen, N. S. (2004). Use of phonological codes for Chinese characters: Evidence from processing of parafoveal preview when reading sentences. *Brain and Language, 91*, 235–244.

Van Orden, G. C. & Goldinger, S. D. (1994). The interdependence of form and function in cognitive systems explains perception of printed words. *Journal of Experimental Psychology: Human Perception and Performance, 20*, 1269–1291.

Van Orden, G. C., Johnston, J. C., & Hale, B. L. (1988). Word identification in reading proceeds from spelling to sound to meaning. *Journal of Experimental Psychology: Learning, Memory and Cognition, 14*, 371–386.

Verstaen, A., Humphreys, G. W., Olson, A., & d'Ydewalle, G. (1995). Automatic (prelexical) phonemic activation in silent word reading? *Journal of Memory and Language, 34*, 335–356.

Wheat, K. L., Cornelissen, P. L., Frost, S. J., & Hansen, P. C. (2010). During visual word recognition, phonology is accessed within 100 ms and may be mediated by a speech production code: Evidence from magnetoencephalography. *Journal of Neuroscience, 30*, 5229–5233.

Xu, B. & Perfetti, C. A. (1999). Nonstrategic subjective threshold effects in phonemic masking. *Memory and Cognition, 27*, 26–36.

Xu, Y., Pollatsek, A., & Potter, M. (1999). The activation of phonology during silent Chinese word reading. *Journal of Experimental Psychology: Learning, Memory, and Cognition, 25*, 838–857.

Yang, J., McCandliss, B. D., Shu, H., & Zevin, J. (2009). Simulating language-specific and language-general effects in a statistical learning model of Chinese reading. *Journal of Memory and Language, 61*, 238–257.

Zhang, S., Perfetti, C. A., & Yang, H., (1999). Whole-word, frequency-general phonology in semantic processing of Chinese characters. *Journal of Experimental Psychology: Learning, Memory, and Cognition, 25*, 858–875.

Ziegler, J. & Goswami, U. (2005). Reading acquisition, developmental dyslexia, and skilled reading across languages: A psycholinguistic grain size theory. *Psychological Bulletin, 131*, 3–29.

Author Index

Subject Index